TRAVELS INTO THE POOR MAN'S COUNTRY

Henry Mayhew in 1851, aged 39. The frontispiece
to volume 1 of *London Labour and the London Poor*, perhaps
from a photograph by Richard Beard. Courtesy
of Columbia University Libraries.

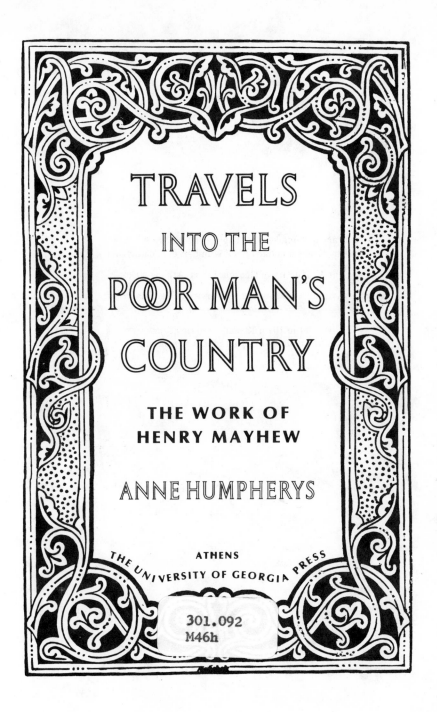

TRAVELS
INTO THE
PŒR MAN'S
COUNTRY

THE WORK OF
HENRY MAYHEW

ANNE HUMPHERYS

ATHENS
THE UNIVERSITY OF GEORGIA PRESS

Library of Congress Catalog Card Number 76–15346
International Standard Book Number: 0–8203–0416–6

The University of Georgia Press, Athens 30602

Set in 10 on 13 point Century type
Printed in the United States of America

FOR JOHN

Contents

What a confession it is that we have all of us been obliged to make! A clever and earnest-minded writer gets a commission from the *Morning Chronicle* newspaper, and reports upon the state of our poor in London: he goes amongst labouring people and poor of all kinds—and brings back what? A picture of human life so wonderful, so awful, so piteous and pathetic, so exciting and terrible, that readers of romances own they never read anything like to it; and that the griefs, struggles, strange adventures here depicted exceed anything that any of us could imagine. . . . But of such wondrous and complicated misery as this you confess you had no idea? No. How should you?—you and I—we are of the upper classes; we have hitherto had no community with the poor . . . until some poet like Hood wakes and sings that dreadful "Song of the Shirt"; some prophet like Carlyle rises up and denounces woe; some clear-sighted, energetic man like the writer of the *Chronicle* travels into the poor man's country for us, and comes back with his tale of terror and wonder.

Thackeray,
Punch, 9 March 1850.

Preface

Henry Mayhew, as E. P. Thompson has said, is a puzzling character. Little biographical information has survived and that which has sometimes seems at odds with what one deduces about the author of *London Labour and the London Poor* from reading the four volumes. In the last decade there have been two attempts to provide a partial solution for the puzzle. John L. Bradley began the task with the biographical introduction to his selection of passages from *London Labour and the London Poor* in 1965. E. P. Thompson and Eileen Yeo continued the investigation in 1971 in the introductory material to their selection of letters from the *Morning Chronicle* in *The Unknown Mayhew*. In addition there have been a number of articles which examine Mayhew's relationship with Dickens. References to *London Labour and the London Poor* in the burgeoning scholarship on Victorian urban history have steadily increased.

Despite this growing interest in Mayhew and use of his work, there is still general ignorance of the way his surveys developed and the dualities of his attitudes toward his subject. As a result more than one historian has misused his findings and inadequately evaluated his importance.

In the light of both the popularity of his books on the poor and the lack of information about them, I try to do two things in the present study: to bring together all the known facts about Mayhew and his surveys, and to explain the enlargements, hiatuses, and abrupt abandonments that characterize his work in terms of his temperament and the ambivalence of his responses to his experiences. It seems to me that there is a pattern to Mayhew's work which reflects what we know of his life, and the elucidation of that pattern shapes the following volume.

In the first chapter I present as completely as possible the biographical and historical background for Mayhew's major work and posit a theory of his personality which will explain the way his career developed and the manner in which his social surveys grew. In the second I concentrate on the development of the *Morning Chronicle* letters—which laid the foundation for his subsequent work on the street folk—and examine their limitation in scope as well as the strength of the individual portraits in terms of Mayhew's responses to his investigations. In the third chapter I continue the discussion by analyzing *London Labour and the London Poor* at length and by focusing on three major areas of Mayhew's achievement: his interviews, his statistics, and his economic views. In chapter 4 I discuss his survey of London prisons, the final part of his investigations, and the one that appears to come closest to his ideal. In the last two chapters I approach the topic from a different perspective. Chapter 5 is a discussion of the characteristics of Mayhew's style of writing on London's working poor and shows how the conflicts within him are reflected in the way he reported his observations. Chapter 6 places him in the context of the literature of the period, particularly in his relationships with Charles Kingsley and Charles Dickens. Out of this combination of biographical narrative, detailed analysis, and literary criticism, I hope will emerge a true evaluation of Mayhew's important contribution to our understanding of his age.

Acknowledgments

I owe debts of gratitude to a number of institutions and individuals. I wish to thank Columbia University, whose traveling grant in 1967 allowed me to complete part of the research for this volume. I appreciate the kindnesses shown me at the Boston Athenaeum Library, where I first read the *Morning Chronicle* letters. I wish to thank Herbert H. Lehman College of the City University of New York for a grant from the George Shuster Fund which helped me in the preparation of the manuscript and in indexing.

I am grateful to Patrick Mayhew of London for permission to use the unpublished manuscript of Mrs. L. M. Coumbe and other family papers. I wish to thank Robert B. Partlow, Jr. for permission to reprint the relevant passages from my article "Dickens and Mayhew on the London Poor" from the fourth volume of the *Dickens Annual* (Carbondale and Edwardsville: Southern Illinois University Press, 1975). This article was an early version of the section on Dickens and Mayhew in chapter 6. I also wish to thank the editors of the University of Georgia Press for a number of excellent suggestions and also for catching several errors in the text.

I wish to express my gratitude to John D. Rosenberg of Columbia University, whose enthusiasm for Mayhew predates my own and from whom I have received much insight and encouragement in my work. It was he who first suggested Mayhew's identification with his subjects. Any scholar who does research on Henry Mayhew and his work owes a primary debt to John L. Bradley and E. P. Thompson, who were first into the field. Although I had covered much the same ground and although I do not agree with their conclusions in all matters, I am happy to acknowledge the contribution of both scholars to my understanding of Mayhew. I owe another kind of debt to my colleague Gerhard Joseph of Herbert H. Lehman College not just for his reading and commenting on an early version of the manuscript but even more for his steady interest and intellectual exchange. Finally I want to acknowledge the many hours and the considerable effort devoted to this work by my husband John C. Mineka, who, over the many years the book has been in the making, has been both a patient critic and an unfailing support.

TRAVELS INTO THE POOR MAN'S COUNTRY

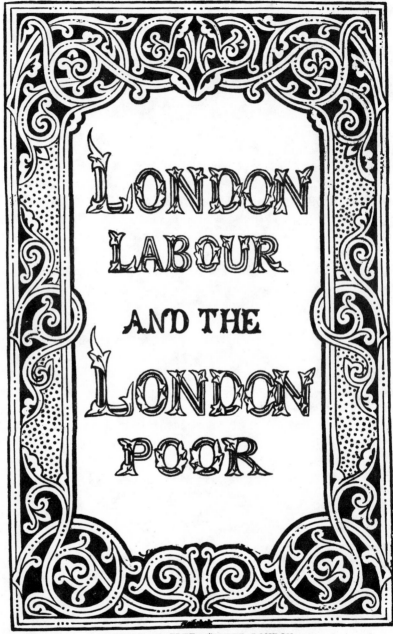

OFFICE: 69, FLEET-STREET, LONDON.

Cover of the weekly numbers of *London Labour and the London Poor*, 1851–1852. Courtesy of the British Library Board.

1

The Making of a Social Historian

London Labour and the London Poor by Henry Mayhew has always had an enthusiastic audience, small in the past, ever more numerous with the surge of interest in Victorian urban and social history of the last decade. Yet Mayhew has remained a badly understood writer. He was never the subject of an assiduously compiled two-volume "Life and Letters" written by a member of the family or a close friend. His son apparently planned such a book at his father's death but in the end produced only a slim volume focusing on his father's role in the founding of *Punch*. Mayhew led an irregular and often hand-to-mouth existence and in addition, for some thirty years after he had abandoned his work on *London Labour and the London Poor*, he lived most of the time in obscurity and seeming inaction. The passage of time and his own undisciplined way of life seem to have taken their toll, and no personal papers of Mayhew's have survived. What we can know about him must be pieced together from scanty and sometimes contradictory reminiscences of acquaintances and from certain family traditions recorded in an anecdotal unpublished family history written by a descendent of one of Mayhew's brothers.[1] There is the one record he left himself—his published work, particularly his contributions to the *Morning Chronicle* and his *London Labour and the London Poor*.

In these heterogeneous sources Mayhew appears to be an unusually inconsistent man in his opinions and achievements, even for an important figure in a period which defined itself in terms of contradictions. He was one of the most energetic and productive of social observers, yet for long periods of his life he produced little and that lacked merit. He was a congenial and good-natured friend, sanguine and humorous, generous and even-tempered, but he could be grossly irresponsible in his relations with his wife and friends, and his publishing history is marred by several petty quarrels and failures to fulfill obligations. Fascinated by speculative schemes of all sorts, he never held onto money once he had it, going bankrupt once and resorting to a variety of expedients for living cheaply all his life. His sincere desire to follow scientific methodology was at times coupled with assertions of blatant prejudice. His great work on London labor and poverty is remarkable for his tolerance for the outcasts of his society—yet when one reads his travel and boys' books one is sometimes overwhelmed by their narrowmindedness and their ignorant and aggressive John Bullism.

These contradictions are all part of the duality in Mayhew's life and work stemming from his uncertain rebellion against the complacent values of middle-class Victorian England, especially as these attitudes were represented by his father. Mayhew's resistance was never absolute, and the tension in him between acceptance and denial of his society's values consistently aborted his talent and frustrated his achievements. Only in one endeavor—his surveys of the working poor of London—did he find a means by which these contradictory drives actually became an advantage.

Mayhew was born 25 November 1812, the fourth son of a successful solicitor (in the firm Mayhew, Johnston, and Mayhew of Carey Street), a headstrong and autocratic man who fathered seventeen children.[2] Joshua Dorset Joseph Mayhew is almost a caricature of the traditional Victorian paterfamilias in both his behavior and his relationship with his son Henry. He required all his sons (Thomas, Edward, Alfred, Henry, Horace, Julius, and Augustus) to address him as Sir and to remain standing until he gave them permission to sit. While loving lavish display, he was obsessive about saving shillings. At his townhouse in London at 16 Fitzroy Square, his servants included a coachman, footman, and page; but he saved pennies by buying umbrellas by the gross and soda by the hundredweight. Nor was he above haggling over pennies. Sutherland Edwards, a friend of the Mayhew brothers, recalls of their father that "having business sometimes to transact at a neighboring police court, he had the distance measured from the court to the square in which he lived. Reckoning from some particular point it was just one mile. But the cabman who drove him to the court thought it was more than a mile; upon which Mr. Mayhew paid for two miles, summoned the cabman, and obtained judgment for eightpence with costs. . . . At last the cabmen in the neighborhood got to know him, and seeing him approach, drove away. Then he took the offender's number, proceeded against him for refusing a fare and re-covered as before."[3]

As this incident shows, Joshua was obstinate. Other anecdotes indi-cate he could become angry when he did not get his way. His wife's collection of jewelry was said to be the result of peace offerings which he made after severe outbursts of temper. (This is about all that is really known about her except that her maiden name was Mary Ann Fenn, that she was married in 1806, and that she died at the age of forty-five.) No such peace offerings are recorded for his sons, however. Instead, if any of them returned home after midnight, he would find the house locked. The furious Joshua would throw down a shilling from an upper window, telling the offender to "go and get yourself a bed somewhere else."[4]

At twenty-one years of age each son was given an allowance of £1 a week and was expected to make his way in the world. (Joshua would sometimes also give them loans, for which he charged interest.) The father seemed to permit his sons some flexibility in their choice of careers: he sent Henry to sea as a midshipman and Alfred to India for a while with the East India Company. The limits of his tolerance were evident in an early clash with Henry, who as a boy wanted to be a research chemist, an inclination which had a crucial influence on his later work on poverty. When he told his father of this desire, Joshua simply offered to apprentice him to his apothecary. Henry was stub-born, keeping his pound a week allowance but spending half of it on chemical apparatus and books. In this he showed determination if not the energy to break completely with his father.

In actuality Joshua wanted all his sons to be solicitors like himself. He had followed his own father's bidding in his choice of a career, and to him it must have seemed reasonable to expect his progeny to do the same. Later Henry recalled that his father, "who thought law was the finest thing in the world," talked to him when a quick schoolboy about how grand it would be to be the lord chancellor of England, an ambi-tion he actually held for Henry—or so his son later remembered.[5]

Despite the fact that Joshua apprenticed each of his sons to himself and charged the cost against their portions of his estate, only one son, Alfred, actually fulfilled his father's desires by becoming a solicitor, and he received the lion's share of his father's estate as a reward. The other sons abandoned their father's offices mostly for journalism. Thomas, the eldest, was associated with the radical press; he was editor of Henry Hetherington's *Penny Papers* and also of the first issues of the *Poor Man's Guardian*.[6] At the time of the Reform Bill, the government reputedly offered £100 for his apprehension.[7] The second brother, Edward, was connected with the theater and wrote as a fine arts critic for the *Morning Post*. At about the age of thirty-five he became a veterinary surgeon and wrote two books on veterinary science, *The Dog* and *The Diseases of the Horse*. Alfred, the dutiful son, and Henry, the family disgrace, were the third and fourth sons. Horace, six years younger than Henry, was a comic journalist, and he remained an intimate of the *Punch* table long after Henry had drifted away. Julius, the penultimate son, was a failure at everything he tried, including art and photography. Later, after his father's death left him independently wealthy, he reputedly married his cook. Augustus, the youngest, was the closest in temperament to Henry, and was his collaborator and friend. On various occasions they shared an exile in the country to avoid their creditors.

That so many of the Mayhew boys made their way as journalists implies that Joshua was not as big a tyrant as Dombey. Yet his sons frequently portrayed him as if he were. Henry and Augustus satirized him several times in their works. In 1848 they ironically dedicated to him the novel *Whom to Marry*, a work in which they portrayed a miserly character who measured the distance between two points in order to sue the cab driver if he overcharged (a detail which appeared again in the characterization of the villainous solicitor in the novel of the same year *The Image of his Father*) and who bought umbrellas by the gross. Henry's resentment was also enshrined in a long and sharply ironic poem written for the *Comic Almanac* in 1848. "A Highly Respectable Man" was uncompromising in its delineation of his father's character and overt in its disdain for his kind of "respectability." Two of the most telling stanzas are the fifth and tenth.

> It is said he's a tyrant at home,
>   That the jewels his Wife has for show,
>   Were all of them salves for some wound—

> That each diamond's heal'd up a blow;
> That his Children, on hearing his knock,
>   To the top of the house always ran—
> But with ten thousand pounds at his Banker's
>   He's *of course* a respectable Man.
> . . . .
> Then he makes a fresh will ev'ry quarter—
>   Or when he's a fit of "the blues"—
> Or his Wife has offended him somehow—
>   Or some Son will not follow his views;
> And he threatens to leave them all beggars,
>   Whene'er they come under his ban—
> He'll bequeath all his wealth to an Hospital,
>   Like a highly respectable Man.[8]

Mayhew senior had nonetheless a strong influence on his sons. Despite their rejection of the career he laid out for them, it was difficult, even impossible, for all of them to deny Joshua's sense of what was respectable and what was acceptable for men of their family and class. Thomas, the radical journalist, committed suicide in 1834 at the age of twenty-seven, apparently depressed by an anticipated bankruptcy caused by the failure of the Penny National Library. That such a young man who had deliberately chosen to ally himself with the working-class press would rather die than face bankruptcy parallels the mixture of social rebellion and conformity that will be characteristic of most of his brothers, particularly of Henry. Thomas's financial problems and their tragic outcome also foreshadowed the difficulties that Henry was to have twelve years later.

Henry's activities from the beginning had brought him into conflict with his father. He seemed unwilling to do as his father wanted but also unable to carry out his own plans completely, even as he lacked the staying power to educate himself as a scientist. At fifteen he disgraced the family by running away from Westminster School to evade what he considered an unjust flogging. As E. P. Thompson points out, the story of this incident, retold in a history of the school, demonstrates both Mayhew's "indolence and his capacity for concentration."[9] It is also the first example of the way he could ruin an impressive achievement by acting on a minor scruple, almost as though the energy he exerted in excelling as expected of him deserted him immediately on achieving his goal. Mayhew had moved from the bottom to the head of the list of candidates in the Latin challenge in a matter of two days. He ran away (apparently ending his formal schooling) to avoid a flogging to be administered for his failure to do some Greek lines at the same time.

Henry's father was willing to give him another chance, and it was at this point that he sent him to India as a midshipman. That did not work either for reasons which are not known. Once again in London in the early 1830s, Henry worked as an apprentice for his father for awhile, but this time his "career" apparently ended in a notable disaster. While working in the paternal office, Henry, either through sheer fecklessness or an unconscious expression of hostility, neglected to file some important papers. According to Sutherland Edwards, the family was interrupted at dinner that night by a bailiff, who had come to arrest Joshua as a result of Henry's forgetfulness. There could not have been a more humiliating blow for a son to level at Joshua. The resulting scene was predictable. Henry rose from the table and soon left the house and apparently did not see his father again for several years.[10]

However strained his relations with his father were at this time, Henry apparently did not lose his pound a week allowance, and by the mid-1830s he seemed reconciled to his family. Indeed the next decade was to be a pleasant one for Henry Mayhew. Cares and responsibilities rest lightly on most young men in their twenties, and on Henry Mayhew they were light indeed. He divided his attention between scientific experiments (in one of which he nearly demolished the kitchen of his brother's house) and the bohemian world of comic journalists, dramatists, and Grub Street hacks. The divergent directions of his energies at this time, in addition to providing a joke or two for his friends ("Literary or scientific today?" they would call from downstairs before venturing a visit to the laboratory above[11]) typify Mayhew's characteristic combination of serious intellectual intentions and of commonplace and even trivial activities.

Though his chemical experiments appear never to have come to anything apart from his claim to have discovered a strong dye similar to aniline dyes,[12] his adventures in middle-class bohemia were more fruitful. His friendships with the journalists and dramatists of the 1830s brought him into contact with some of the best literary talents of the age, including Thackeray, Dickens, and Douglas Jerrold. This group of humorous and devil-may-care wits formed numerous clubs for socializing, the most famous of them being The Rationals, founded in the late 1830s. Meeting in taverns over tobacco and punch, they hatched publishing schemes of all sorts and wrote verses satirical of their friends as well as farces and burlettas. In the last activities Mayhew joined with Mark Lemon and Henry Baylis and perhaps others.[13] At times contributing to established journals, they also founded newspapers and periodicals, some with as little capital as £5. The names of these early magazines, such as the *Censor* and the *Thief*, reflect their popular combination of triviality, wit, and seriousness, while their contents mixed middle-class conservatism and liberal political sentiments. Mayhew and his friends insisted on the need for reform in many areas of life—in factories, in schools, in prisons, and in "the hearts of men," but they did not countenance radical changes and never strayed far from the center. They had little if any connection with working men's groups despite the example of Mayhew's older brother Thomas. The Chartists made them uncomfortable.[14] Though most of these journals were short-lived, Gilbert à Beckett and Mayhew were fairly successful with *Figaro in London*. It appeared regularly for eight years on the strength of good dramatic criticism, a political cartoon every week (some by Seymour and some by Cruikshank) and political commentary. Mayhew edited this journal from 1835 through August 1839.[15]

Punch, founded in 1841, was the culmination of all their comic journalistic efforts. Cautious in its criticism but supporting most reform, comic and facetious but also serious in its social satire, it was the most prominent landmark of Mayhew's early career. By most accounts the project was his idea.[16] At first the magazine was a joint effort of a small group: Mark Lemon, Stirling Coyne, and Mayhew (the original three proprietors) with Douglas Jerrold, Thackeray, à Beckett and others as contributors. Mayhew is credited by some historians of the journal for insisting that the satire not be personal nor scurrilous, that the humor be "kindly" and the political positions without regard to party. After a transfer of ownership of the magazine in 1842, however, Mayhew was eased out of the editorship; and though he continued to make suggestions for articles and cartoons for several years, he ceased to have any direct say in the running of the journal. M. H. Spielmann said Mayhew's last contribution was in 1845. His failure to stay with the project beyond its early years is another example of the pattern which asserted itself throughout his career: personal success followed by some kind of incident or conflict which led him, usually suddenly, to abandon the project.

While Mayhew was actively involved with *Punch* he was reputed to have contributed one of the magazine's most famous jokes: "Worthy of Attention. Advice to Persons about to Marry,—Don't." Written a year after his marriage in 1844 to Jane Jerrold, oldest daughter of Douglas Jerrold, this old saw might have provided a warning for Jane. So might the satirical poem Henry Baylis wrote for Jerrold on the announcement of the marriage which began "What a jolly fine thing to be father-in-law / To a blasted philosopher not worth a straw."[17]

Mayhew probably had met Jerrold in Paris in early 1835.[18] Mayhew, aged twenty-three, may have been abroad to live cheaply and to evade his father's displeasure. Jerrold, aged thirty-two, with his wife and daughter Jane, then ten years old, was avoiding arrest in consequence of a lawsuit.[19] Their convivial association in the following months also included Thackeray, studying art, and John Barnett, a minor English composer who had been Mayhew's music instructor. At their first meeting (according to Athol, Mayhew's son) the older writer feared that Henry was representing his father, the solicitor in charge of the case against him. Henry however indignantly denied having any connection with the law, and he offered to act as a go-between for Jerrold and Joshua, indicating that the quarrel with his father was not completely acrimonious at this point. The negotiation was successful, and to this Athol attributed the friendship between the two men.

In the late 1830s Mayhew and Jerrold renewed their friendship in London, where they were joined again by Thackeray. Out of this close association grew Mayhew's attachment to Jerrold's oldest daughter. The marriage occurred after the founding of *Punch* and on the crest of Mayhew's expectations, but it was followed in less than three years by the disgrace of his bankruptcy. Jane then returned to her father for a stay in the Channel Islands, where she was apparently so ill that Jerrold later declared: "She had made 'a runaway knock at death's door!'"[20]

Mayhew's bankruptcy in 1847 grew out of his attempt to capitalize on the railroad mania with a newspaper entitled the *Iron Times*. During the years 1844–1847, over nine thousand miles of new railways had been authorized by the government. Ever willing to exploit the issue of the moment, Mayhew joined with Thomas Lyttleton Holt, part proprietor of the earlier Mayhew journal *Figaro in London* and one of the most prolific of popular publishers, to found a daily journal full of railway news and gossip. What seemed a good speculation in the event turned out to be too late to take advantage of the boom. Indeed the *Iron Times*'s failure in mid-1846 foreshadowed the devastating bank failures a year later, which were partially caused by the excessive speculation in railways and which ushered in the panic of 1847.

Holt himself went bankrupt in 1846,[21] and Mayhew was to follow him shortly. On a salary of approximately £300 a year he had bought a new house in Parson's Green for his bride, and had accumulated debts totalling £2000. Called The Shrubbery, and lavishly furnished in the style of his father, it was his first and last effort at this kind of respectable establishment. When the *Iron Times* failed, Mayhew's unpaid bills forced him into bankruptcy. He just missed going to prison because the bankruptcy laws had been recently changed to allow private debtors to go into bankruptcy.

Though Mayhew bounced back quickly, writing novels[22] and launching into his major work two years later, the humiliation of his having appeared in the *Gazette* poisoned the relations between him and his father for the rest of the latter's life. Joshua died in 1858 at the age of seventy-nine with his anger enshrined in his thirty-three page will which meted out rewards and punishments to his heirs. The ne'er-do-well Julius, as well as Horace, received good settlements with few restrictions. According to tradition Julius had maintained his father's goodwill by being home by eleven at night; and Horace, by paying his father interest on even the most trifling loans.[23] Henry, however, was excluded from the paternal largesse. Out of the £50,000 estate he received £1 a week for personal maintenance, support, and clothing, to be forfeited if he were to use it for anything else or to anticipate it, or if he ever were bankrupt again. His wife received a separate sum of £2 a week for herself and her children. Finally all the money which the elder Mayhew had given for support of Henry's two children was to be considered a debt to be charged at 5 percent interest. Joshua's justification for this disinheritance contained implicit reference to the bankrupty: "To my son Henry I cannot make any personal bequest because he cannot possess any property to his own use."

Though the bankruptcy was a severe blow to his father and though in much of his behavior as a young man Henry Mayhew seemed to rebel against his father's bourgeois response to life, the son also frequently accepted and even glorified some of the very attitudes and values that he at times appeared to oppose. He was never able to assume a consistent position as a rebel against bourgeois values nor on the other hand to become their unqualified advocate.

This aspect of Mayhew is exemplified by a startling anecdote of a scene between himself and his father in the mid-1850s when Henry was a successful journalist in his mid-forties. He and some friends organized a combination lecture and comic recitation which exploited *London Labour and the London Poor*. Henry spoke about his work and imitated various London street-sellers. James Hatton accompanied him on the piano and sang comic songs. The performance was given with some success in London at St. Martin's Hall on 27 June 1857. (Some version of it may have been performed two months earlier at Brighton.) The success in London tempted an expansion of the project, and Thomas Willert Beale arranged a tour of three months in the provinces. On the first night the show played in Brighton, Mayhew was struck dumb almost at the start of the performance by the sight of his sternly disapproving father sitting in the front row.[24]

Even though he knew that his friends would be damaged by the failure of the project, Henry left the stage immediately. According to George Hodder, Joshua then "made such a solemn appeal to [Henry] as to his compromising the respectability of his family by continuing so 'degrading' a pursuit, that he determined to abandon it" (p. 213). After this incident he left Brighton the same night, and his partners had to make excuses to the entrepreneurs in London who had backed the project. Mayhew himself apparently never apologized nor referred to the event at all. Though generally resisting his father's way of life, he was nonetheless vulnerable to Joshua's appeal to conventional respectability.

The tensions resulting from these conflicting responses might account for his repeated pattern of success followed by a seemingly self-induced failure. In trying to maintain two positions at once, those of rebellion and respectability, Henry Mayhew made it difficult for himself to finish anything significant since completing a project often necessitated taking a final position.

His contemporaries recognized this duality in him. Henry Vizetelly said Mayhew "would scheme and ponder all the day long, but he abominated the labour of putting his ideas into tangible shape."[25] He was "a genius, a fascinating companion, and a man of inexhaustible resource and humour," M. H. Spielmann wrote, but "indolence was his besetting sin, and his will was untutored."[26]

Most of Mayhew's works exhibit the results of these contrary tendencies. Many things he undertook—his works on education, his surveys of labor and the poor, his children's books—were intended as innovative approaches to major Victorian concerns. Yet each of these works, as well as all his deliberately trivial novels and travel books, was also designed to exploit trends and popular taste. As John Bradley expresses it, Mayhew's work shows "his extraordinary awareness of the needs of his readers, an awareness he exploited in his writings from one decade to the next."[27]

With the exception of his social surveys Mayhew never approached his topics rigorously. He took no part in the serious intellectual life of his time; he was not even a member of the Statistical Society. He generally opted to write on "serious" topics in the simplified form of children's books or popularized cheap pamphlets. Such forms not only had the potential of making money, but they also did not necessitate that Mayhew engage in consistent intellectual application.

His early works on education prove one of the first examples of the resulting mixture of sound intelligence and uncritical acceptance of old platitudes. The first, *What to Teach and How to Teach It: so that the*

Child may become a Wise and Good Man (published in 1842 and dedicated to Mark Lemon), was issued in a one shilling edition and written simplistically. Nonetheless it appears to have been intended as a serious effort to reform Victorian educational principles. Its sequel, *The Prince of Wales's Library* (1844), supposedly a practical application of the principles in *What To Teach*, is, as Bradley says, only "a characteristic early Victorian manual of instruction,"[28] with a heavy stress on conventional moralism. *What to Teach* itself was also uneven in the soundness of its argument, most of which Mayhew said he drew from some lectures entitled the "Philosophy of the Human Mind" by a Dr. Brown. At the same time Mayhew's own criticism of Victorian education grew out of his own experiences. At Westminster School, he later said, "we were not even taught our own language, nor even writing nor reckoning, but bored to death simply with the dead tongues . . . we were sent into the world to get our living out of the elements by which we were surrounded . . . in the same beastly ignorance as any Carib—not only of the physical world about us, but of our own natures and our fellow-creatures, as well as of all that was right, true, beautiful, or indeed noble in life."[29] In reaction to the impracticality of Victorian middle-class education, Mayhew suggested that the curriculum include science, history, and modern languages, and that students be educated in one specific area. He also examined ways to inculcate a love of learning for its own sake, the best way being, he thought, by practical experience and the encouragement of the emotion of wonder and curiosity. He accepted the utilitarian idea that pleasure was the sole motivation for men, but at the same time breezily asserted that what gave the most pleasure was giving pleasure to others. Sympathy, he asserted, was an instinct. *What to Teach* was thus a combination of some intelligent practical suggestions for reform of the current mode of education and conventional assertions.

1851, a novel that he wrote with George Cruikshank to exploit the interest in the Great Exhibition of Industry of All Nations, not only shows the same combination of intelligence and banality, but in comparison to Mayhew's articles on the exhibition for the *Edinburgh News* is also the clearest example of the intellectual flabbiness that his failure to reconcile the opposing impulses in himself could produce. The novel appeared at the time of the opening of the exhibition when Mayhew was writing a series of weekly reviews for the *Edinburgh News* on various parts of the exhibition. (Both these projects were aborted, apparently because Mayhew was ill.)

1851 recounted the comic misadventures of a couple of country cousins and their two children who "Came Up to London to 'Enjoy Themselves', and to See the Great Exhibition," in the words of the subtitle.[30] One part of the novel, however, deviated from the comic intention. Parts 5 and 6 (May and June) of *1851*, written roughly at the same time as the articles for the *Edinburgh News*, minimized the humor and instead turned to a discussion of the strengths and weaknesses of the exhibition, and most important the attitude of the lower classes toward it. After the June number this subdued note disappeared completely.

There were a good number of correspondences and even identical passages in these portions of *1851* and the articles in the *Edinburgh News*. There was also one striking difference in the treatment of the working class response to the exhibition. In the first weeks of its existence the exhibition had had relatively high admission prices. Not until May 26 were "shilling days" introduced Monday through Thursday to bring the exhibition within range of the pockets of the working classes. The sponsors of the exhibition were apparently disappointed by a drop in attendance on shilling days.[31]

Mayhew threw himself into the debate over why the working classes appeared to be staying away from the exhibition. On June 21 he wrote a piece about the question for the *Edinburgh News*, many paragraphs of which also appeared in the June number of *1851*.

In *1851* Mayhew theorized complacently that "the reason why the shilling folk absented themselves from the Great Exhibition at first was, because none of their class had seen it, and they had not yet heard of its wonders, one from another" (p. 155). The article in the *Edinburgh News*, on the other hand, reached a much different conclusion, one critical of the exhibition itself. The working classes kept away "simply because they have no faith in the Exhibition itself. It is *not* an Exhibition of the Works of Industry, say they, but the works of traders." And further: "Glance your eye through the whole catalogue and see if you can find in any place the mention of any one working man's name as having been even *partly* concerned with his employer in the production of the articles exhibited."[32] It is impossible to know whether Mayhew was simply adapting his conclusions to his audience, thus demonstrating a cavalier attitude toward the question, or whether he actually did not recognize the contradiction between two explanations which must have been written within weeks if not days of each other. In either case the disparate conclusions reflect Mayhew's ambivalent stances.

After *London Labour and the London Poor* Mayhew's work tended to lose this duality for the most part and to become outright propaganda for middle-class prejudices. In *The Upper Rhine* (1858), he trumpeted violent anti-Catholic sentiments and just as violent chauvinism about England: "Englishmen can say with justice that there is no nation, either past or present, which will, for a moment, admit of comparison with their own" (p. ix); or "British veins may be said to contain the essence, as it were, of all the noblest tribes the world ever saw" (pp. 351–352). Though in his boys' books of this period he displayed his familiarity with basic experimental science, Mayhew also demonstrated a paucity of innovative ideas. In *Young Benjamin Franklin* (1861), he preached living by the golden mean and passively accepting one's station in life because poverty and suffering were part of God's inscrutable plan for mankind. The theory of human personality which he advanced in this volume was based on the four humors.

Even though Mayhew's ambivalent responses to his society had negative effects on all his other works, in his great books on labor and the poor the result was almost entirely positive. On the one hand his rebelliousness and unconventionality permitted him to sympathize with his subjects and to encourage an unusual and productive relationship. At the same time the restraining influence of Victorian values provided a form of distancing and balance. Because the subjects of labor and the poor gave him an outlet for both sides of his personality, Mayhew's full energies were released in his social surveys.

The tensions took their toll even on these volumes. None of his social surveys were finished as projects, and they periodically displayed the intellectual laziness characteristic of his other work. Though he lavished almost pathological care in gathering and computing his statistics as well as in questioning his informants and reporting their responses, in reprintings of his work he never corrected mistakes, even those of which he was aware; and seldom did he make any effort to update material when he used it again in later years.

Apart from the role of Mayhew's ambivalent attitudes and the originality of his approach, the genesis of his surveys is of interest. Beginning with a journalistic project for the *Morning Chronicle* Mayhew set out to exploit the popular interests of the day. In the ten or so years preceding his first social survey, Victorian public opinion had been schooled to respond quickly to exposés of social conditions. The numerous parliamentary investigations into the condition of women and children in factories (1832), in mines (1842), and in potteries (1843) when published in their familiar blue covers had presented much information about the lives and working conditions of industrial workers to the public as had the reports on sanitary conditions by Dr. Kay Shuttleworth (*The Moral and Physical Condition of the Working Classes Employed in the Cotton Manufacture of Manchester*, 1832) and Edwin Chadwick (*An Inquiry into the Sanitary Condition of the Labouring Population of Great Britain*, 1842). In addition revelations which came out after 180 children died of cholera in the Tooting Infant Pauper Asylum in 1848–1849 stirred public concern about dirt and overcrowding in these institutions. As a result of all these developments and despite a fear and distrust of the Chartist movement (which had actually collapsed in 1848), there was a spirit of reform abroad in London in the months preceding the *Morning Chronicle* investigations.

As the major competitor to the *Times* the *Chronicle* had a large audience and good resources. From the paper's founding in the late eighteenth century it had had a list of impressive contributors: Hazlitt and Dickens had been parliamentary reporters, and J. S. Mill contributed a series of articles on the famine in Ireland between 1845 and 1847. In 1847 Sir John Eastlake, a supporter of Palmerston, sold the paper to a group of influential Peelites. John Douglas Cook, "a hard-headed Aberdonian,"[33] became editor. In the 1840s as the *Times* became more conservative, the rivalry between the two newspapers created a large audience for the *Chronicle*. Throughout this part of its history the *Morning Chronicle* was vigorous in support of various reforms, particularly those related to sanitation and health. In fact the immediate background of Mayhew's *Morning Chronicle* investigations was the concern over sanitary conditions in the slums which resulted from the cholera epidemic of 1848–1849.

Despite the potato famine in 1846–1848 in Ireland, the panic of 1847 in London, and the revolutions of 1848 in Paris and Vienna, a chief concern in England in 1849 was cholera. The first outbreak of this terrible disease, which attacked its victims suddenly and after a few days left them dead of vomiting and diarrhea, their bodies blue and wizened, was in Sunderland in October 1831. Within a year over 5000 Londoners had succumbed to the disease. The epidemic of 1848–1849 was much worse. From September 1848 to September 1849 some 14,000 people died in London alone, and probably 53,000 in the whole of England and Wales.[34] Furthermore it was clear to nearly everyone that the worst outbreaks were in the filthiest slums. At this time there was no real understanding of the way that the disease spread (by infected water) although many people believed it had something to do with bad vapors and that these vapors were linked somehow to the filth, overcrowding, and neglect in the slums.

In September 1849 Mayhew, who later said he undertook his initial investigation of Jacob's Island for the registrar general,[35] went to Bermondsey, the center of the leather industry and an area that had been hard hit by the cholera, for a firsthand report on Jacob's Island, a pesthole made infamous ten years earlier in *Oliver Twist*. The place had hardly changed since Dickens's famous exposé: Mayhew found the same rotting houses and the same filthy ditch. His report of this visit appeared in the *Morning Chronicle* on 24 September 1849. Soon afterward the cholera subsided, and Mayhew expanded his subsequent reports to cover much more than sanitary conditions.

By most accounts Mayhew's report on Jacob's Island was the genesis of the "Labour and the Poor" series. The editors of the *Chronicle* claimed in 1850 that Mayhew had had nothing whatsoever to do with formulating the plan for the series, but Mayhew himself stated that he had originated the idea for the "Labour and the Poor" project even before his trip to Bermondsey.[36] Whatever the truth, almost immediately after Mayhew's article on the slum appeared in the newspaper the *Morning Chronicle* announced the publication of an enormous three-part investigation into the condition of labor and the poor throughout England. Different correspondents were to report on various parts of the country. Provincial correspondents included Angus Reach, who wrote from the manufacturing districts; Alexander Mackay, from the rural districts, and later Charles Mackay, who surveyed Birmingham and Liverpool;[37] and Shirley Brooks, who picked up from Alexander Mackay when he left the *Morning Chronicle* staff.[38] Mayhew himself was the "metropolitan correspondent."

The London that he undertook to survey in 1849 was a city of stunning contrasts between rich and poor. Slums and elegant squares were frequently back to back; ironic juxtapositions, such as Tothill Fields prison (which Mayhew was to visit in March 1850 and again in 1856) being a stone's throw from the Royal Palace, were visible all over town. By 1849 the expression of these contrasts was a literary commonplace. The opposition between big houses for a single family and a single room for several families was particularly remarked, for one of the main evils of London was the overcrowding in lower-class neighborhoods. Not until the 1860s did workers' trains enable large numbers of lower-class men and women to move a distance from their employment. In 1849 workers had to live within walking distance of their jobs, and thus the densest and most miserably housed population in the metropolis was in the old parts of London where industry was centralized and buildings the most decrepit.

In addition, aggravating these conditions, the "rookery" of government regulations and separate and conflicting administrations made even the most elementary services to these neighborhoods very difficult. Collecting human waste in London, for example, until 1848 had been in the hands of eight independent commissioners of sewers. At that point, under the impetus of the indomitable Edwin Chadwick, the General Board of Health and the Metropolitan Commission of Sewers were established. These two bodies were unable to do much, however; and a central drainage system for London was not possible until 1855 when the Metropolitan Board of Works took over the project.

Servants comprised almost 20 percent of the metropolitan working population in 1851. The largest trades were the building, clothing and food workers.[39] Other skilled workers were mainly involved in traditional crafts such as furniture-making, precision instrument-making, printing, tanning, currying, engineering, and shipbuilding. Below the regularly employed was a large substratum of unskilled workers who lived hand-to-mouth, working on the docks, selling items in the streets, begging, cadging, and barely scraping together enough to live.

In 1849 workers in a number of these trades were facing a sharp drop in their wages. The causes were varied. Some occupations, like the Spitalfields handloom weaving, were obsolete; others, such as tailoring and furniture-making, were facing competition from large mass producers who had their goods worked up more cheaply by a process of subcontracting. A large influx of Irish had poured into London and other big towns following the famine years 1846–1848, and these workers sometimes undercut the wages of their English counterparts by agreeing to work for less. Nonetheless, "because of the enormous variety of trades and occupations practised in London, the impact of trade depression there was not as universally disastrous as it was in areas of less diversified employment."[40] Because of this very variety in London, however, the residents of the metropolis had a harder time comprehending the situation of the lower classes at any given moment than did the observer of the northern industrial towns. This partially explains why, after a decade of royal commissions, select committees, and harangues by ministers, doctors, and politicians, the readers of the *Morning Chronicle* responded to Mayhew's revelations, many of which were not new, as if he had told them something they had never known. He was the first to succeed in bringing the condition of the metropolitan workers into focus for the rest of the urban population.

Mayhew's year at the *Morning Chronicle* was probably the best in his life. His talents flourished and his energies found outlet without obstacle. Sutherland Edwards said that he was highly paid and that he "had an army of assistant writers, stenographers, and hansom cabmen constantly at his call" (p. 60). Public response was more than generous. Praise for his articles was almost universal, the conservative *Economist* being a persistent nay-sayer. The articles by the metropoli-

tan correspondent were not only lauded by the most established journals, clergymen, and philanthropists; but they were also praised by
those members of the working classes who read them, including some
of the most radical. In the same number of the *Red Republican* which
attacked an article in *Household Words* advocating education as a solution for working class grievances, the editor of the *Red Republican*,
Julian Harney, reprinted excerpts from Mayhew's articles, continuing
to do so through the year-long duration of the journal. G.W.M.
Reynolds followed a similar practice in his *Political Instructor* in
1849–1850. Individual readers sent so much money into the *Chronicle*
office that a special "Labour and the Poor" fund was incorporated, containing at one point as much as £869 for the relief of the poor. Most of
this money was earmarked for specific hardship cases interviewed by
Mayhew.[41]

The influence of Mayhew's letters was not limited to its strictly
charitable results. The metropolitan correspondent was soon in demand as a speaker at meetings of workers and benevolent societies. In
addition to meetings which he called himself, he also addressed independent groups of tailors and longshoremen and philanthropic middle-
class groups.

This public response to Mayhew's *Morning Chronicle* letters
reached its highpoint in December. In the next year interest lagged
and verbatim transcripts of the new session of Parliament in January
ate up the pages. By April 1850 Mayhew's letters, which had been
published three times a week, were now appearing only once a week.
Finally in December 1850 they stopped altogether, although the series
on the rural districts and manufacturing cities continued for a number
of months.

At exactly which point Mayhew's written contributions ceased is a
puzzle. According to him he was no longer employed by the *Chronicle*
by 4 October 1850, even though ten letters from the metropolitan correspondent were published after that date. Since two of these were
later reprinted in *London Labour* and since he seems to have kept at
least four letters ahead, some contributions from him were clearly published in the period after he left the paper. He claimed to have refused
to do two articles on metal workers which in early October the editor of

the *Chronicle* had suggested as his final contribution, but a little over two weeks afterward the metropolitan correspondent contributed a new series on dressmakers followed by ones on hatters and the London markets, one of which Mayhew later in *London Labour* claimed as his. This last survey dwindled away and finally stopped in late December 1850 without editorial explanation.

The break between Mayhew and the *Chronicle* was marked by bitter exchanges on both sides. As early as February 1850 Mayhew expressed annoyance about alterations which he contended weakened statements attacking free trade made by bootmakers, traditionally one of the most politically conscious trades in London. This disagreement flared up again some four months later in Mayhew's investigation of the timber trade. In this case the editors systematically removed every reference to the adverse effects of free trade on wages.[42]

For their part the editors of the *Chronicle* admitted some censorship, claiming it was normal editorial practice. The remarks which they had cut out were "neither more nor less than the hacknied common-place about the 'untaxed' foreigner, which the journeyman bootmaker probably learnt from one of Mr. G. F. Young's speeches." Furthermore, "our Special Correspondents were distinctly instructed to confine themselves as much to facts, and not to trouble themselves about opinions or inferences" (31 October 1850).[43]

The quarrel between Mayhew and the *Chronicle* editors burst into the open over a matter unrelated to free trade and censorship, however. Beginning in September 1850, a full one-column advertisement appeared on the first page of the *Morning Chronicle* for Messrs. H. J. & D. Nicholl, on Regent Street, a very large firm of ready-to-wear tailors making a popular paletôt coat, who had periodically placed smaller advertisements in the *Morning Chronicle* during the preceding year. Since Mayhew never used names of firms in his articles, readers of the *Chronicle* could not know if Nicholl employed exploited labor or not. The firm did use the "contract" system which Mayhew had roundly denounced, and in a March 1850 meeting of metropolitan tailors reported in the *Chronicle* on the 29th, the Nicholls were attacked specifically. Within weeks after this firm had placed its first costly advertisement, a long laudatory article on the firm and on the "contract" system of labor appeared in the *Morning Chronicle* under the general title of "Exhibitors at the Great Exhibition."[44] Mayhew may have already severed his connection with the paper at this point, but he still took this praise of the Nicholls as a personal affront.

Upon seeing the article, he later claimed, he "wrote to the editor, stating that as he, Mr. Mayhew, was generally known to be the author of the letters on the subject of the 'Labour and the Poor of the Metropolis,' he would feel obliged by his stating in the *Chronicle* that he was not the writer of the article alluded to. To this request the editor's answer was 'No!'"[45] Following this refusal Mayhew made public both his grievances against the *Chronicle* editors and his feelings about Nicholl at a meeting of London tailors. A few days later the editors of the *Chronicle* denied all the charges that he made against them, although they did not try to refute Mayhew's point-by-point attack on Nicholl and on the contract system in general.

The controversy which followed led to vicious attacks on Mayhew by the *Economist* and by his old colleague at the *Chronicle*, Angus Reach.[46] Mayhew was undaunted by these assaults. He answered the charges in the *Economist* with a letter to that journal (21 December 1850), but he then turned to his new project, an independent weekly publication called *London Labour and the London Poor*, priced at two pence.[47]

After such a brilliant beginning for Mayhew as the *Morning Chronicle*'s metropolitan correspondent, the end of the story is disappointing and frustrating. No matter how one sifts the evidence one cannot help but sense that in the summer of 1850 Mayhew had finished the project and was seeking an excuse to quit. In the story of his various quarrels with the editors of the *Morning Chronicle*, there is a pettiness— admittedly on both sides—that jars with the magnanimity and humanity of the metropolitan correspondent's normal stance. He may have simply become tired; the demands on his time and physical energy had been enormous for almost a year. Perhaps the free and easy bohemian who chafed at school and at parental authority could no longer brook the probably heavy-handed editorial control of the newspaper. Probably it was a combination of these factors which made Mayhew take affront at the conflicts between himself and the editors. It is also possible that he may have had his eye on the main chance and may have wanted to capitalize on the reputation that he had made at the *Chronicle* by striking out on his own. James Grant, an early historian of London, noted the desire of many authors in the 1830s to publish their own books after they had become known to the public in order to reap higher profits.[48]

Since it meant financial insecurity for his wife, the collapse of Mayhew's work at the *Morning Chronicle* could also have been the cause of the final break with his old friend and father-in-law Douglas Jerrold which occurred at this time. In early 1850 Jerrold wrote to an American correspondent that Mayhew "will cut his name deep. From these things [the *Chronicle* letters] I have still great hope." Yet even this praise was ambiguous, for the "still" might suggest that Jerrold had all but lost his hope that Mayhew would amount to anything. Only a few months later Jerrold was writing to John Forster that he must come to London *"in re* Mayhew, whom God make wiser!" Two weeks later he wrote again to Forster, saying that he would not come to London again: "sons and son-in-law have finished me."[49] At the time of Jerrold's death in 1857 the two were completely estranged. Asked on his deathbed by Horace Mayhew if he were friends with H——, "referring to an estrangement that existed between him and a relative," Jerrold said yes.[50] His son-in-law, though present at the funeral, was not one of the pallbearers, even though Horace and a number of Henry's former friends were. Mayhew later wrote an article in praise of Jerrold, which was quoted at length by one of Jerrold's subsequent biographers but which seems to have disappeared.[51]

The quarrel between Mayhew and Jerrold must also have affected Jane Mayhew, although few details of her relationship with her husband are known. There seem to have been a number of separations, none of them proving permanent until sometime after the late 1860s. We do get one indirect glimpse of her long-suffering patience in the years of the *Morning Chronicle* in "Our Pet Thief," a quasi-humorous piece in the *Comic Almanac*. Appearing in 1851, during Henry's editorship of the magazine and surely written by him, it recounted, from his wife's point of view, the domestic disappointments and disasters that resulted when Mayhew brought into his home a lad who had changed some money for him in a poor lodging house. (The story is told in Letter V.) The moral was "that the bosom of a quiet family is not exactly the place in which to foster and reclaim a London pickpocket."[52]

Though life with Mayhew could never have been easy for Jane, by all accounts she was devoted to him. She bore him two children, a daughter, Amy, and a son, Athol. She took care of his mail (the legend is that he never opened a letter), and settled his accounts with his perennial creditors as best she could. As he acknowledged in an appreciative but condescending dedication to her in *German Life and Manners*, she also acted as amanuensis for his books. "Many a time, too, when on completion of one of our books, you have played over the drawing-out of the title-page, and laughingly wished to know whether 'our *joint* names' were to be inscribed thereon, I have felt at once the justice and the impudence of the joke; and would willingly have acknowledged the partnership had I not so long traded on a different footing—without the public having a suspicion that there was so much as a 'sleeping member' in the firm" (1:IV).

Jane and the children accompanied Mayhew on at least one of his later retreats to Germany[53] to live cheaply, and the glimpses that one gets of the Mayhew family life in Saxony in the early 1860s are warm-hearted and affectionate. Nonetheless Mayhew's final years brought a more or less permanent if friendly separation. His granddaughter remembered his weekly Sunday dinner visits to her house, where her grandmother lived, as happy occasions;[54] but Mayhew was not at his wife's deathbed, and her tombstone announced her as the daughter of Douglas Jerrold. There was no mention of her husband.

Before this sad end, however, Mayhew had yet to write his second major work, *London Labour and the London Poor*. Certainly there is no evidence that the energy Mayhew poured in "Labour and the Poor" had been dissipated in 1851. While launching *London Labour* he also edited the *Comic Almanac* and contributed an article composed from rehashed *Morning Chronicle* material to *Meliora*, Viscount Ingestre's anthology for the Society for Improving the Dwellings of the Working Classes (1851). He and Gus planned a sequel to *The Greatest Plague in Life—The Shabby Fammerly*—which apparently never got beyond the advertisement on the wrappers of *London Labour*. He also started the simultaneous projects connected with the Great Exhibition of Industry of All Nations.

Mayhew's main effort at this time, however, was the series which eventually became *London Labour and the London Poor*. In this venture he displayed the same combination of energy, determination, intelligence, and plain foolishness as he did in the *Chronicle* series. Mayhew started this new project with a survey of London's costermongers, and in the beginning the new publication ran smoothly. After his disagreements with the *Chronicle* editors, he probably enjoyed the power of having all the decisions in his own hands. Little capital was needed for this type of weekly publication; the income on one issue paid for the next and "unsold weekly parts could be stitched together to be offered as monthly parts, then bound and sold as a normal volume."[55] His reputation as the metropolitan correspondent gave him an immediate audience, though the price of the weekly parts indicates he did not plan to expand his public to the working classes.[56] An American edition of the 1851 numbers, however, shows that Mayhew's reputation extended beyond English shores. The weekly circulation in England, while quite high, never reached the level of the popular monthly publications of Dickens and others. According to the lawsuit between Mayhew and Woodfall, *London Labour and the London Poor* sold around 13,000 copies weekly. Reynolds's *Mysteries of London* and the fifteenth number of the *Pickwick Papers* both reached circulations of nearly 40,000.[57]

London Labour and the London Poor was prospering and held the opportunity for even greater success when it foundered in consequence of what seems to have been a minor scruple of Mayhew's. The publication stopped in midsentence in late February 1852. Mayhew's financial problems had again reached the law courts. The case was almost unbelievably petty. Under the terms of his contract with Mayhew, the printer of *London Labour*, George Woodfall, was to be paid after all the other bills and set office expenses, including salaries for Mayhew and John Howden, the publisher, had been paid. In March 1851 Woodfall filed a suit in chancery demanding that Mayhew and Howden be prevented from selling any more numbers of *London Labour and the*

London Poor on the grounds that this contract had been violated. The conflict was as complicated as the sums were small—in one case a matter of an unauthorized £1 a week raise for Howden. Woodfall seems to have made several attempts at a settlement, but Mayhew either refused or neglected to cooperate. Even though four years later Mayhew claimed that "the interruption in the publication arose from matters over which he had no control,"[58] his behavior here, as in his bankruptcy five years previously, seemed to be a case of deliberate self-delusion. Not only did Mayhew not respond to Woodfall's attempts at a settlement, but he also did not contest the law suit, thereby assuring the death of *London Labour and the London Poor*.

It is impossible to know exactly why Mayhew allowed *London Labour* to abort in this way when it seems that with a little effort he might have saved it. The sad story of the end of *London Labour and the London Poor* is only the most dramatic of the apparently self-induced abortions of his work, and the one most frustrating because the work promised so much. As in the *Morning Chronicle* affair, perhaps he was tired of the project, for potentially even more exhausting than the research itself were the psychological tensions released in him by his survey of the street folk. As will be seen, Mayhew had a tendency to identify himself with these subjects—the down and out, the antisocial, the arrogantly rebellious—and at the same time to resist the identification. With this kind of internal conflict, his daily encounters with the cadgers, the wanderers, and the poor could have taken a toll on his emotional energies that made him unconsciously relieved to find a means to end the whole endeavor. It could also explain why he never made a serious effort to finish the project. The one volume of bound-up parts and the weekly parts of volume 2 plus a few new interviews in 1856 were destined to be the end of *London Labour and the London Poor*.

One loses sight of Mayhew in the years between 1852 and 1854. It was a period of apparent inactivity and retrenchment. In 1853 he surfaced in the agitation to have the Crystal Palace opened on Sunday so the working classes could visit it.[59] He was probably out of England in 1855 when the issue reached its height with the riots against the sabbatarians. The preface to his children's book *The Wonders of Science* (a biography of Sir Humphry Davy) is dated 25 November 1854 in Bonn, Germany, where he was probably trying to live cheaply. The book itself was published in 1855. Internal dates of his two travel books on Germany (*The Rhine and Its Picturesque Scenery*, 1856, a descriptive volume, and *The Upper Rhine and Its Picturesque Scenery*, 1858, a collection of descriptions and evaluations of Germany), imply that Mayhew extended his stay in Germany through part of 1855. He probably returned to England in the last months of 1855. Although the letterhead of his stationery in 1856 carried the legend *Labor Vincit*, there is little evidence that Mayhew had much to show for his efforts from 1852 to 1855.

Shortly after his return, he revived his old connection with the publisher David Bogue,[60] making possible the last attempt to continue the work of *London Labour and the London Poor*. During the 1840s and 1850s Bogue had published many of the works by the Mayhew brothers, and this association probably led to the plan in March 1856 for Mayhew and Bogue to resume the *London Labour* project under the new format of "The Great World of London," a general survey of the city and its occupations. Despite the more general topic, after one and a half monthly numbers, Mayhew shifted to a detailed survey of the prisons of London. While Mayhew toured the prisons he and Bogue made additional publication plans. In March 1856 Mayhew announced that the old suit in chancery was in the process of settlement and that Bogue would soon reissue the first two volumes of *London Labour*. While he did not seem to want to take on any completely new survey of work or poverty, Mayhew was expanding his five *Chronicle* letters on street entertainers into a third volume to be issued at the same time. In September on the wrappers of the monthly part of "The Great World of London" he reported that volume 2 was in type and that a large part of the manuscript of volume 3 was in the printer's hands.

All these plans with Bogue were fully underway at the end of September 1856, and Mayhew's fortunes once again curved in the ascendant. As in the period 1849–1852 the more work he sought the more he found to do. The number of activities remind one of the exuberant days of his youth. He may have returned to the theater.[61] He also revived his convocations of lower-class people, holding a series of meetings with various criminal groups from March 1856 through February of 1857. His stated purpose in these meetings was to create an association to assist the men in reformation, but the notoriety associated with such gatherings was also a means of self-advertisement. In fact, according to Henry Vizetelly, who was an associate of Mayhew's at this time, one parolee warned his fellows that Mayhew's "object in calling us together is to sell his books!"[62]

Mayhew also returned to straight journalism at this time. He established some connection with the *Morning News*, a penny-daily offshoot of the *Morning Chronicle*, which began in March 1856 when the stamp tax was removed. In May 1856 Mayhew and Gus worked for the *Illustrated Times*, a newspaper begun in 1855 by Vizetelly. They covered the trial of Palmer, a notorious poisoner, becoming embroiled in an argument over some remarks Mayhew made about the frequency of poisoning.

In addition to the theater and reporting, his involvement in practical reform-movements resumed briefly. He addressed a committee favoring the abolition of capital punishment in July 1856; he was active in a group trying to set up a series of "concerts for the people" in September 1856.

Unfortunately Mayhew's revived fortunes suffered a reversal when his publisher Bogue died suddenly at the age of forty-four on 17 November 1856.[63] "The Great World of London" stopped in midsentence, probably in December. [64] The plans to finish and reissue *London Labour and the London Poor* succumbed with Bogue.

There is no evidence that Mayhew tried to find another publisher or to continue either "The Great World of London" or *London Labour*. Instead he became absorbed in other interests, none of which provided sufficient engagement for his energies or scope for his talents. One cannot escape the feeling that the end of "The Great World of London" was the death blow to Mayhew's intellectual and physical recuperative powers. His social surveys had called forth the best in him, and hereafter his works were desultory and jejeune efforts inspired by the need to make a living. In April 1857 he began another novel with Gus, *Paved with Gold*, but dropped out of the project after the first five numbers. At about the same time he began his series of lectures and dramatic readings which ended in the humiliating confrontation with his father at Brighton. In this context perhaps this final defeat by his father, who was to die shortly, was both a sign of Mayhew's enervation and a contributing factor to his inability to rally.

After this he picked up one thing and another, but nothing seems to have seriously engaged his interest. He edited the *Morning News* in January 1859, after which the paper folded. He wrote the most interesting of his boys' books, *Young Benjamin Franklin* (1861), in which he revealed his opinions about all kinds of topics from Dickens to Rembrandt in long footnotes. In 1861 Mayhew returned to Germany where he stayed for two or three years, trying, he said later, to complete the research for a book on Martin Luther.

At this time the publishing company of Griffin, Bohn undertook to finish and issue four volumes of *London Labour and the London Poor* as well as "The Great World of London," now called *The Criminal Prisons of London*, in book form in 1861–1862. When Mayhew's major work reached this "final" form, its impact had long since been dissipated, and little public notice of the volumes was evident. Nonetheless the 1861–1862 edition was successful enough to justify the publication by Griffin and Company of another edition of *London Labour* in 1865.[65]

Little survives to suggest what Mayhew was thinking and doing after 1863. All of his works of the 1860s and 1870s were weak, with little of the vitality and insight of his surveys of labor and the poor. During his time in Germany he converted his original project on Luther to a short moralistic book for children, *The Boyhood of Martin Luther* (1863). At this time he also produced his last travel book, *German Life and Manners as Seen in Saxony at the Present Day*. Back in London in 1865, almost as if to prove how completely he had repudiated his identification with the lower classes, he edited for a short time *The Shops and Companies of London*, a view of commerce from the employers' point of view, at times fulsomely laudatory. For this journal, modelled on a French publication *Les Grandes Usines de France*, Mayhew surveyed wide varieties of London businesses and industries that he had ignored in his earlier works, such as food manufacturers, engineering toolmakers, auctioneers, makers of musical instruments. His object was "not only to exalt work and manufacturing skill, but to uphold the dignity of Trade itself" (p. 3). While Mayhew had never downgraded work nor denied the importance of trade, it is disappointing to see with what enthusiasm he hobnobbed with the manufacturers (a real pleasure he said), and with what breezy indifference he treated the workers' conditions. He portrayed all the employers he interviewed as models, and he made no effort to check their stories against those of the workers at the factories. He merely mentioned in passing the poisoning that resulted from the leading of mirrors. In an establishment which made mourning clothes he said sanctimoniously that "we see no cause for the howl of sympathy of the Dressmakers' Association" (p. 220), a remark of astonishing condescension.

With the further passage of time, his career becomes very indistinct. Late in the 1860s Mayhew may have tried unsuccessfully to start a rival to *Punch*.[66] A letter shows he was living in London at 230 Regent Street in late 1867; in 1870 George Augustus Sala said that Henry and his son were correspondents covering the war between France and Prussia.[67] Bradley says that Mayhew also tried to "interest a publisher in the 'ghost-writing,' on behalf of a well-known trainer of horses, of a volume of equestrian lore"[68] in the early 1870s. Mayhew brought out the single issue of *Only once a Year*, a kind of popular annual, in 1870. Sometime in late 1870 or early 1871 he wrote a report for the licensed victuallers on unlicensed working men's clubs, and his perspective again was that of the established businessmen. In 1874 he contributed some rehashed material from the *Chronicle* and *London Labour* to a second edition of *London Characters*, a potpourri of sketches by different hands with illustrations by W. S. Gilbert.[69] In the same year he and his son wrote *Mont Blanc*, a play "freely adapted from the popular Voyages de M. Perrichon," which failed miserably.[70] A letter requesting a duplicate reader's ticket for the British Museum dated 1878 shows that he was still actively working at that date, but nothing remains to tell us what he was working on.

Mayhew's last years were probably solitary and sad. His obituary in the *Illustrated London News* noted that he "moved in a rather small circle."[71] Despite his conviviality and his earlier friendships with many of the wittiest and most charming talents of his age, his life after

1856 seemed to be a shedding of responsibilities, of old ties, of opportunities and possibilities, even finally of his own talent and genius for social observation. Accounts of Mayhew in his later years give evidence of his continued good humor and sanguine temperament, but it is hard not to think of him as a disappointed man.

Mayhew died of bronchitis on 25 July 1887 at the age of seventy-four in London. Only his son-in-law Phillip Allen was present; his son Athol may have been out of the country. He was buried at Kensal Green, leaving no will. His effects were not administered for another ten years when Athol received £90 10s. At the time of his death, Mayhew was almost completely forgotten. The *Times* gave him a one-paragraph obituary, and even the most complete obituary, that of the *Illustrated London News*, was laconic in its praise: "If the author of 'London Labour and the London Poor' had died earlier, many people would have been present at his funeral. . . . As it was, those for whose cause he had valiantly contended seem to have forgotten him."

The neglect lasted well into the next century. V. S. Pritchett records a revival of interest in Mayhew in the 1930s,[72] but until the last decade any such revival has been very limited. In the early 1950s Peter Quennell brought out a three-volume series of selections from *London Labour* which sold well and introduced many new readers to Mayhew's work, but not until Bradley's selections in 1965 was there any attempt at serious discussion of Mayhew and his work. Over one hundred years passed before his four volumes on the street folk were reprinted in full. Even the London County Council waited until 1955 to honor Mayhew with a commemorative blue plaque at 55 Albany Street, the house where, living with his brother Alfred in the 1830s, he almost blew up the kitchen with a hydrogen-oxygen experiment. This plaque makes Mayhew's role in founding *Punch* his primary claim for recognition. As we shall see, there should be much more to his reputation than that.

The Metropolitan Correspondent

In 1849, the same year that Mayhew began his major work on labor and the poor, John R. McCulloch distinguished the role of the economist from that of the statistician in his *Principles of Political Economy*:

> The economist . . . takes the facts furnished by the researches of statists; and after comparing them with each other, and with those deduced from other sources, he applies himself to discover their relation and dependence. By patient induction, by carefully observing the circumstances attending the operation of particular principles, he discovers the effects of which they are really productive, and how far they are liable to be modified by the operation of other principles. It is thus that the various general laws which regulate and connect the apparently conflicting but really harmonious interests of every order in society, may be discovered, and established with all the certainty that belongs to conclusions derived from experience and observation.[1]

When Mayhew gave his own definition of his position as social investigator in 1851, he made the same distinction between the role of "statist" or collector of facts, which he was fulfilling at the time, and that of "economist" or theoretician, which he hoped to be in the not-distant future. "Mr. Mayhew is neither Chartist, Protectionist, Socialist, Communist, nor Co-operationist; but a mere collector of facts, endeavouring to discover the several phenomena of labour with a view of arriving ultimately at the laws and circumstances affecting, and controlling the operation and rewards of the labourer," he wrote.[2]

Juxtaposition of these two passages—one from a spokesman for the standard political economy of the Manchester school and the other from a journalist with a crusading reputation—reveals intentions in Mayhew's work on labor and the poor not immediately evident. He did not plan solely to write an exposé of bad living conditions or sweated labor. Instead he saw his work as a step-by-step "scientific" inquiry into the laws of political economy. Of course he had polemical purposes

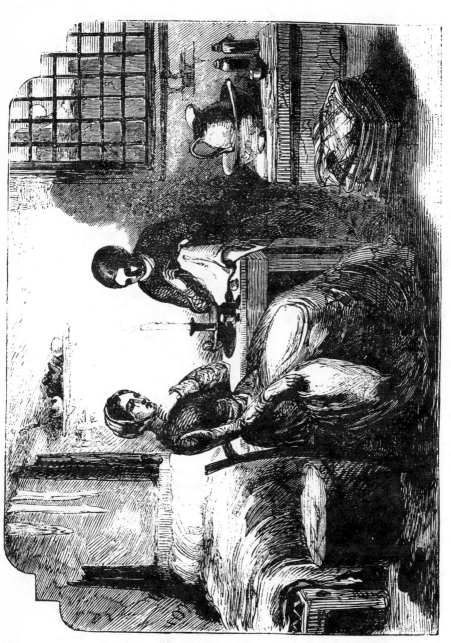

THE LABOUR QUESTION—NO. I: THE NEEDLEWOMEN OF LONDON

Mayhew's letters for the *Morning Chronicle* on "Labour and the Poor" were frequently excerpted in other news-papers. The *Penny Illustrated News*, one of the many short-lived journals for the lower classes, ran a four-part series of reprints in early 1850 accompanied by pictures, such as the above (5 January 1850), which illustrated a letter of as well. Continuing his description of his role in the same passage he stated that he also wanted to show "the importance of the poor and the working classes as members of the State." While propagandistic intentions were common enough among statisticians and economists of the period and did not necessarily taint the quality of the facts uncovered, the clear bias toward labor in this quotation separated Mayhew from other reformers and investigators of his class, and that bias points to what was special in his work.

Mayhew's intentions have been unclear to readers in later generations because in the event he did not fulfill his plan. Indeed he never got beyond the first stage, the collection of facts. Nonetheless it is crucial to remember what he hoped to do, for only with that in mind can we understand what he in fact did. Furthermore investigation of the way in which his interviews grew out of his search for "facts" and the manner in which this part of his "scientific" inquiry soon subsumed his larger intentions can clarify elements in Mayhew's puzzling personality as well as aspects of his investigations which have seemed confusing or contradictory.

The overall plan of "Labour and the Poor" as announced by the *Morning Chronicle* was not markedly innovative. The description could have prefaced many other Victorian social inquiries: "It is proposed to give a full and detailed description of the moral, intellectual, material, and physical condition of the industrial poor throughout England" (18 October 1849). The four areas of interest sketched by the editors in this opening editorial, and the order in which they were presented, showed the Victorian bias. The first concern was the "morals" of the working poor, the second their thoughts and ideas, the third their living conditions, and the fourth their health. The title of the series further demonstrated a disjunctive sense of the subject, for it was by no means clear if labor was to be considered equal to poverty or if there was any relationship between labor and poverty at all.[3] Angus Reach, the reporter from the manufacturing districts, tended to see two parts to the survey: the "labor" part—the type of work done—and the "poor" part, the living conditions of the workers. Mayhew sometimes seemed to suggest the same separation, but finally he came to realize that some types of work created their own living conditions—that poverty could grow out of work.

The information the *Chronicle* sought thus was a mixture of statistics, objective descriptions, and highly dubious evaluations of character. Such a mix mirrored the elastic notion of "facts" and the uncertain motivations for collecting them typical of the period. As Asa Briggs recently noted, not only did the early Victorian statisticians seek information about material progress, which usually could be quantified; but they also tried to solve problems which could never be reduced to numbers, such as the numerical relations of demography to social class, to economic structure, or to moral behavior. Many of these early statisticians, furthermore, "were anxious not merely to present information but to propound a message, sometimes a gospel."[4]

This statistical method developed largely in response to the spirit of reform of the early Victorian age. During the two decades before the series began, many legislators and practical reformers who wanted to begin the task of ameliorating the worst results of England's industrialization had been continually frustrated because of the lack of concrete data on which to formulate policy. In 1835 McCulloch, writing the "State and Defect of British Statistics," said: "There are no authentic accounts of the qualities and current prices of articles in any great market, the rent of houses and lodgings, the rate of wages in proportion to the work done, and a variety of particulars, indispensable to be known before any one can pretend to estimate the condition of the bulk of the people, or to compare their state at one period with their state at another."[5] In 1839, even Carlyle, who believed statistics could never provide an answer, admitted the problem: "A Legislature making laws for the Working Classes, in total uncertainty as to these things [facts about conditions] is legislating in the dark. . . . The simple fundamental question, Can the labouring man in this England of ours, who is willing to labour, find work, and subsistence by his work? is a matter of mere conjecture and assertion hitherto; not ascertainable by authentic evidence."[6]

To answer this strongly felt need, many new sources of statistical information opened up in the 1830s and early 1840s. G. R. Porter made public much data in the annual returns of prices, wages, and production which he published for the Board of Trade beginning in 1833. McCulloch himself gave many figures on trade and production when he edited the "Statistical Account of the British Empire" in 1837. The Statistical Society of London was founded in 1834 (the one in Manchester preceded it by one year), and from both poured numerous statistical articles on all manner of subjects from marriage to crime and education. The government itself also collected much material through the various parliamentary investigations and through royal commissions. The census was a source of statistics as well, though not until it came under William Farr's direction in 1851 was it very reliable.

Despite all the resulting statistical information from these official and private sources, there was still doubt in 1849 as to the actual condition of the working classes. (There is still debate about the subject today.[7]) The editorial in the *Morning Chronicle* announcing the "Labour and the Poor" series reflected this uncertainty openly: "In the course of our earnest endeavours to solve or settle the great social problems of our day, and to ascertain whether any (and what) legislative measures can be adopted to improve the moral and physical condition of the poor, we have been invariably stopped, embarrassed, thrown out, or compelled to pause and turn aside, by the want of trustworthy information as to the facts" (18 October 1849).

Even though the journalists had always been in the forefront of the investigation of urban life, that a newspaper should undertake a task that the government had found very difficult reflected both the energy and the naiveté of the period. The *London Times* had run a series on Ireland in 1845–1846 by sending special correspondents to the area, and a number of letters to the *Morning Chronicle* made a comparison between these two investigations. Mayhew's contributions to the *Chronicle* series were quite different from the *Times*'s reports, however, because Mayhew relied mainly on interviews with workers while the *Times*'s correspondents described what they saw narratively. Mayhew's contributions were more reflective of the methods of the parliamentary select committees than of any journalistic models, for these committees took direct testimony from individual workers as well as from doctors, ministers, managers, and district workers. On the other hand "Labour and the Poor" differed from the blue books, for the newspaper had to appeal to a popular audience and to keep it interested day after day. Its correspondents thus tried to combine the lightness, drama, and wit of the London journalists with the theoretically dispassionate presentation of information of the government investigations. Mayhew's first piece for the *Chronicle* which was directly related to the "Labour and the Poor" series, the article on Jacob's Island, was a good example of this mixture. He dramatized what he saw through dialogue and vivid description, but his purpose was the presentation of facts about housing and sanitary conditions, and so he tried to avoid personal judgments or evaluations. Even so, though his report from Bermondsey was effective both as journalism and as social investigation, he immediately abandoned its format in his following contributions in order to turn to a procedure which he considered more "scientific."

His mode of reporting was the result of his intentions for his investigations. In his role as metropolitan correspondent he wanted to find answers to two questions, one specific, one general. First, what was the condition in London in 1849 of the working classes in terms of the ratio of their wages and their expenses? And, second, what factors were responsible for this condition, both in specific trades and in general? Regarding the latter he was particularly interested to know how the repeal of the corn laws in 1846 had affected wages. Mayhew was not able to answer these questions definitively in his year's investigation because he was not able to collect enough information. His major achievement was to result from what was initially almost an afterthought: that, in addition to the statistics of wages and costs, he wanted also to report what individual members of the working classes thought were "the real or fancied wrongs of their lot."[8]

There was perhaps something deliberately provocative in Mayhew's decision to give voice to the opinions of the lower classes in this way, and the length of the interviews and the increasing amount of space that they absorbed in his reports reinforced his implication that these opinions were important, a feeling certainly not shared by the majority of his contemporaries. The editors of the *Morning Chronicle* later repudiated this aspect of his plan during the public part of their quarrel with Mayhew, but their rejection of its significance was shortsighted. The long interviews by which Mayhew sought to get these opinions were to be the most important contribution that he made to the social history of his time as well as the source of both his contemporary and his modern reputations.

Mayhew himself apparently did not consider these interviews unusual or of singular importance. Instead he justified them to his readers on the grounds of a more scientific methodology, by which he, like many Victorians, meant the inductive method. Almost from the very beginning of his official role as metropolitan correspondent, this "scientific" orientation of his reports was evident. He stated in a letter to the editors in February 1850: "I made up my mind to deal with human nature as a natural philosopher or a chemist deals with any material object; and, as a man who had devoted some little of his time to physical and metaphysical science, I must say I did most heartily rejoice that it should have been left to me to apply the laws of the inductive philosophy for the first time, I believe, in the world to the abstract questions of political economy."[9]

Mayhew's sense of the inductive process ultimately derived from his early enthusiasm for chemistry. Although when at first he tried to apply the process to social investigation, his procedure was vague, and the order in which he intended to set about the various parts of his investigations confused, the need to solve specific practical problems soon forced him to develop a more systematic procedure. His first formulation of method was that "it is my intention to visit the dwellings of the unrelieved poor—to ascertain, by positive inspection, the condition of their homes—to learn, by close communion with them, the real or fancied wrongs of their lot." He also planned to give "the weekly amount of income derived from each [group of poorly paid workers], together with the cause—if discoverable—of the inadequate return." Each of these generalizations would then be compared in "a catalogue of such occupations in London as yield a bare subsistence" (I, 19 October 1849).

As outlined in this order, Mayhew's method was a reasonable representation of the inductive method. However, when he announced this process to his readers in his first letter, he mentioned each of the three steps in the inverse order to that which I have given here, thus outlining a deductive process rather than an inductive one. At the beginning

Mayhew expected to be able to collect all the facts in advance and to draw all the conclusions before he wrote up his report. Of course this was impossible, and the actual form of the reports as well as the investigations themselves were inductively organized for the most part. Though he quickly realized his reports would have to be of "undigested facts," he continued throughout his work to hope that he would discover the "laws" which determined the condition of the lower classes.

Mayhew's "scientific" conception of the "Labour and the Poor" project provides one answer to the question of how a ne'er-do-well middle-class bohemian, who had very little to his exclusive credit by the age of thirty-six, suddenly became both a trenchant social observer, able to establish remarkable empathy with people quite alien to himself, and a journalist of seemingly inexhaustible energy and resource. The *Morning Chronicle* project enabled Mayhew to combine his "philosophical" interests with an easy and intellectually less demanding mode of expression, namely journalistic reporting.

The "Labour and the Poor" survey accordingly allowed a number of different streams in Mayhew's talent to combine for the first time. The investigatory intentions of the series gave him exactly the position that he needed to resolve the tensions between class-identification and incipient rebellion—the role of the seemingly disinterested scientist. Assuming that role, he could give expression to direct and implied criticism of the social system through quoting other observers, but he himself did not have to take any position at all. At the same time the role gave him the distance necessary to avoid sentimentalizing, exaggerating, or surrendering entirely to his sources of information. This balance was maintained as long as he himself was not called upon for a personal commitment one way or the other, and it is responsible for the strengths of his work on the poor.

The early development of his contributions to the *Morning Chronicle* show this combination of journalism and social science in the making. At the beginning the conventional journalistic source of his reports was obvious. In his first official article as the metropolitan correspondent, he drew a standard "literary" picture of the contrasts of London with the aid of statistics culled from Porter, from McCulloch, from the Report of the Poor Law Commissioners, from Smirke's *His-*

tory of London,[10] and from the Constabulary Commissioners' Report on Crime, among others: "A vast bricken multitude, a strange incongruous chaos of wealth and want—of ambition and despair—of the brightest charity and the darkest crime, where there are more houses and more houseless, where there is more feasting and more starvation, than on any other spot on earth—and all grouped round the one giant centre, the huge black dome, with its ball of gold looming through the smoke (apt emblem of the source of its riches!) and marking out the capital, no matter from what quarter the traveller may come" (I, 19 October 1849). Visualizing London's contrasts this way was a cliché by 1849, and even though Mayhew's variation of the convention was effective, his literary talent did not lie in the ability to generalize through symbol. His skill was in rendering particulars, and not until he had specific experiences to relate did the artist in him begin to demonstrate his powers.

In this very first letter Mayhew also began the "scientific" part of his survey by taking several paragraphs to define the term *poor*, giving a theoretical distinction much like that later used by both Charles Booth and Seebohm Rowntree[11] later in the century. "All those persons whose incomings are insufficient for the satisfaction of their wants—a want being, according to my idea, contra-distinguished from a mere desire by positive physical pain, instead of a mental uneasiness, accompanying it." Although this was a relatively value-free definition, when he next tried to classify the causes of poverty he used as his criterion a typically Victorian value judgment. The poor could be distinguished "as they *will* work, they *can't* work, and they *won't* work."

After this uneven beginning Mayhew moved to personal investigation. His direct experiences had started with the trip to Bermondsey in September, if not earlier, but the first report of them in the "Labour and the Poor" series proper was Letter II, a visit to the homes of several handloom weavers in Spitalfields. This was the only survey Mayhew made of the weavers and what he uncovered was already well known since the government had conducted an inquiry into the handloom weavers in London's East End in 1840. Mayhew probably began his investigations with them exactly because the situation was familiar, for he had not yet uncovered any new material. Since the weavers lived in a small area, he could see a number of them in a short space of time. His method of locating his informants was to contact someone familiar with the residents of Spitalfields, who in turn introduced him to individual families.

In his early letters the methods Mayhew used gradually lost some of their more obvious journalistic conventions. In this second letter his characteristic style of reporting his interviews developed, reflecting in miniature the unfolding of his opus as a whole, from the general descriptive approach of the first letter of the *Morning Chronicle* to the lengthy "street biographies" of *London Labour and the London Poor*. Stating that "hardly a line will be written but what a note of the matter recorded has been taken on the spot" (II, 23 October 1849), Mayhew first gave a general summary of the workers' words. Next he repeated a little dialogue, and finally quoted several statements in some detail with the phraseology and personality of the speakers made evident.

In the first and second kind of interview Mayhew combined direct quotation and third-party (the interviewer's) interpretation: "His master had been a-losing terrible, he said, and yet he'd just taken a country mansion. They only give you work just to oblige you, as an act of charity, and not to do themselves any good—oh, no! Works fifteen hours and often more." In the very last interview of all in this second letter, however, Mayhew evolved a new form of reporting, a fusion of himself, through his questions, and the respondent, whose answers were reported in the first person, in a long uninterrupted monologue, with the questions absorbed into the replies. This combination of his perspective and his informant's was to prove a catalyst for Mayhew's latent energy and talent, and its expression soon dominated his reports.

Nonetheless these early interviews were quite limited in scope, for Mayhew simply wanted to test a hypothesis, and the only questions he asked were to that end. What he wanted to find out from the weavers was whether their poverty was caused by low wages, high prices, improvident habits, or by some combination of these. He did, however, also inquire as to their explanations as to what was responsible for "the depreciation in the value of their labour." "The spirit of competition on the part of the masters," they replied, though Chartist weavers attributed it to their lack of suffrage. Mayhew, true to the "disinterested" role that he had adopted, reported both answers but made no comment himself.

In Mayhew's next letter, later reprinted in *London Labour*, we see the first stages of his self-education in economics, which was to culminate in about ten months when he abandoned his unqualified support for the idea that supply and demand determined the rate of wages. Referring to the previous letter, he pointed out the discrepancy between the statistical evidence on wages offered by previous investigators and the wages quoted by the weavers themselves. The higher wages noted by other reporters were incorrect, he concluded, because these previous compilers had not averaged in the days during the year when the weaver was out of work—"at play." Thus, though one job of weaving might net twenty-six shillings, if, as was likely, the weaver was out of work for the two weeks following, his average weekly wage was only eight or nine shillings a week. At this early point Mayhew simply noted the discrepancy; later he would systematize his method of determining the "real" wage for any trade.

Now, however, the discovery of "at play" time of the Spitalfields weavers led him to investigate a type of employment quite different from that of the highly-skilled handloom weavers, namely the heavy labor of the dockworkers. The connection was logical if not immediately obvious: when the weavers were out of work, how did they live? One answer Mayhew found was that they tried to get work on the docks. So to the docks he went. While there he discovered that many of the casual dock workers lived in "low" lodginghouses in the neighborhood, and he tried to investigate these places. His desire was frustrated at this point because the proprietor of one took him for a government spy, and he had to beat a quick retreat; later he launched a full-scale investigation of lodginghouses and other refuges for tramps and vagrants.

Mayhew recognized the apparent randomness and possible confusion of the picture which resulted when he moved from Spitalfields weavers to casual dock laborers to low lodginghouses. He also admitted that he had been forced to give up his plan to report his findings deductively.

"I would rather have pursued some more systematic plan in my inquiries, but in the present state of ignorance as to the general occupations of the poor, system is impossible. I am unable to generalize, not being acquainted with the particulars—for each day's investigation brings me incidentally into contact with a means of living utterly unknown among the well-fed portion of society" (III, 26 October 1849). Later he found another reason to justify the method of investigation dominating the form of his reports: "I thought it better, even at the risk of being unmethodical, to avail myself of the channels of information opened to me rather than defer the matter to its proper place, and so lose the freshness of the impression it had made on my mind" (V, 2 November 1849).

Mayhew's third letter also showed a further development in his general methodology, this time in his mode of descriptions. As we saw, in the initial article on Jacob's Island, a middle-class commentator controlled the description; in Letter I the view of the contrasts of London, while more detached, was undistinguished. In Letter III Mayhew developed a way to describe the docks only hinted at in his earlier efforts. After making some general but precisely detailed remarks about the neighborhood, Mayhew described his visit to the London docks in the early morning before the call to work. "He who wishes to behold one of the most extraordinary and least known scenes of this metropolis should wend his way to the London Dock gates at half-past seven in the morning. There he will see congregated within the principal entrance masses of men of all grades, looks, and kinds. Some in half-fashioned surtouts burst at the elbows, with the dirty shirts showing through. Others in greasy sporting jackets, with red pimpled faces."

I will have more to say about the style of these descriptive passages, but let me note now that, although marred by some stilted phraseology and the air of a set piece, the description of the docks reflected the normal pattern in his work on labor and the poor: a general survey of a specific scene at a specific time, a series of selected but carefully specified particulars, and a final remark rounding off the whole. While the observer of the scene remained distant (Mayhew often removed himself physically, viewing a scene from high above), the preciseness of the details which he observed in the individual people that he selected to specify brought the reader into close contact with the scene. As in his reported interviews the form of his descriptions combined detachment and involvement.

The interviews themselves followed the pattern of fused question and answer which Mayhew had first used at the end of Letter II. This interview form was now reinforced by his understanding of the "scientific" inductive method of investigation. Mayhew believed, like other fact-collectors of the period, that the condition of the workers could be determined absolutely through statistics and "factual" descriptions; but the inductive method gave little direction as to just how many "facts" were needed before the "laws" governing economic and social conditions were manifest. This uncertainty led Mayhew to include more and more long interviews. In addition, since in reality he was writing his articles inductively, it was also not clear what in any given exchange might turn out to be relevant in the end; nothing could safely be omitted, and so he committed himself to including random remarks that grew out of the conversations. We can never know definitely, of course, how completely the reported interviews reproduced the actual ones; but the fact that Mayhew himself insisted that his reports were verbatim and the number of irrelevant remarks that he included lend some support to his assertion that "the story of the people's sufferings is repeated to the public in the selfsame words in which they were told to me" (VI, 6 November 1849).

Part of the process of reporting "scientific" investigations is to give the complete data so that others can check the results. By reproducing the whole interview in the apparent words of the respondent and by including seemingly irrelevant remarks, Mayhew allowed his readers to draw their own conclusions after going through the "raw" data themselves.

One other characteristic of his interviews resulted from Mayhew's conception of his reports as parts of a scientific investigation. Because each interview was only to be a single piece of data and did not need to represent a whole class, he could allow expression to the most individual, even idiosyncratic of his subjects' experiences. Although he insisted that he did not seek unusual cases and his first three letters did seem to favor representative interviews, it must have occurred to him before too long that extreme hard-luck cases and radical opinions, far from distorting the picture, actually supported his general view of the condition of the workers. The more individual each worker's experience the more convincing was his information when it confirmed the figures about wages from another worker totally different in abilities, background, and individual situation. Mayhew had thus a perfectly good reason to seek out the most antisocial and the most exploited of the lower classes and to allow full expression to their lives and their opinions.

Nevertheless as a reporter he also tried to maintain a clear distance between himself and his subjects by devising methods of checking their statements for accuracy. At the same time that he was gradually giving more and more space in his reports to the expression of the opinions of the poor, he recognized the dangers in relying solely on their testimony. He was aware that the workers whom he questioned might try to shape their answers to what they thought he wanted to hear; he could be steered to untypical cases, and he worried about his subjects' inaccuracy of memory and their imperfect accounts. In addition by the third or fourth week he had moved toward the second stage of his inquiry, the generalizations about wages in a given trade, by developing his method for determining the "real" wage of the average worker. (Mayhew asked for piece-work prices, the "nominal" wage, and for the number of hours worked each day. He deducted from the nominal wage the various charges and fines which were levied against the workmen, and he added any extra money or perquisites. He then averaged these earnings on a weekly and yearly basis to get the "real" wage. Finally he averaged all the individual "real" wages in order to arrive at the "general" wage for a given trade.) He knew that he needed many different examples in order to be conclusive in these generalizations. Therefore in his early reports we can see him struggling to find a way both to check the accuracy of the individual figures that he received from his informants and to maximize his contacts with members of a given trade.

Before he arrived at a solution which satisfied him, Mayhew tried several different techniques, and in the first weeks of his work he carefully reported on the success of each method to his readers. He tried to check the workers' information with the facts derived from masters and management, but disillusionment with this effort set in almost immediately. Most masters were unwilling to cooperate: employers hid their figures in order to keep their profits unknown, and the middlemen would hardly give him the time of day, let alone any information about wages they paid (VI, 6 November 1849).

He soon abandoned the effort to pry data out of a reluctant management and devised other means of checking. He consulted "a gentleman who is thoroughly conversant with the character of several of the operatives" and together they visited a workroom where many tailors were employed (VI, 6 November 1849). One month later he asked "several of the most experienced and intelligent workmen" in the tailor trade "as to the best means of arriving at a correct opinion, respecting the state of the trade" (XVI, 11 December 1849). They all agreed that in order to get a fair estimate of wages, Mayhew should interview one man in each of the different branches of the trade. "After this I was to be taken to a person who was the captain or leading man of the shop; then to one who, in the technicality of the trade, had a 'good chance' of work; and, finally, to one who was only casually employed." He was not content to rest here, however. "To prevent the chance of error," he continued, "I begged to be favoured with such accounts of earnings as could be procured from the operatives." In spite of his persistent search for figures, he remained committed to the personal history. "I was anxious to arrive at something like a criterion of the intellectual, political, and moral character of the people, and I asked to be allowed an interview with such persons as the parties whom I consulted might consider would fairly represent these peculiar features of their class to the world." Some of these people he interviewed in their homes, and some were brought to him at the *Chronicle* office. In both cases, apparently, a stenographer took the interview in shorthand.

These methods by themselves still did not satisfy Mayhew's desire for thorough cross-checking of his informants. The interviews were neither numerous nor random enough. Toward the end of his first major exposé, that of the conditions of tailors and seamstresses, he finally hit on a solution which would increase both. Instead of his going to the workers, he arranged large and apparently well-publicized meetings where they came to him at meeting halls such as the Hanover Square Rooms or the hall of the British and Foreign School in Shadwell. At these gatherings members of a particular trade or group were invited to give information about their work and wages. The men and women told their stories orally, and Mayhew instructed the others at the meeting to correct any errors or exaggerations which they heard. Frequently a stenographer from the newspaper took the statements.

The range of these meetings was remarkably varied. The first was really a dinner for the residents of a low lodginghouse where Mayhew was shocked by the angelic face of one incorrigible thief and where he picked up the "pet thief" whose story he later recounted in the *Comic Almanac*. Other meetings included one attended by a large number of tailors—the *Chronicle* said two thousand, but perhaps that was journalistic exaggeration. Another was convened for twenty-five needlewomen who had been forced into prostitution by low wages. He also met with coal-heavers (originally laborers who unloaded coals from ships by heaving them from one stage to another; in Mayhew's time simply laborers who unloaded coal) and in another time and place with some wives of ballast-heavers (laborers who unloaded the gravel or other material placed in the hold of a ship in order to prevent her from capsizing when in motion) turned into drunkards by the publicans' control over their pay. He held a meeting of 166 vagrants, "the greater part of whom were thieves, and none above 20 years of age" (XXX, 29 January 1850). As the series went on, the large meeting ceased to play such an important role in Mayhew's reports. Probably this was in part because of the difficulty of getting together people in professions such as peddling. Mayhew never completely abandoned the device, however. While writing *London Labour*, he convened a meeting of street sellers and in 1856–1857 he held a series of gatherings of swell mobsmen (swindlers who dressed as gentlemen) and ticket-of-leave men (or parolees).

The accuracy of the information collected by means of this mass "interviewing" was of course not necessarily any more reliable than that collected individually. Group pressure would undoubtedly have led to some exaggeration in answer to such questions as "how many had been compelled to pledge their work to obtain necessaries?" More informative were the individual life-stories reported at the end of the meetings, though these too might have been influenced by the large audience listening to them.

Nonetheless the large meetings, and the manner in which information gleaned from them tallied with that from individual private interviews, finally convinced Mayhew of both the accuracy of the working people and of the effectiveness of his methods of checking their stories. By January 1850 he eliminated from his reports the details of how he tested the information he received from his sources. Whenever an unusual practical problem arose, he still gave the particulars of his solution. At one point, for example, he invited the reader to compare the testimony of two ballast-heavers, one who was reluctant to speak, the other eager to volunteer his information.

Despite the fact that Mayhew's accuracy of information will never be completely demonstrable, nearly all readers from 1849 to the present have trusted him. This trust grows out of the apparent inclusiveness of his reported interviews and the number of different life stories that he published. Individual statistical generalizations might be inaccurate; individual workers might have exaggerated; Mayhew might have been fooled in some instances, but one senses that the total picture, limited in scope as it might be, is accurate. Thus the "experimental" part of his inductive investigation did indeed provide the "proof" for the general hypothesis that exploitation and neglect took place in individual trades.

By 6 November, when Mayhew began his survey of tailors and seamstresses, his methods of generalization, description, and interviewing were by and large established. In his reports he first classified each trade into its various categories, breaking down major groupings as necessary. After the initial division of a trade he then gave a general factual survey of it, frequently including its history and such details culled from police reports and government figures as the relative amount of criminality, the average age, and so on. Next he produced the interviews, sometimes with interpolated descriptions. When the data from the initial interviews suggested new avenues of investigation, Mayhew followed them up. Finally, if the data clearly pointed to certain conclusions, Mayhew drew them.

Mayhew's rapid discovery of such an effective form for his descriptions and, more important, for his interviews probably resulted as much from his enthusiasm for his encounters with the working classes as from his natural sharpness of mind and his respect for the inductive process. As early as the end of the first week the articles mainly consisted of a series of personal conversations between him and the individual workers. Because of the way the interviews were reported, however, the contacts seemed to be between the reader and the worker. The reader's resulting involvement with individual poor people soon became the most notable difference between the letters from the metropolitan correspondent and those from the manufacturing regions. In Mayhew's pages the interviewer gradually recedes into the background, but in those of Angus Reach there was seldom more than a sentence or two from a worker and those hardly ever without a qualification, either direct or implied, regarding its reliability. Although Reach and Mayhew came from the same class (both were sons of solicitors) and had much the same journalistic background, only Mayhew was able to encourage his subjects in his reports to upstage him and to make their doing so a matter of principle. As a result he was praised by the *Morning Chronicle* readers for his intimate portraits and for his own objectivity while Reach was criticized for lacking both.[12]

As Mayhew moved through the various investigations, he accumulated knowledge which affected the form of future investigations. The tailors' survey was disorganized, and it shifted confusedly between the exploited part of the trade usually located in the East End, called the "slop" or "sweated" branch by Mayhew, and the "honorable" part in the West End where wages and conditions were good. The sweated laborers were piece workers who frequently had to labor cruel hours to make a pittance. Mayhew's subsequent investigations were more coherent and organized from the beginning because he expected to find the same division between sweated and honorable workers in different trades, and he initially set up his investigations and his questions to fit his expectations. In this way he carefully built up the evidence which would finally force him to make a cautious criticism of popular explanations for low wages.

Rather than continuing to analyse each of Mayhew's articles in order, let us now consider the scope of all of his contributions as metropolitan correspondent. Of the eighty-two letters two were miscellaneous "descriptive" articles; thirty-three were devoted to workers in skilled and semiskilled trades; nine to dock workers and longshoremen; nine to the street sellers and performers; seven to beggars, thieves, and vagrants; five to the transit system; and the remaining seventeen to low lodging-houses, the merchant marine, an attack on the "ragged schools," and a survey of London markets. Thus roughly a third of the articles of the metropolitan correspondent were concerned with skilled workers, over half of these involved in occupations connected with the making of clothing.

Of the four principal branches of this trade—one of the most important in London—Mayhew thoroughly covered three: tailoring, the production of shirts, blouses, and underwear, and shoemaking. The fourth, women's dressmaking, he surveyed cursorily. By also investigating furniture-making—the other major London skilled trade and after the clothing makers one with the most exploited piece workers—he completed a thorough exposé of the situation of sweated labor in London. But of all the other skilled workers in the metropolis—the engineering workers, and those involved in food manufacture or the production of highly finished goods such as watches and jewelry—there was barely a hint. Nor was there any mention of the largest working class group of all, the nearly quarter-million men and women working as servants. Ironically in Mayhew's later survey, *The Shops and Companies of London*, by abandoning his concern for the workers' condition and concentrating only on a description of the work done, he was able to be much more inclusive in his investigations of London industry.

This breakdown makes the limits of Mayhew's survey clear. Despite the fact that many of his readers in their letters of approbation to the *Chronicle* stressed the scope and inclusiveness of his material, the value of his contributions lay in the particularity of their portraits and not the breadth of the coverage. The extension of these human particulars to the whole of the working class occurs only in the mind of the reader.

Mayhew had larger intentions, of course, and he did not relinquish them until many years later. Yet to have covered all trades, all unskilled vocations, all labor of every kind in the depth and minuteness of detail with which he examined the state of the tailors and seamstresses would have taken several years, much money, and limitless energy. To have achieved his final goals any other way would have involved severe condensation. The articles on dressmakers and hatters which appeared after he officially left the *Chronicle* show the negative results of such abbreviated coverage. The pressure to wind up the series in a hurry produced shallow interviews done secondhand and short and enervated reports.

Far from wanting to limit his survey, Mayhew was continually expanding it, a characteristic that became the main mode of development in *London Labour and the London Poor*. He started with grandiose expectations but almost immediately became obsessed with the immediate situation in which he found himself. Throughout "Labour and the Poor" he promised a number of surveys which never appeared. In January 1850 he announced a new plan to cover an additional six categories of longshoremen in addition to the three whom he had already interviewed. He no sooner announced this plan than he had to postpone it because he was unable to accumulate enough information. A survey of prison labor was also frequently promised but never produced.

These unrealistic extensions of his work not only point to Mayhew's impracticality but also show that he did not think through his projects before he began them, and they are another sign of the intellectual laziness we have seen earlier. In this case his inability to recognize in advance the problems which underlay his practical task is one reason for his incapability of finishing his work.

In the first half of "Labour and the Poor" Mayhew never let the impracticality of his plans deter him. Stumped by a difficulty in collecting material for a scheduled series, he turned to another more readily available source, all the time trying to give some theoretical justification for the abrupt change. While data on the tailors was being collated, he investigated the costermongers, he said, to determine if the poor were overcharged as well as underpaid. When the longshoremen series was frustrated, he turned to a survey of the vagrants and houses of refuge because that was the time of year the places were open and full. After January 1850 the most common reason for these modifications of plans was that he would turn to a short "fill-in" series while collecting and collating material on larger topics, nearly all of which failed to appear in print. On one occasion the idea for a new series which interrupted an ongoing survey seemed to grow out of a current issue. Mayhew said he investigated the merchant marine in order to ascertain "among other matters, the opinions of the men" (XL, 7 March 1850) about the merchant service bill currently being debated in parliament. (This bill, among other provisions, would have given the Board of Trade the superintendence of matters relating to the Merchant Service and would have established government shipping-offices to hire and pay sailors and to regulate wages.)

However inevitable his unrevised goals made such an untidy way of proceeding, the random development disturbed Mayhew, for he had planned a much more directed investigation. Yet as we have seen, his earliest efforts at general classification had been crude. As early as the third article he was forced to admit that "all I can at present assert is, that the poor appear to admit of being classified, according to their employments under three heads—Artisans, Laborers, and Petty Traders." In May 1850 in Letter LII, he was finally able to project a more rigorous approach. By this time he had gained a broader perspective into which he could fit the particulars of his earlier work; experience now enabled him to evolve a system of classification which would determine in advance the form of his surveys.

This new classification was still rough in its differentiations, but it was more helpful than the three-part division. He now decided to classify the workers according to the materials they worked on, lumping together all those who worked with the same raw materials. There were thus to be large diverse groupings under "workers in wood," in metals, in glass, and so forth. Mayhew planned to take up each large category seriatim, investigating all the associated occupations one after another. In the *Morning Chronicle* he began with the "timber trade" or "workers in wood."

The investigation based on this new classification did not survive this first series, probably because of Mayhew's increasing difficulties with the editors of the *Morning Chronicle*. He implied he would move on next to the workers in metals, but instead he took up the transit system. The reason was never given, but perhaps because of the 1846 Royal Commission on Metropolitan Termini, there was a body of easily available material at hand. The metal workers would have involved more original work, and he was probably unwilling to undertake it at this point.

Mayhew paralleled his more rigorous classification and his stronger sense of direction in these later letters with some thoughts on the wage question in general, even though in the summer of 1850 he had not completed his projected survey. He was ready nonetheless to venture a few observations because of the undeniable thrust of some of his numerical data. Perhaps he also seized the opportunity to provoke the editors of the *Chronicle*, whose political commitment to free trade was in opposition to Mayhew's conclusions.

Mayhew's investigations had demonstrated that many workers were receiving lower than subsistence wages. Serious and perceptive political economists like J. S. Mill continued to debate the various possible causes of these low wages. In the popular mind, however, the explanation was simply that they resulted from a surplus of labor or "overpopulation." Sidney Herbert believed this, for example; and he stated it without qualification in his prospectus for the Female Emigration Society.

This assertion grew out of standard supply-and-demand theories which stated that only if the demand for labor were high, relative to the supply of labor, would wages be high. Under this analysis, if there were no loss in demand for goods and wages still fell, the only possible explanation was that there were too many workers. At this point the received opinion fell back on Malthusian principles. High wages encouraged the working classes to expand their numbers and thus to force their wages lower and lower.

Mayhew was noncommittal about evidence which seemed to contradict this theory when it first appeared in the letters on the boot and shoemakers. He balanced opinions from both sides. Some workers felt competition from the importation of cheap French goods reduced their wages rather than "overpopulation." Others laid the blame on competition between workers who undercut each other's wages, and there were other explanations. Mayhew was cautious: "It should be borne in mind—lest we mistake what is a matter of opinion for a matter of fact—that these are simply the notions and sentiments of the workmen, and that they are here given in a spirit of fairness to them" (XXXIII, 7 February 1850). He was nonetheless puzzled by evidence which seemed to support the notion that supply and demand was not working in wage determination, and remarked in passing that "not a trade have I investigated where cheap prices have been maintained by the ordinary operation of the laws of commerce" (XXXV, 14 February 1850).

By June 1850 Mayhew was convinced that supply and demand did not determine the level of wages. The resulting position that he adopted was his first unequivocal break from received economic assumptions of the period even though later, in an investigation of scavenging, he refused to extend this generalization to another trade without corroborating evidence. The nominally uncommitted observer, nonetheless, had stepped closer to a view of the wage question which was expressed by many of the working classes themselves.

Indisputable data contradicted the theory that an excess of workers caused low wages. Mayhew had determined that "though the London carpenters have increased 4 per cent less than the general population of the metropolis, still each of the operatives has been compelled of late years, either by the strapping masters [who forced their men to do extra work], or a reduction of wages, to get through twice or three times as much work as formerly, and thus the trade has become as overstocked by each hand doing double work, as it would have been if the hands themselves had been doubled" (LX, 11 July 1850). The theory of supply and demand in terms of wages held true only if one ignored where the increase in the labor force came from; it could as easily come from working conditions and low wages themselves as overpopulation.

Mayhew had further statistical evidence. The number of London cabinetmakers declined 32 percent from 1831 to 1841; yet, although the demand increased during the same period, the wages of the nonsociety or non-union men had been 300 to 400 percent higher in 1831 than in 1841 (LXIII, 1 August 1850). Mayhew now saw that supply-and-demand theories of labor illuminated only the process of production but showed nothing about how the national wealth was to be distributed among labor, capital, and landholders. "Wages depend as much on the distribution of labour as on the demand and supply of it," he said (LXVI, 22 August 1850). Mill in *Principles of Political Economy* made a similar discovery that the country could distribute its produce as it wished. Mayhew, who had probably read Mill by this point, may have been influenced by Mill's analysis of distribution. Whatever the source his adoption of this idea, as Robert Heilbroner said of Mill's discovery of it, lifted the economic debate "from the stifling realm of impersonal and inevitable law and brought it back into the arena of ethics and morality."[13]

On the basis of this discovery Mayhew formulated his own "law" of low wages: "Overwork makes underpay." In addition the lower wages got, the more work each man had to do to live and the more men would be thrown out of jobs: "Underpay makes overwork." In his recognition that the supply of labor could be increased without any addition to the population simply by requiring more work of an individual worker, Mayhew foreshadowed the point that Marx would make with great force in his discussion of the working day in *Capital*.

At this point Mayhew stopped at the brink of a full analysis of the causes and cures for low wages, though he would take the subject up again the next year in *Low Wages*. In fact suggestions for reform of the abuses that he had detailed in "Labour and the Poor" were scant from all sources. Despite the outcry over his revelations of sweated labor, not until 1888–1889 did a select committee even inquire into the practice. At the turn of the century the Factory and Workshops Act (1901) finally ended the worst abuses, but exploitation of piece workers itself lasted well into the twentieth century.

Two minor reform-movements did grow directly out of Mayhew's series, however, although neither of them appears to have lasted very long. The first was a scheme to send poor seamstresses of impeccable character to the colonies, and the second, an organization which tried (unsuccessfully) to change the method of payment for ballast-heavers who were at that time hired and paid through publicans. (The corresponding laborers, coal-whippers, men who raised coal out of a ship hold by means of pulleys, had been protected from publican extortion since 1843.) Mayhew was also influential in setting up a Friendly Association of Costermongers, which appears to have died when the treasurer of the association absconded with the scanty funds.[14]

The Female Emigration Society was the most successful direct result of his "Labour and the Poor" series. Mayhew's revelations of the terrible pay and working conditions among needlewomen evoked a vigorous and widespread outrage which was surprising since the conditions were generally known already. (*Punch* had published Thomas Hood's "Song of the Shirt" to great outcry in 1843.) Still the detail and the numbers in Mayhew's exposé touched the public conscience. Carlyle is an example. *Latter-Day Pamphlets*, written during the latter months of the *Chronicle* series, has as one of its leitmotifs the thirty thousand poverty-stricken seamstresses which he said he learned of from Mayhew's reports. The professional philanthropists were activated by the revelations as well. As reported in the *Chronicle* (Mayhew himself never mentioned it), one evening early in December as Mayhew was chairing a meeting called to elicit statistics from some destitute needlewomen, Sidney Herbert and Lord Ashley (the future Lord Shaftesbury) suddenly appeared and took over the chair. They announced their intention to solicit funds to enable distressed needlewomen to emigrate to the colonies where women were few and their chances both of earning an income and of finding a husband would be increased.

It is not surprising that the first response to Mayhew's revelations was an emigration scheme, since shipping the unwanted, unneeded, and "excess" population to the colonies was a favorite panacea for England's ills at this time. Dickens was to send the Micawbers and L'il Emily to Australia for a miraculous rehabilitation in 1850. Gibbon Wakefield had published one of his major works, *A View of the Art of Colonisation*, earlier in 1849; and there was much public debate about various emigration schemes. Herbert and Ashley themselves were members of the Canterbury Association, Wakefield's last emigration scheme; and this may be one reason they had the colonies on their minds.

After sketching in their plans at Mayhew's meeting, the two philanthropists left him and his associates to pick up the pieces as best they could, and two days later a letter from Herbert appeared in the *Chronicle* detailing the plan. In the weeks following much public attention and many private funds were absorbed by the Female Emigration Society. By mid-January, according to the *Morning Chronicle*, which enthusiastically supported the project, £17,000 had been pledged. The first group of women sailed 25 February 1850. In all twenty groups were sent out, about seven hundred women, the last ship leaving in January 1852. The association at this point "probably merged with the Family Colonisation Loan Society."[15]

Mayhew himself was undoubtedly annoyed about what he could consider Herbert and Ashley's interference and scene-stealing. In 1851, when he was editor, an anonymous humorous piece in the *Comic Almanac* ridiculed the Female Emigration Society specifically, although Mayhew himself never openly opposed either emigration or the society. His attack on the ragged schools in spring 1850 however probably did reflect some latent antagonism toward Lord Ashley, the chairman of the Ragged Schools Union since its inception in 1844.[16] In these letters, for one of the few times during his career as social observer, Mayhew's attacks on a popular middle-class institution were not coupled with qualifications, contradictions, and a refusal to draw a final conclusion. He expressed his negative judgments on the ragged schools strongly and in his own person. The position he took, though generally well-founded, was too extreme, perhaps because of his feelings about Ashley, more likely because of his unqualified trust in statistical evidence.

The significance of Mayhew's series in "Labour and the Poor" on the ragged schools goes beyond his possible annoyance with Ashley, for his attack on two of the most popularly supported cures for bad social conditions—education and private philanthropy—was bound to stir up trouble for him. Out of the controversy which followed his conclusion that the schools did not reduce juvenile crime but might even increase it came serious charges against his reliability and honesty. In the acrimonious exchanges involved in this affair Mayhew emerged from behind the screen of disinterested scientist to provide us with a few tantalizing glimpses of the way he worked.

Mayhew's criticism was based on the assumption that the purpose of the ragged schools was to reduce the amount of juvenile crime by teaching poor children to read and write. He had long ridiculed the notion that literacy improved morals, and in his pamphlet *What To Teach* he spent considerable space exposing "The Fallacy of the Supposed Connexion Between Reading and Writing, and Morality and Intelligence," as the title of the first chapter put it.

His assertion that the only purpose of the ragged schools was to do this was too bald, and Ashley denied it outright. It was nevertheless true that the Ragged School Union was more interested in rehabilitation than education, reflecting a general early Victorian attitude. J. J. Tobias has noted a widespread belief from 1830 onward that education was a means of preventing crime, and he attributed to this feeling the sharp rise in public expenditure on schools after 1830.[17]

If Mayhew's premise had some validity, the judgment he made on the basis of it was a little unfair. He claimed that because the statistics showed that juvenile crime had increased since the founding of the ragged schools, the schools were worthless, and even more, they might have contributed to the rise in crime[18] by bringing boys of "vicious propensities" together.

The Ragged School Union did not take his criticisms silently, and in the end their rebuttal challenged more than his use of statistics. Ashley first defended the schools, saying they were only intended to keep the situation from getting worse, but Mayhew quoted the 1848 report of the ragged school commissioners against him: the report claimed that "it is clearly proven that in addition to the good done to the children and parents as individuals, the public are benefited by improved neighbourhoods and diminution of crime" (XLV, 29 March 1850).

The *Chronicle* reported a flurry of meetings of various boards of ragged schools in the weeks that followed. The statements made by all denied Mayhew's charges, but little evidence was introduced to support these denials. One defender asserted that Mayhew "forgot the conservative power of love, by which these schools were animated, and which was sufficient to preserve the good children from harm" (9 April 1850), while another noted that "thieves, rogues, and vagabonds" had congregated before now "at the gin-shops and lodging-houses, the alleys and crowded thoroughfares. How much better, then, to meet at school?" (12 April 1850).

Finally on 22 April 1850 the *Chronicle* published a long letter from Alexander Anderson, secretary of the Ragged School Union, which sought to refute Mayhew's charges by discrediting him as a reporter. While noting other factors which would account for the rise in official rates of crime, especially the 1847 Larceny Act which allowed magistrates to send children under fourteen to prison, Anderson tried to cast doubt on Mayhew's honesty by going back to question some of the people whom he had originally interviewed.

The resulting indictment was severe. Anderson charged Mayhew with leading his witnesses and with omitting information which contradicted his own point of view. The former accusation involved a boy in prison who had told Mayhew he had first met thieves while attending a ragged school. Anderson himself then spoke to the boy who "confessed the lie," excusing himself because he had hoped Mayhew would put in a good word with the governor of the prison if he got the information he was seeking. Mayhew in turn introduced a letter from the governor which supported the original version of the interview and which reaffirmed Mayhew's disinterestedness in his interviewing.

Another charge by Anderson seemed more damaging than that involving the duplicitous witness. (After all the boy could also have lied to Anderson for hope of gain.) The secretary returned to a London policeman quoted by Mayhew. The policeman told Anderson that when he informed Mayhew that every Sunday the children brought the Bibles given them to church and paid them off in installments, Mayhew said, "Ah, well, never mind that; we don't want to put that down," presumably because he was looking for evidence that the children sold the Bibles. Henry Wood, who had been present at the original interview (as well as at others) and who apparently took some notes and even asked some questions, flatly denied that Mayhew had uttered such a remark. Mayhew also introduced a personal vindication from Richard Knight of the City Mission who had helped him locate some of his informants.[19]

In the actual report of Mayhew's interview with the policeman, both men were more circumspect than Anderson's rebuttal would lead one

to assume. "The gentlemen who manage the Ragged School do everything they can to instruct and encourage the children in well-doing,"
the officer was quoted as saying; "they make them presents of Testa-
ments and Bibles." At this point Mayhew inserted parenthetically: "I
find by the Reports (of the Ragged School Union) that they are sold"
(XLV, 29 March 1850). Once again he only quoted the union against
itself.

Though the subject soon dropped from the columns of the *Morning
Chronicle*, the charges against Mayhew lingered. In 1851, in a review
of volume 1 of *London Labour*, the *Athenaeum* in its generally de-
rogatory remarks on his contributions to the *Morning Chronicle* used
the controversy as its main supporting evidence: "An attack on the
Ragged Schools, [was] based, as our readers know, on statements
which could not afterwards be sustained; and the proved exaggeration
in one case helped to throw a degree of doubt over the whole series"
(15 November 1851).

Despite the *Athenaeum*'s doubt Mayhew's criticisms were not fully
answered, and his honesty as a reporter was not undermined. Yet
even if we can criticize his conclusion, though not impugn his honesty,
the censure cannot apply to the rest of his work. In his next controver-
sial series, his critical evaluation of the Sailors' Home, he was at great
pains to show all sides of opinion; but this time the complaints about
the home were quoted from others rather than made by Mayhew.

In an earlier investigation he even went out of his way to uncover
opinions contrary to his own. Along with other reformers Mayhew was
convinced that the lower classes' dependence on spirits and beer was
injurious both to their health and to the possibility of bettering their
lives. He was anxious to promote temperance among them if not
teetotalism. The majority of the workers, particularly the unskilled
laborers, did not agree. They believed that they had to drink before,
often during, and after work to "keep up their strength." Mayhew
gave full coverage to this point of view even though it contradicted his
own and was bound to offend many of his readers, who were, as Francis Sheppard has said, much more affronted by drunkenness than by
bad housing or unemployment (p. 368). "Sartainly, a drop of 'short'
(neat spirit) does one good in a cold morning like this," a coal porter, or

a man who carried coal from the place of unloading to the customers, told him. "Beer—four pots a day of it—doesn't make me step unsteady. Hard work carries it off, and so one doesn't feel it that way. Beer's made of corn as well as bread, and so it stands to reason it's nourishing." Mayhew also sought the opinions of a coalbacker (one who carried coals on his back from ships to wagons) "who worked hard and drank a good deal of beer, and who had the character of being an industrious man" (XXI, 28 December 1849).

Doubts raised in the ragged-school controversy as to how leading questions determined his results are also relieved by considering Mayhew's work in the perspective of his period. He sometimes did ask what we would now consider to be leading questions; all the Victorian social investigators did. Today there is an entire profession devoted to the science—still an inexact one—of constructing questionnaires which will not predetermine the answers by the wording of the questions. In the search for an unbiased questionnaire we are perhaps overscrupulous in an area where early Victorian social investigators had few scruples at all. The blue books were full of leading questions. During an investigation of children in factories, for example, a seventeen-year-old girl who had worked in a Leeds factory since she was eight years old was asked:

> You were exceedingly fatigued at night, were you not? —Yes, I could scarcely get home.
> Had you to be carried home?—Yes, to be trailed home.
> How were you waked in the morning?—The bell in Mill-street rang at half past 5, and we got up by that.
> That was not a pleasant sound to you? —It was not.
> Was the fatigue gone off in the morning? —No; I was worse in the morning.
> You thought the bell a very doleful sound? —Yes, it was a doleful sound to me.[20]

Mayhew used leading questions of this sort, but his eagerness to let his informants expand on their answers and his apparent reporting of all their additions minimized the interviewer's control over the information. The answers to obviously leading questions were usually validated by the larger context in which they appeared. One might justifiably suspect the responses that Mayhew got in a meeting of young vagrants to such questions as "Are not you all tired of the lives you now lead?" and "Do not the parties who keep these places [low lodginghouses] grow rich on your degradation and your peril?" (XXXI, 31 January 1850). Yet in a longer interview with a young pickpocket in a previous article, Mayhew reported not only the yes or no answer to such questions, but also all that preceded and followed the direct answer. As a result the negative effect of the leading questions was blunted. "I would be glad to leave this life, and work at a pottery. As to sea, a bad captain would make me run away—sure. He can do what he likes with you when you're out at sea" (XXX, 22 January 1850). Details such as his desire to work at a pottery make us feel that the interview represented not only the leading questions of the interviewer but also many honest feelings of the boy. The inclusiveness plus the number of such examples in Mayhew's work reinforces one's confidence in the truth of particular cases.

Despite the possibility of fragmentation in so large a collection of particulars, a general picture of London's poorly paid workers does emerge from Mayhew's interviews. We sense a group of people who did not have much notion of the causes of their suffering and even less idea of how to improve their lot. They seemed to be mainly reliant on their own hard work, and when that failed, on their own charity to each other; only occasionally did they benefit from the benevolence of their "betters." The men and women in Mayhew's reports inspire our respect because their monotonously similar hard-luck stories were understated, for the most part, without bitterness and without censure, either for others or for themselves.

Mayhew's achievement was to find the means by which these qualities of openness, humanity, self-reliance, and patience could find utterance. He did so by partly identifying himself with his informants, his questions giving expression to their experiences. Also crucial were his tendencies towards ever-smaller details and classification. "It was, in one sense," his colleague Charles Mackay wrote later, "as if a mighty microscope were applied to the festers, social sores, and diseases of humanity; and in another, as if some unparalleled photographic apparatus was brought to portray fresh from the life the very minds, rather than the bodies of the people" (2:152). In this evaluation Mackay found exactly the right comparisons not only to describe the sense the reader gets from reading Mayhew's work but also to depict his process of writing it. The photograph with its combination of verisimilitude and artistic selection and arrangement was what Mayhew aimed at in his extended interviews, and in *London Labour and the London Poor* he would actually use photography to help achieve it. More significant is the analogy of the microscope, which points to Mayhew's characteristic method of working by looking at smaller and smaller parts of the whole. This mode was just starting toward the end of "Labour and the Poor," but in *London Labour and the London Poor* Mayhew's categorizing and classifying mind was liberated to look ever closer at each segment of his topic and to magnify every aspect with the result that particulars were revealed but the general picture was blurred.

Mayhew's "microscopic" technique had a very positive effect as well, for in the magnification of facts in the life histories he reported each individual grew in stature until he became a full-size human being for the reader. This quality explains why Mayhew's contemporaries were so astounded by his revelations, why many thought his reports were stranger than fiction. Lower-class men and women were very like middle-class readers of the *Morning Chronicle*! "The pictures which these Metropolitan letters exhibit, draw from God's own storehouse of Fact," the reviewer for *Fraser's* wrote, were "stranger, sadder, terribler than all fiction," a sentiment echoed by Thackeray in *Punch* and by an enthusiastic article on *London Labour and the London Poor* in the *Eclectic Review*.[21]

Yet from our vantage point we can see that Mayhew's method of magnification affected his ability to generalize. One has only to think of Marx, or Frederic LePlay, or Friedrich Engels to recognize that Mayhew's contributions to social history remain in the realm of brilliant observations. Compared to Engels, for example, Mayhew's understanding of the situation of labor in England at midcentury was shallow. The comparison nonetheless is an important one for a proper evaluation of both Mayhew and Engels's work. Engels's achievement is a profound general view, as Steven Marcus has shown: "What Engels has perceived [about Manchester] and created is a general structure; its form is that of a coherent totality, a concrete, complex, and systematic whole, each of whose parts has a meaning, and more than one meaning, in relation to all the others."[22] In dealing with London, Engels had the same breadth of vision. Though he opened his chapter "The Great Towns" with a conventional reworking of the contrasts of rich and poor, he almost immediately saw in this cliché a profound truth. "The disintegration of society into individuals, each guided by his private principles and each pursuing his own aims has been pushed to its furtherest limits in London," he said.[23] Engels thus recognized in 1844 what Robert Nisbet has called one of the major sociological phenomena of the nineteenth century: the increasing individualization or separation of the individual from communal or corporate structures.[24]

This level of observation was beyond Mayhew in "Labour and the Poor." Yet it is important to note that even though he did not generalize in this way, his work implied exactly the same sense of alienation as Engels noted about London. As each life history followed upon the next and Mayhew exposed the general pattern of low wages, he also projected a picture of men and women as cut off from one another in life as they were in the form of the reports Mayhew made of his interviews. However moving and however human—indeed the more moving because their humanity was so powerfully evoked—the individual portraits were, the long string of unintegrated interviews in "Labour and the Poor" details a story of essentially isolated individuals.

While Engels must be praised for knowing the significance of what he saw, Mayhew also deserves much credit for providing the proof of Engels's insights. With all its power of generalization Engels's work did not contain individual men and women with "minds" in addition to bodies, in Mackay's phrase. Missing from *The Condition of the Working Class* were individual human beings with their own dignity and their own worth. Thus the contributions of Mayhew and Engels are complementary, even essential to one another. In some ways this finally is Mayhew's importance. His work cannot stand by itself as an insight into labor and the poor in mid-Victorian England; it is, however, a necessary corollary to nearly every other major work of social commentary in the period.

During the year he had worked for the *Morning Chronicle*, Mayhew had personally traversed many of the streets in the ring of established trades which extended from Clerkenwell through St. Pancras, St. Marylebone, Westminster and southward to Stepney and the East End. The form of his reports, particularly the interviews, combining journalism, social investigation, and "scientific" intentions, enabled Mayhew to merge with his informants without losing his own status; and this fusion in turn increased his will to work and gave him the chance to discover where his real strengths lay. Theoretically his readers were to be educated by his mission. Instead his year at the newspaper turned out to be, as Thompson has said, a slow and partially achieved education for himself.[25] He started "Labour and the Poor" with the unusual and provocative intention of giving a voice to labor's side of the story of low wages. Early in his survey he was forced in spite of himself to limit his investigations to that side. By the end of "Labour and the Poor" he emerged much closer to the working classes' view of their own situation than to that of the editors of the *Chronicle* and their readers. This sense of connection between Mayhew and his subjects was to underlie his achievement in *London Labour and the London Poor*.

On the practical side he had made many personal contacts among the working classes. The praise given him by radical working-class journals like the *Red Republican* and *Reynolds Political Register* meant that the better-informed workers would have some confidence in him and thus open up new sources of information to him. In his year as metropolitan correspondent he had also learned how to conduct and how to record interviews and how to compile statistics. He moved on to his next project with characteristically monumental designs and unsullied hopes. The regrettable fact, however, is that he applied all of these newly released powers of observation, interviewing, direction, and control to one small, albeit fascinating, part of London labor—the men, women, and children who sold an astonishing variety of food and objects in the streets of London.

3

The History of a People

The development of *London Labour and the London Poor*[1] was similar to that of "Labour and the Poor." Both surveys began in one place and ended moving toward another; both were subjected to several significant derailments along the way; both were aborted before achieving their stated goals. The contents of the four volumes of *London Labour* as we know them were meant as a prelude to a larger survey which ultimately collapsed for various reasons. Among them were Mayhew's obsessive classifying tendency, which we have glimpsed in his classification of workers in Letter LXII in the *Morning Chronicle* series, and his growing fascination with the details of his subject.

The work was projected as a continuation of the investigation of the three "Labour and the Poor" categories—"Those that Will Work," "Those that Cannot Work," and "Those that Will Not Work." The street sellers were to be covered in a short introductory series. After six months of reporting on their condition and their earnings Mayhew expected to return to the survey of skilled and unskilled workers in the manner he had finally come to in the *Morning Chronicle*, taking up in turn the "Workers in Silk, Cotton, Wool, Worsted, Hair, Flax, Hemp and Coir [coconut fiber used to make rope] as well as the Workers in Skin, Gut, and Feathers, comprising both the Manufacturers and Makers-up of these materials" (wrapper 5, [11 January 1851?]).

Mayhew had turned to the street folk before when he needed time to sort out his statistics on the tailoring trade, and so his return to them now was natural. In addition street sellers were as old and as functional as any institution in London. They had traditionally supplied the lower classes with their food and goods, for these groups did not like to make the rounds of shops where they might be treated huffily and where shopkeepers normally refused to sell them their sugar, tea, or fish in the small quantities they could afford. Street traders were also frequently the only source of supply in the growing suburbs. The

YOUNG PHILIP JOINS A SCHOOL OF CROSSING SWEEPERS

The antics of young crossing sweepers, who entertained as well as cleaned crossings and begged for tips, were detailed by Augustus Mayhew in his part of *London Labour and the London Poor* (2:494–505) and again in *Paved with Gold*. The illustration by Hablot K. Browne ("Phiz") is from the novel. Courtesy of the British Library Board.

amount of food they handled was enormous, some estimates running as high as two million pounds a year.[2]

The world of the street folk was changing, however, even as Mayhew wrote, and a desire to mark the changes and capture current conditions also increased the scope of his project. Despite their obvious economic importance, the street sellers in Victorian London were harried by competitive shopkeepers and eternally "moved on" by policemen. Ordinary citizens, even those dependent on them, were suspicious of them because they lived in neighborhoods frequented by criminals, and undoubtedly the street folk were in periodic conspiracy with the criminal elements of society. As a result, under pressure from big shops, new laws had recently been passed affecting street trades. The most damaging to them was the law which prevented the costermonger, a seller of fruits, vegetables and fish, from standing still. If he did so he was liable to be arrested and to lose his wheelbarrow and his stock of goods. For this reason, between November 1849, when Mayhew first wrote the description of the New Cut Saturday market and December 1850 when the description appeared again, expanded and revised in *London Labour*, "the mob of purchasers has diminished one-half,"[3] and "within these three months," many costers with regular stands had been removed (1:59). Yet some version of the lively street scenes that he evoked did linger for another decade: Alfred Bennett, recalling his youth in Camberwell in the 1850s, remembered a "diorama of the streets" much like Mayhew reported;[4] but the sharp reduction of the "diorama" in the 1860s made Mayhew's revelations seem quaint when they were finally issued as books, and this is one reason they were less remarked than his *Morning Chronicle* letters.

As he approached his new work, Mayhew indicated that he had learned something from the difficulties that he had had with the organization and detail in his earlier survey for the *Chronicle*. He now expected to be more selective, announcing that his earlier contributions to "Labour and the Poor" would be "so condensed and revised as to be made bookworthy," although "a large amount of wholly original matter" would be added (wrapper 9, [8 February 1851?]).

In the event the more he reorganized his earlier material the more he had to say and the longer the survey of the street folk became. As he looked closer, he magnified the details and the plan to shorten and select from his collected data was undermined by his passion for categorizing and by his devotion to "autobiographical" interviews. In the first two volumes of *London Labour* the subject, though initially compressed, inflates like a balloon. For example he apparently intended the two early interviews with a costerboy and girl to stand alone and to represent the whole costermonger class. This intention soon disappeared as he included ever more "street biographies" in each weekly number, and finally at the end of volume 1, he found it necessary to include a separate section entirely devoted to children who made a living selling on the streets.

Part of the reason for his inability to select only one or two representative life histories and let them stand for the whole was the limitless curiosity released in Mayhew by the alien world of the street folk. The role of "disinterested" social scientist once again, giving him as it did an opportunity to lose himself vicariously in the lives of the lowest classes without threatening the loss of his own middle-class status, deflected the search for the general in a fascination for the particular. When it came down to it, Mayhew was interested by the data, the individual men and women, and not by the search for a theory, although he never recognized that in himself. Unfortunately this lack of self-knowledge together with the energy released by his "scientific" contacts with the lower classes contributed to the way his grand intentions for *London Labour* faded away to nothing, and resulted in expansion of the topic of the street folk to a finally unmanageable size.

Nonetheless Mayhew's growing interest in the world of the street folk did not drive his original goal from his mind. In his column "Answers to Correspondents" printed on the wrappers of *London Labour* each week (and itself a sign of the way that his topic was burgeoning), he consistently referred to the upcoming survey of skilled workers. These wrappers have a more important role in Mayhew's work than as indications of his intentions, however. They are also the source of much of what we know about his opinions and methods since he discusses both matters on the wrappers much more openly than in *London Labour* itself. (The earliest wrappers were simply brief answers to miscellaneous queries or periodic acknowledgements of money sent in for the relief of some particular street seller, such as the crippled nutmeg-grinder seller whose situation provoked much sympathy.) Mayhew refused to have anything to do with these donations, and turned them over to his publisher John Howden, who served as secretary of a "loan office for the poor." By 28 June nearly £30 had been received, "£4 10s. of which have been dispensed as gifts, and £24 10s. advanced as loans to 19 people, to be repaid in small installments, with interest, at the rate of 5 per cent per annum" (wrapper 29). The small number of donations compared to the over £800 sent into the *Morning Chronicle* reflects both the smaller circulation of *London Labour* and the fact that Mayhew's readers were less moved by the plucky street folk than by the sweated laborers.

The provisional nature of the "Answers to Correspondents" part of Mayhew's expanded survey gave him added protection in his role as "scientist." He did not have to accept responsibility for his opinions in this context. He explained that he "merely avails himself of the *waste* pages of this periodical as a means of recording the opinions which are forced upon him in the course of his investigations. . . . He reserves to himself . . . the right of changing or modifying his sentiments as often as a more enlarged series of facts, may present new views to his mind" (wrapper 16, 29 March 1851). Nonetheless most of his opinions on social and economic questions appeared first, and sometimes exclusively, on the wrappers; and there are few cases where "a more enlarged series of facts" altered his view.[5]

Reading *London Labour* wrappers and text together in chronological order clarifies some of the confusion in the structure, order, and intentions of the four volumes. While interviewing costermongers and street sellers in his text, Mayhew was expressing his opinions and arguing the questions of political economy which grew out of his projected survey of skilled and unskilled workers. This disparity in subject between wrapper and text later resulted in a major disruption of his subject when he inserted into the survey of street cleaning in volume 2 a badly organized discussion of the causes of low wages. At that point Mayhew thought he had found an opportunity to link the concerns of the wrappers and the current subject of *London Labour* itself.

In addition to the survey of changing conditions in the street trades and the exchange of ideas between him and his readers in the "Answers to Correspondents," Mayhew expanded the weekly numbers of *London Labour* in another, very attractive way. Each issue began with a woodcut, usually of one of the street sellers interviewed. Most of these woodcuts were engraved from daguerreotypes by Richard Beard, an early London photographer who opened the first portrait studio in Europe in 1841 and who held the patent of the daguerreotype process in England.

Photography was in the early stage of its development in 1851; the census of that year listed fifty-one professional photographers in Great Britain. At this point it was seen mainly as a branch of the graphic arts; one had one's photograph taken as one had one's portrait painted, a parallel underlined by the long sitting time necessary for the daguerreotype. This long exposure time also meant that there were few photographic representations of ordinary people and their work. Though the possibility that the photograph could have a documentary value in social investigations was realized by a few people, not until the end of the century, when photographs could be used in newsprint, was the possibility exploited.[6]

Mayhew's use of photographs as the basis of a social record even before they could be reproduced as such in print is a tribute both to his prescience about the application of modern technology to social science and to his concern for a rigorous precision in his own work. Unfortunately the original photographs have been lost,[7] but the woodcuts themselves represent some of the most accurate pictures that we have of the actual facial features and dress of the people making their living in the streets of London at midcentury, and are thus a valuable contribution to the social history of the period.

In the beginning of the *London Labour* series, Mayhew appeared confident of his ability to condense his material, although this control soon evaporated. The opening pages of the series do show us for the first and last time what he meant to do with each sector of the laboring classes as he revised the material in the *Morning Chronicle*. We have seen how in the initial plan for "Labour and the Poor" Mayhew had intended to report his findings deductively but was forced to do the opposite by the way his research unfolded. In the earliest numbers of *London Labour* he was finally able to achieve his desired structure. Later in volume 2 he summarized his sense of this way of proceeding. When one compares this late method with his initial one as given in Letter II, one can see that even his sense of his subject had broadened considerably by this point. Opening his discussion of scavengers, or the men who collected the garbage, he said: "First, I shall give an account of the class employment, together with the labour season and earnings of the labourers, or 'economical' part of the subject. I shall then pass to the social points, concerning their homes, general expenditure, &c., and then to the more moral and intellectual questions of education, literature, politics, religion, marriage and concubinage of the men and their families. All this will refer . . . only to the working scavagers[8] in the honourable or better-paid trade; the cheaper labourers I shall treat separately as a distinct class; the details in both cases I shall illustrate with the statement of men of the class described" (2:216–217).

This mode of development was carried out in the early numbers of *London Labour and the London Poor*. Mayhew proceeded with his survey of the street trades, starting with a theory which would explain the details that followed. Rather than turning to economic or social theories, though these were implicit later in the volumes, Mayhew seized upon a weak anthropological analogy. Quoting the work of Dr. Andrew Smith, probably the man who was medical supervisor to the army and a recognized expert on South Africa, Mayhew asserted that there were two races of men—the civilized, stationary ones and the "wandering" tribes.[9]

Mayhew's original—and from our point of view rather crude—application of this theory was to use it to describe and to understand those members of Victorian society who did not partake of the prevalent social values of domestic stability and of law and order. In this class of wandering tribes he included not only the habitual vagrant and the rural itinerant pedlar but also the "urban and suburban wanderers, or those who follow some itinerant occupation in and round about the large towns." He supported this dubious association by pointing out that the "outcasts" and "vagabonds" of England shared the characteristics of the uncivilized nomadic European tribes, namely that they possessed "nothing but what they acquire by depredation from the industrious, provident, and civilized portion of the community;—that the heads of these nomades are remarkable for the greater development of the jaws and cheekbones rather than those of the head;—and that they have a secret language of their own . . . for the concealment of their designs" (1:2).

Such an explanation of low life by innate qualities was not an uncommon theory, and Mayhew had leaned toward it from the very beginning of his investigations. In Letter V (2 November 1849), talking about young pickpockets he met in a low lodginghouse, he had remarked that "their errors seem to have rather a physical than either an intellectual or a moral cause," yet what Mayhew considered "physical" causes hardly fit the category as we would understand it. The pickpockets "seem to be naturally of an erratic and self-willed temperament, objecting to the restraints of home, and incapable of continuous application to any one occupation whatsoever." In subsequent letters he rendered the same judgment on hucksters and street performers.

Such assertions as Mayhew made here indeed support Gertrude Himmelfarb's charge that Mayhew contributed to the idea that the poor were a class apart.[10] But Mayhew's general explanation of street life was less important than the rest of his work; it occupied only two pages out of all his volumes, though he periodically referred to it and it did color some of his judgments about costermonger life. Mayhew himself partially abjured the theory in one of his later summaries in volume 1 as well as the introduction to volume 2, drawing a three-part distinction among those "bred" to the life, who could be civilized if society made the effort, those who "took" to the streets and who were the real rovers by choice and temperament, and those poor workers "driven" to a nomadic occupation by their inability to get any other kind of work. Even many in the second group, he said, "are in no way distinguished from a large portion of even our wealthy tradesmen—our puffing grocers and slopsellers" (1:322).

More important the inclusion of the "raw" data of the interviews which Mayhew had developed in the *Morning Chronicle*, while it eventually destroyed the original intentions of the new series, also undercut the force of his dubious hypothesis. The reader received not only the general theory but also the particulars on which it rested. As with the several series in the *Chronicle* the particulars proved to be more instructive than the theory and in some ways contradictory to it.

The anthropological analogy, emphasizing the animalistic and stupid, sat uneasily on the sharp and aware street folk whom Mayhew actually quoted. Despite very large differences, they were still much closer to his readers than to the aborigines of Australia, and he implicitly recognized this in the interviews with them which followed the general introduction. For example, in his opening remarks on the patterers, street sellers who depended on a lively spiel to entice customers, Mayhew portrayed them as an almost subhuman species in their insusceptibility to kindness, their suspiciousness, their trickery, and amorality. Yet in the series of interviews which followed the opening remarks, and in the integration of the words of the patterers into Mayhew's own discussion, one finds very little moralism or negativism. Mayhew, and hence his readers, forget the general hypothesis in the revelation of the details. In fact, at the end of the long subsection, almost as if the experience of his data had made him change his mind, Mayhew turned around and blamed the patterers' "betters" for the same sins: "Until the 'respectable' press becomes a more healthful public instructor, we have no right to blame the death-hunter [who sold fake 'last confessions' of well-known criminals], who is but an imitator—a follower—and that for a meal" (1:230). The theory of the "dangerous classes" which Mayhew elucidated in his work was intended to move his readers to press for reform by making them see how different the poor were from themselves. The interviews produced the opposite effect. "That [the costers and other street sellers] partake of the natural evil of human nature is not their fault but ours,—who would be like them if we had not been taught by others better than ourselves to controul the bad and cherish the good principles of our hearts" (1:213).

Perhaps an unconscious response to this contradiction in his feelings about his subject reinforced Mayhew's increasing reliance on the long interview. As his investigations continued he may have become less convinced of the validity of his overview and thus retreated into the particulars which he could trust. Certainly in the early pages of *London Labour*, when his theory was most confidently asserted, he relied on these long interviews less. The early pages of volume 1 are nearly all in Mayhew's voice as narrator, though he included much quotation of single phrases and sentences.

Mayhew's ability to posit a theory about the street folk was the result of the large number of particulars he had already collected in his earlier four letters on "hucksters" (a word he seldom used in *London Labour*) written in November and December of 1849. While the theory he found did not add much to his treatment of his subject, he was able to organize the details of his earlier series more coherently. The initial surveys had been skimpy and disorganized, and they contained only a few extended interviews. The first letter did end on a biography of a hot-eels seller (reprinted in *London Labour*, 1:162–163), but the rest of the letter was made up of generalized remarks and statistics, occasionally punctuated by single quoted remarks from his sources. As he said "all this information . . . I had direct, not from one, but several of the class" (XIII, 30 November 1849).

When he used this material in *London Labour* Mayhew organized it in a series of ever-narrowing subdivisions. This made the report more understandable and "scientific," but it finally enlarged the topic of the street folk to epic—or mock epic—proportions. The subject was first divided into six groups; then each of these was subdivided into smaller units. One of the six main groups, the sellers, for example, was subdivided eight different ways.[11] Following this general division and subdivision Mayhew returned to the larger survey by discussing costermongers, the sellers of fish, fruits, and vegetables. His classifying mania was applied to all aspects of their life. The costermonger class was itself broken into general subtopics, including their varieties, history, habits, and amusements, their politics and social arrangements, their religion, education, literature, and economic situation. Short interviews and directly quoted comments were used in this part of his work to support and to explain generalizations, as when Mayhew quoted "one smart costermonger" who told him, regarding artisans reduced to street trading, "They don't find a living, *it's only another way of starving*" (1:7). Finally Mayhew included two representative lives, given in the long interview form, one of a costerlad and the other a costergirl.

In addition to the general material and the two extended interviews, there were a few scenic descriptions in this early section such as those of the Saturday-night and the Sunday-morning markets. In all but that of the "penny gaff" Mayhew followed the practice he had developed in the *Morning Chronicle* series of reporting in the present tense the experience of a specific night or morning. In the penny gaff, entertainments housed in store fronts and frequented by the lowest classes, he was so shocked by the obscenity of the performance that he suppressed the details which normally made up his descriptions. His moralistic response in that description shows the limits of his tolerance of the lower classes, although, in that it is atypical of Mayhew, it also emphasizes the scope of his acceptance.

After going into some detail about the costermongers as a group, Mayhew began his investigation of each subdivision of the class. As he got into each one, the subject widened out again. He began with some general statistics on the kinds of fish bought and sold at Billingsgate and a description of the market, with a glance at the peculiarities of the trade laced by short quotations and statistical charts. Then the topic swelled once more as he subdivided the group into the people selling each type of fish—i.e. sprats, shellfish, oysters, periwinkles, and "dry" fish. Each of these divisions was supported by long individual interviews (sometimes two or three to a subsection) in which Mayhew reported not only the statistical details of each category but also the mode of life of this type of street seller.

Mayhew maintained the same method of subclassification in each of the larger groupings of costermongers. In doing this, he spent some five weekly numbers, a little under one hundred pages. The next seventeen numbers, about three hundred pages, he devoted to the street sellers who hawked things other than fish, fruits, and vegetables. At this point Mayhew's classification had destroyed the perspective of his survey. The costermongers numbered some 30,000 by Mayhew's count while other street sellers totalled only 11,000.[12] Yet he devoted over two-thirds of volume 1 to long interviews with this minority. The disparity between numbers and space was not deliberate but the inevitable result of his decision to give one representative interview for every subclassification of the larger group. There was one interview with an oyster seller, who might represent hundreds, and one interview of the same length and scope with a seller of spectacles and eyeglasses, who represented on the average only thirty-five men. Mayhew tried to restore the balance by beginning each subsection with figures which gave the total numbers of each subclass, but these figures were lost in the details of the individual interviews.

The later sections were not as well organized as those on costermongers either, for Mayhew's increasing interest in the minutiae of his subject led him into a number of long digressions much like those of the early *Morning Chronicle* letters. His source for the information on patterers, for example, gave yet another exposé of low lodginghouses, and later an interview with a blind street seller turned into a second eighteen-page attack on low lodginghouses, which itself contained a flock of inserts from *Morning Chronicle* sources and an account of a meeting of vagrants misleadingly entitled a "Meeting of Thieves."

From about the middle of the first volume it seems evident to the reader of *London Labour* as it unfolds that the investigation of the street sellers had become so particularized that it would take many months, even years, to finish it and to turn to the artisans again. Mayhew as usual remained sanguine. In May 1851 he announced that he "purposes giving the results of his inquiries into the state of the working classes immediately the excitement of the Great Exhibition has lulled a little" (wrapper 23). But throughout volumes 1 and 2 he referred to other impending surveys of street folk such as one on street Italians. By June he foresaw the duration of *London Labour* as five or six years (wrapper 29), a considerable expansion over the smaller span announced at its inception. In September, after remarking that he would get to "those who need not work" at some point, he added "though really the subject he has undertaken is so vast that it becomes almost fearful to contemplate" (wrapper 39). Apparently unaware of why this had happened, he remained unable to compress his material.

Sometime in the second half of 1851 all the twenty-six numbers which made up volume 1, minus the wrappers, were issued bound in a cheap blue cover. For this first publication in book form, Mayhew added an index, a list of errata (typographical errors in figures), a dedication to his father-in-law Douglas Jerrold, and, most important, a preface.

In this preface, really an afterword to volume 1, Mayhew made some acknowledgments. First, in recognition of his informants, he asserted that personal experience of "some thousands of the humbler classes of society" in the last two years had proved to him the reliability of the poor as sources of information. He also gave credit again to Henry Wood, who had "contributed so large a proportion of the contents of the present volume that he may fairly be considered as one of its authors," and to Richard Knight of the City Mission.

The preface also projected further growth of the survey. Mayhew outlined the contents of the upcoming volume 2; the list of topics he gave expanded the list in the opening of volume 1 by including street Jews, Italians, and other foreigners; and street mechanics. Only three of the eight subdivisions listed in the preface were eventually surveyed, even though the title page of volume 2 of *London Labour* in 1861 repeated the misleading catalogue.

The first number of volume 2 followed one week after the last number of volume 1, and it began with another short introductory section. In this one Mayhew made some suggestions based on the data that he had collected. He recommended a series of poor men's markets modelled on the Old Clothes Exchange in the East End which would allow the sellers freedom to operate and at the same time keep the streets clear. Mayhew's growing concern for the interests of labor, which started in the *Morning Chronicle*, again surfaced in his plan for the management of these poor men's markets. He wanted the consumer and the seller to have equal say to that of the middle-class shareholders: the markets should be directed by "a committee consisting of an equal number of shareholders, sellers, and working men—the latter as representatives of the buyers" (2:4).

In this introduction to volume 2, Mayhew also advanced a theory to explain what he saw as an increase in the number of street folk. While the theory itself was not particularly enlightening, it was based on ideas that contrast interestingly with those of Thomas Carlyle. Unlike Carlyle, Mayhew believed that a revulsion toward work was a natural response in man. Although Mayhew's first expression of this idea preceded Carlyle's *Past and Present* by less than a year, his reiteration of it in *London Labour* sounded as if it might be directed toward Carlyle's great polemic.

In *Past and Present* Carlyle argued that to find his proper work and to do it religiously was the best action a man might perform. His argument in support of this idea was a biting condemnation of the idle ruling aristocracy and a warning to the selfish middle classes. Ideally all work, especially that of the governing classes, should be seen as service. Carlyle knew that the life-destroying labor of the industrial classes was not uplifting, and he said so.

Mayhew's argument was based on a different definition of work. The son of a rich London solicitor, he defined work as the lower classes did—as precarious, exhausting, life-consuming labor. In his introduction to volume 2 he expressed this indirectly but unequivocally: "We are taught to regard all those who object to work as appertaining to the class of natural vagabonds; but where is the man among us that loves labour? For work or labour is merely that which is irksome to perform, and which every man requires a certain amount of remuneration to induce him to perform. If men really loved work they would pay to be allowed to do it rather than require to be paid for doing it" (2:5).

Mayhew's own responses as well as his observation of others reinforced this definition for him. It was stated simplistically but it was similar to one of Marx's insights. Most men's labor, Marx said, "is not voluntary but imposed, *forced labor*. It is not the satisfaction of a need, but only a *means* for satisfying other needs. Its alien character is clearly shown by the fact that as soon as there is no physical or other compulsion it is avoided like the plague."[13] Mayhew was groping toward some notion of the alienation of labor but his uncertainty about his own position and his mental laziness prevented him from finally understanding the significance of his own reactions.

In *London Labour* his application of his sense of the alienation of labor led to a shallow conclusion. Despite the evidence he had collected showing that street trading was very hard work, Mayhew cavalierly judged that, in its freedom of movement and liberation from society's strictures, it was less demanding than a respectable trade. Thus when pay was low in the trades, men would naturally take to "easier" occupations such as street selling. While this assertion has little in intrinsic value, it does show once again the implicit attraction street life held for him.

Though Mayhew did not make direct reference to Carlyle in his remarks about work, he did refer to the Victorian prophet two times on the wrappers. These references are some of the most disturbing evidence about Mayhew that we possess. Carlyle, as we have noted, spoke favorably of Mayhew's revelations about distressed seamstresses. Mayhew never returned the compliment. He apparently had no respect for Carlyle. In one of his comments his scorn could perhaps be justified, but in the other it was so wantonly wrong that one's faith in Mayhew's accuracy is almost shaken.

Both references occurred within a week of each other. This might suggest that Mayhew was reading Carlyle in January 1852, but since in neither case did he quote accurately, it seems more likely that he was simply responding to Carlyle's reputation in the winter of 1852. The first reference came in a discussion of the bad effects of machinery on employment. In the course of an ironic discussion of what would become of the men thrown out of work in mechanized trades, Mayhew remarked: "You could not exactly do with them as Mr. Carlyle humanely recommends, 'shoot them and sweep them into the dustbin'" (wrapper 57, 10 January 1852). This was undoubtedly a reference to Carlyle's remark in "Model Prisons": "If I had a commonwealth to reform or to govern, certainly it should not be the Devil's regiments of the line that I would first of all concentrate my attention on! . . . to them one would apply the besom, try to sweep *them* with some rapidity into the dustbin."[14] The exaggeration in Mayhew's paraphrase was perhaps forgivable since Carlyle's fulmination against prisoners in this essay was quite distasteful. He was not referring to workers, of course, and Mayhew's suggestion that he was was unfair.

A more incomprehensible distortion of Carlyle's remarks appeared the next week in "Answers to Correspondents": "If there were no labourers and labourers' children to keep, then machinery and economy of labour might be a national blessing, but so long as society *will* permit labourers to have children—so long as the 'painless extinc-tion' of every poor man's child, as soon as it is born, which Mr. Carlyle advocates 'in grim earnest!' is not part and parcel of the law of the land—so long must the invention of machinery and the economy of labour be a national curse instead of a blessing" (wrapper 58, 17 January 1852).

How could Mayhew have so missed the point of Carlyle's *Chartism*? With the bitterest irony imaginable Carlyle had attacked Malthusian explanations of the "condition of England" by referring to a pamphlet he saw by one "Marcus." It was this "Demon Author" who made the brutal suggestion that "all children of working people, after the third, be disposed of by 'painless extinction.'" Carlyle "applauded" this suggestion— the apotheosis of a view from "a Benthamee Malthusian watchtower, under a Heaven dead as iron"—and suggested that "there might be 'beautiful cemeteries with colonnades and flower-plots,' in which the patriot infanticide matrons might delight to take their evening walk of contemplation; and reflect what patriotesses they were, what a cheerful flowery world it was."[15] One can only assume that Mayhew was so revolted by the hysterical tone in *Latter-Day Pamphlets* that he could not attribute a single decent sentiment to Carlyle, nor could he bother to check his memory of a work written a decade before he quoted it. It remains a disquieting example of Mayhew's mental laziness.

After his short introduction to volume 2 with its suggestion for poor men's markets and his explanation for the high number of street traders in 1851, Mayhew continued his carefully categorized investiga-tions of street life. In its devotion to details about tiny segments of the whole, volume 2 became even more disorganized than had the latter part of volume 1. The subject of the first volume, the sellers, spilled over into the opening numbers of the second with a survey of the sellers of secondhand goods and of mineral productions and natural curiosities. These sections themselves contained several digressions.

Even Mayhew's careful classifications began to break down under the weight of their subdivisions. The sellers of secondhand items were not easily separable from the "street buyers." One of the sub-categories of this division, buyers of umbrellas and parasols, led to further digression on the Jews—not just those who earned their living in the streets but all who lived in the East End. In this discussion Mayhew echoed the kind of casual prejudice against Jews which existed at almost all levels of Victorian society and which led to Disraeli being known in some quarters as the "Jew d'esprit."[16] In *London Labour* the discussion was tinged with bias, although he praised Jewish charities. He described Jews as greedy, unpolitical, nonintellectual (because they preferred the theater and concerts to reading), and fond of gambling. Mayhew was never really interested enough in this minority, with whom he felt nothing in common, to go beyond a restatement of some of the milder conventionalities.

Finishing the discussion of the Jews abruptly to turn with ludicrous effect to the street buyers of hogwash and tea leaves, he finally took up the third large division of the street folk—the street finders and collectors who earned a "living" by what they gathered on the streets. Classification of this group was more difficult than might have been expected as was interviewing so Mayhew devoted only twenty-three pages to them, compared to the 500-odd pages given to the street sellers.

Next came his last major expansion. Mayhew extended the category "street finders and collectors" to a group who only vaguely fit the label, all those whose official business was to dispose of the city's refuse, the "dustmen, nightmen, [chimney] sweeps, and scavengers" (2:159). These groups were not treated in this order in the following text, again showing his changing plans; nor apparently did Mayhew intend at this time the survey of crossing-sweepers which closed the volume in 1856.

This final enlargement of his subject did not result either from his increasingly detailed breakdowns or from his long interviews. This time the loss of control over the direction of his work resulted from a plethora of available statistical information. The large number of official figures on this subject available to Mayhew grew out of the same concern over sanitary conditions which led to his very first investigation—that of Jacob's Island. Yet it is curious that in the long discussion in *London Labour*, Mayhew did not describe directly the sanitary problems connected with refuse disposal which most concerned his contemporaries and which resulted in the limited reform at the time. Instead he became a prisoner of the statistics; he could not focus his picture on the most important of the multitude of details.

Despite this final explosion of his material Mayhew's opening remarks in this last section showed that he had never lost sight of the goal in his initial plan. "I have now to deal with what throughout the whole course of my inquiry into the state of London Labour and the London Poor I have considered the great object of investigation—the condition and characteristics of the working men; and what is more immediately the 'labour question,' the relation of the labourer to his employer as to rates of payment, modes of payment, hiring of labourers, constancy or inconstancy of work, supply of hands, the many points concerning wages, perquisites, family work, and parochial or club relief" (2:216).

The subject of street cleaning proved to be a debilitating one for Mayhew's survey, nonetheless. The proliferation of information on this subject resulted in an overgrowth of long and tedious statistical studies on the physical makeup of the street, the traffic which dirtied it, the mud which formed on it, the water which flowed over it, and the several ways of cleaning it—machines, paupers, or orderlies who cleaned it before it got dirty. (Not surprisingly Mayhew approved the last.) The subject of scavenging, however, did provide an opportunity for a complete if unsystematic expression of Mayhew's thoughts on free trade, the "small master" or subcontracting system of employment and the remedies for low wages. This spreading of the discussion from the wrappers into the text was not enough magnification of it, and soon Mayhew began *Low Wages*, a new weekly, to take the overflow and to allow him finally to systematize his ideas on political economy.

Even *Low Wages* was not the final branching out of his work in 1850–1852. During the same period that he was beginning it and surveying refuse collection, he was also publishing an extra volume to *London Labour and the London Poor*, a survey of "Those that Won't Work." The decision to embark on this volume must have occurred to him fairly late in his investigations. According to his remarks on the wrappers, as of 22 March 1851 he had no intention of dealing with prostitutes or other criminals. These subjects appeared recurrently in "Answers to Correspondents" nonetheless, and in late August 1851 the first number of the new volume appeared. Subsequent numbers show that this work was also becoming distended. Mayhew himself wrote only the first thirty-seven pages, and in late 1851 it was bogged down in a historical survey of prostitution through the ages, written by Horace St. John (1832–1888), a friend of Mayhew's and later a journalist and editorial writer for the *Daily Telegraph*.

The prospectus for the extra volume had promised a more immediate investigation of the London prostitutes, but Mayhew was probably too busy with all his other projects to begin work on that topic at that moment. His official explanation, however, made no mention of his other work. Instead, drawing himself up to the full height of conventional moral dignity and at the same time using the excuse of his disinterested pursuit of knowledge to justify the titillating subject, he solemnly declared that a history of prostitution was necessary in order to prove whether the moral abhorrence of it was innate and universal or if it was culturally induced. Mayhew himself was reasonably certain that it was the former. Unfortunately he never made his promised systematic survey of London prostitutes. Early in 1858 he made another stab at the subject, probably in response to the "minor flood" of articles in the press from late 1857 through March 1858 urging the government to get involved in suppressing prostitution.[17] Mayhew was reported in April 1858 to have proposed to Lord Derby, recently in power with Disraeli, that the government send him on a visit to "all the great centers of civilization on the Continent for the purpose of testing the relative merits of the interference and non-interference systems" of dealing with prostitution.[18] It is not surprising that Derby did not take him up on this grand scheme.

Mayhew opened the first number of the extra volume in August with an attempt "to classify the different kinds of labour scientifically" (4:4), this one another expansion of his classifications in the *Morning Chronicle* letters. This long chart was the last extension of Mayhew's subject, the ultimate magnification of his plan. For sixteen pages he struggled with a final effort to control the subject of the "Workers and Non-Workers of Great Britain."

He began by justifying the classification of the workers in the metropolis by their attitudes toward work by appealing to a biological need of all animals for sustenance collected either by themselves or by others. Next he looked for a way to order a comprehensive picture of those who will work "so that the mind may grasp the whole at one effort" (4:4). For two years this will-o'-the-wisp had evaded him. He dismissed all previous attempts at the classification of labor, particularly that which Prince Albert had devised for the Great Exhibition. Mayhew had more respect for the system of classification created by John Stuart Mill in *Principles of Political Economy*, and he actually adopted three of Mill's categories for his own system. Mayhew made one crucial addition to Mill's analysis.

This qualification turned out to be the most significant aspect of his new classification. Once again Mayhew's examination of his subject suddenly brought him to a striking insight closer to the view of the working classes than to that of his own class. He thought that Mill confused the labor picture by not discriminating from the "Enrichers" (the producers of goods), a group which, rather than producing utilities directly, was "occupied in *fitting other things* to afford utilities." He thus disagreed with Mill, who included capitalists among the enrichers. To Mayhew they were only "auxiliaries." Their function was "merely *auxiliary* to the labour of the producers, consisting principally of so many modes of economizing their time and labour" (4:9). The only true producers or enrichers of the nation were the actual workers who made the goods.

A stronger bias in favor of labor could hardly be imagined, but Mayhew was not willing to go beyond his classifications to attack the economic system of the country. "Whether the gains of some of these auxiliary classes are as disproportionately large, as the others are disproportionately small [manual laborers were also auxiliaries], this is not the place to inquire," he said (4:9).

Mayhew's inclusive classification of workers had few other surprises. He included "authors, editors, and reporters" among the enrichers of the country, and his ambivalence about the establishment found a harmless outlet in his classification of servitors. This group, he said, destroying class distinctions with one blow, included not only servants and amusers, but also, grandly, the sovereign, the House of Lords and Commons as well as all judges and executive and administrative officers from the cabinet to the street keepers.

Perhaps the most informative part of Mayhew's new classification was that of the nonworkers, where all the varieties of begging styles were duly catalogued, and where each variety of cheat and thief was given his slang name. Here we learn that "bouncers and besters" defrauded "by laying wagers, swaggering, or using threats" (4:24) and that their accomplices were called "jollies" and "mobsmen." We also discover that "snow gatherers" stole clean clothes off the hedges, while "noisy-racket men" thieved china and glass from bins outside china shops and "bluey-hunters" purloined lead from the tops of houses. This group of nonworkers was intended to be the actual subject of the extra volume. Since his discussion of the general characteristics of the nonworkers, particularly of the prostitutes, was expanded (yet again) in *The Criminal Prisons of London*, the analysis of his ideas on these subjects will be taken up in the next chapter.

It was thus that *London Labour and the London Poor* unfolded and gradually lost its original direction in the continual amplification during the years of 1850–1852. What Mayhew accomplished in these three volumes, two of them aborted, was not extensive in its scope, covering only an estimated 40,000 persons out of a population of nearly 2,500,000 residents in London. *London Labour* does nonetheless give the reader the sense of a much larger sample. One tends to forget in reading it that the subject was "only" the street folk.

This "failure" is a response to *London Labour* as a work of art rather than as a piece of social science. Indirectly we learn much about working-class life, through a process of extension and inference. After all, that mammoth poundage of food sold on the streets was *bought* by somebody. Who were the buyers if not the working classes themselves? Thus in an analogous way we can learn not only what they ate but about their reading habits, the amusements of their children, their medicines, their pets, the decorations for their houses, their household utensils, their favorite foods. We discover what piqued their curiosity and their pity, what bored them, what excited them. Mayhew himself recognized this potential when in volume 1 he tried to determine the diet of the poor through the statistics of food sold in the streets, concluding that herrings and sprats provided most of the protein for the working classes, who spent one-fifth on vegetables what they spent on fish. The most popular vegetable was potatoes (because of the Irish) and next, onions (1:118–120).

We also learn something about the social structure of the lowest classes from *London Labour*. The street sellers were a hierarchical society, not markedly different from the rest of Victorian England. All the English sellers disliked the Irish, whom they despised for being able to live on half what an Englishman needed. The costermongers looked down on the sellers of green stuff like watercress or food for cage-birds, while the sellers of ready-made food like sandwiches and coffee who were frequently ex-artisans, kept apart from the coster-mongers. The patterers who sold "stationery, literature, and fine arts," in many ways the most cunning and frequently the most dishonest, considered themselves the "haristocracy of the streets," to quote one of Mayhew's informants (1:213). Furthermore, despite the snobbery of such fine distinctions, all the lower classes were bound together in a "cash nexus." A street seller sold tea to the artisan for his dinner; the artisan's wife sold the used tea leaves to a woman who in turn sold them to a rag-and-bottle shop (the cheapest sort of second-hand shop) and ultimately they were made into "new" tea and sold again to the costermonger's companion. Moreover a decrease or increase in the artisan's wages was felt all along the chain.

In the relationship between buyers and sellers we also see something of what Mayhew would have called the "social and moral characteristics" of the working classes. Mayhew himself never generalized from his findings beyond the costermongers; but a modern social anthropologist, Oscar Lewis, whose techniques were similar to those of Mayhew's, tried to formulate a "culture of poverty" based on his own investigations of the Mexican urban poor. His most general evocation of his subjects' lives might have been quoted from Mayhew.

> The stories in this volume reveal a world of violence and death, of suffering and deprivation, of infidelity and broken homes, of delinquency, corruption, and police brutality, and of the cruelty of the poor to the poor. These stories also reveal an intensity of feeling and human warmth, a strong sense of individuality, a capacity for gaiety, a hope for a better life, a desire for understanding and love, a readiness to share the little they possess, and the courage to carry on in the face of many unresolved problems.[19]

Having traced the development of *London Labour and the London Poor* in 1851 and 1852, we can now turn to a closer analysis of three key elements in Mayhew's work: first, his methods of interviewing, particularly as developed in *London Labour*; second, his collection and use of statistical data; and, third, his various modifications of the political economy of his time as evolved on the wrappers, in volume 2, and in the unfinished *Low Wages*.

In his process of interviewing, Mayhew's commitment to detail, while damaging to the coherence of his overall plan, had more positive effects. Just as the fusing of himself and his subjects in the *form* of the reported interviews, as developed in the *Morning Chronicle* series, provided a resolution of sorts for Mayhew's conflicts, so did the *act* of interviewing itself in *London Labour*, at least as we can deduce it from the finished product. His conversations with the street folk gave him a creative outlet for his bent toward minutiae. His inability to let go of any small portion of his work, justified by the "scientific" need to report the uncensored material, as well as his tendency to broaden and deepen every part of any topic resulted in interviews which ranged over a wide variety of subjects and created incomparable individual portraits.

Rather than analysing the form of the reported interviews in *London Labour*, which was the same as that in "Labour and the Poor"— namely a fusion of the reporter's questions and the respondent's replies given in the "voice" of the subject—we will try to unravel the way in which Mayhew conducted the interviews themselves. This must remain speculative, for we have only his word that he changed little if anything when he wrote up his interviews for publication. He stated this unequivocally. He gave "a literal description of [the people's] labour, their earnings, their trials, and their sufferings, in their own 'unvarnished' language" (1:iii). If this was true, then a pattern in Mayhew's interviewing does emerge.

Although the specific situations of each interview probably varied, the intention in each was to put the subject at ease and to encourage his expansiveness. Mayhew began this process with the introduction of himself by someone whom his sources would trust. We have seen how he tried to secure someone who was familiar with a neighborhood or trade to provide him with names and addresses of representative and trustworthy individuals that could give him the information he needed.

Occasionally he selected workers or street folk at random. In *Chronicle* Letter LXV, for example, he met on the street a man carrying a cabinet he had made on speculation for the cheap furniture trade and interviewed him on the spot.

Familiar surroundings could also put his informants at ease and thus encourage their candor, and so Mayhew liked to hold the interviews in the home of his informant. This was not always feasible, and sometimes he brought his subject into his own home, which gave the interview an overtone of friendliness. One beggar told him: "I was afeard to come to you at first because I had been 'a starving' on the pavement only a few days ago, not a hundred yards from your door, and I thought you might know me" (XXXI, 31 January 1850). Some conversations took place on the move: he watched a packman work (1:379) and went on rounds with a turfcutter (1:156). At large meetings he tried to induce an easy atmosphere by provoking a sense of community among the informants. His efforts had a disconcerting effect at least once. When in answer to the query of how many boys had been in prison, one nineteen-year-old announced that he had been in prison twenty-nine times, "shouts of 'brayvo!' lasted for several minutes, and the whole of the boys rose to look at the distinguished individual" (XXXI, 31 January 1850).

Once with the person or persons to be interviewed, Mayhew or his companion made notes on the appearance of the informant and the place of the interview, and then began to ask the questions. In November 1851 Mayhew detailed the twelve areas of investigation which he believed were essential: 1) the division of labor in the given trade with a description of the work performed by each class; 2) the hours of labor; 3) the mode of attaining employment; 4) the tools employed and who found them; 5) the rate and mode of pay to each different class of workman; 6) the deductions from the pay; 7) the additions to wages in the shape of perquisites; 8) a history of the wages in the trade; 9) the brisk and slack season of the trade; 10) the rate of pay to those who were "taken on" only during the brisk season; 11) the amount of surplus labor in the trade and the cause of it; 12) a description of the badly paid trade (wrapper 48, 8 November 1851).

It is doubtful that any individual interview followed this outline exactly, nor did Mayhew consistently follow it in the written reports, particularly since most of the questions were relevant mainly to the skilled and unskilled trades. But most of his information on the street folk was clearly gleaned from responses to similar questions. Nonetheless, because the street folk were quite a different class than the artisans, Mayhew asked further questions of them which were aimed at revealing the psychology of street life. "Poor, ignorant, or prejudiced men may easily be mistaken in their opinions," he said, "or in what they may consider their 'facts,' but if a clear exposition of their sentiments be obtained, it is a guide to the truth" (2:245). The desire for this kind of information finally made his obsession with detail a creative advantage, for out of his compulsive use of his "microscope" developed his special mode of questioning. In turn this mode reinforced the unusual and sympathetic relationship which grew up between him and his subjects during the course of an interview. Mayhew was able to provoke an astonishing candor in his individual contacts as the general separation between investigator and subject was forgotten in the welter of immediate details. The persistence and direction of his questions multiplied the kinds of information that he received.

Although Mayhew sometimes asked unusual questions in his efforts to get at the sentiments of his subjects, his most effective means of helping the poor and the illiterate express themselves was to follow through on any promising line of inquiry. What do you know about the condition of poor tailors, he asked a scavenger. "O, as to poor journeymen tailors and sich like, I knows they're stunning badly off, and many of their masters is the hardest of beggars. I have a nephew as works for a Jew slop, but I don't reckon that *work*; anybody might do it." Mayhew disagreed. "Werry well," the scavenger answered politely, "it's all the same." Do you think you could make a weskit, Mayhew apparently asked. "No," the man admitted, "but I've sowed my own buttons on to one afore now" (2:225). In an interview with a casual dock laborer, the man, in the process of describing the ups and downs of his wages, remarked that once he was well-heeled enough to drink wine. Mayhew asked what kind of wine he drank and which kind he liked best. "The port was like rather rough beer, but stronger, certainly," the man answered. "Sherry I only had once or twice, and liked good old ale better" (LVIII, 27 June 1850). A "quick-witted street seller" who was astonished at the idea of selling ice-cream in the streets told Mayhew, "Aye, and there'll be jellies next, and then mock turtle, and then the real ticket, sir." Mayhew asked what was the difference between real and mock turtle. "I don't know nothing of the difference . . . but I once had some cheap mock in an eating-house, and it tasted like stewed tripe with a little glue" (1:206).

Mayhew possessed great skill in adapting his questions to individuals and in inserting incongruous questions which might provoke a humanizing detail. Thus he led a half-literate seller of birds' nests to give a recipe for cooking snails and another street seller to instruct him on the method of broiling fish on an "Irish gridiron" or fire tongs.

With some of his more responsive subjects Mayhew asked personally revealing questions directly, choosing the most promising line of inquiry. For example he asked a seller of birds who was crippled in hand and foot if he dreamed at night. "Sometimes," the man answered, "but not often." Mayhew continued by asking him what he dreamed about. "I often have more than once dreamed I was starving and dying of hunger. I remember that, for I woke in a tremble. But most dreams is soon forgot." Still persisting, Mayhew asked if he were a cripple in his dreams; and when the man answered in the negative, he asked how it felt not to be crippled. "Well, I can't explain how, but I feel as if my limbs was all free like—so beautiful" (2:68).

Even with the most unpromising subjects Mayhew's determined questioning enabled the subject to express the elements of his life, including its intellectual limitations, in his own words. Do you know who the pope is, Mayhew asked a thirty-year-old costermonger. "I don't know what the Pope is. Is he any trade?" the man asked in turn (1:22). The two long interviews with a costerlad and a costergirl provide one example after another of the manner in which Mayhew's individualized questions gave a voice to the inarticulate and the illiterate. Do you think this world could go on forever, he asked the girl. "No," she answered, adding: "There's a great deal of ground in it, certainly, and it seems very strong at present; but they say there's to be a flood on the earth, and earthquakes, and that will destroy it." When is this earthquake to take place, Mayhew inquired. "The earthquake ought to have took place some time ago, as people tells me, but I never heerd any more about it" (1:46). Did God Almighty make the world, he asked the boy, who indignantly replied: "In coorse God Almighty made the world, and the poor bricklayers' labourers built the houses arterwards—that's *my* opinion" (1:40).

The openness with which this boy and girl spoke to Mayhew points to the most important aspect of his interviews, namely the special relationship between him and his subjects. This feeling was possible because, in the first place, Mayhew shared with his subjects a number of important characteristics. In his remarks on patterers, for example, he noted an incapability of working regularly, a predilection for ludicrous amusements, and a relish for all that was ingenious (1:214) very much like his own. He repeatedly noted his informants' desire "to shake a leg," and Mayhew's insistence that working was neither natural nor enjoyable gave to the reiteration of this characteristic a tone of envy.

When Mayhew came into contact with these people, many of whom spoke of, and acted upon, some of his own latent desires, an unconscious recognition must have taken place which enabled him to identify himself with these lowliest members of Victorian society.[20] This sympathy in turn projected interest without condescension, and it disarmed the natural suspicions of his informants. In addition, Mayhew's apparent lack of superiority was reinforced by his method of interviewing. He took notes on what his subjects said, and he entered into exchanges with them, which made of the interviews conversations rather than interrogations. He was interested in their thoughts and their feelings. ("I have endeavoured to elicit the *feelings* of the several paupers whom I conversed with," he said at one point [2:245].) Their revelations stimulated a limitless curiosity, its scope extending with each new detail.

His curiosity was whetted in proportion to what they told him. A mutually encouraging relationship developed in each interview as a result. Mayhew's interest, strengthened by his sympathy and freed to a large degree from the anxiety of losing status by his role as scientific investigator, made the informant feel that he could trust the reporter with the most brutal or bizarre details. The more they told him the more questions he asked; the more he wanted to know the more important his subjects appeared in his eyes and the less superior he seemed to them. So the interviews progressed, with the sympathy and curiosity of the investigator and the candor and garrulousness of the subjects reinforcing each other, producing one engrossing detail after another.

The street folk, vagrants, and petty criminals gave him not only the details of their lives but also those of the "dodges" and "slangs" by which they cheated their customers, who were frequently as poor as if not poorer than themselves. Not only the more intelligent, such as the patterers whose livelihood depended on their ability to talk, revealed themselves in this way. One pathetic mudlark, a miserable waif who made his living by rummaging in the shallows of the Thames for pieces of coal, responded in such detail that within a few paragraphs he had sketched in a psychological profile of himself.

Concrete evidence that this relationship did exist is found in Mayhew's longstanding friendships with some of the people he interviewed. When Old Sarah, a blind hurdy-gurdy player whom Mayhew had met during his investigations for the *Chronicle*, was hit by a cab two years later, he visited her in the hospital for several months until she died. He kept contact with some of his informants, and so as late as 1874 could inform his readers that the faithful daughter of a crippled mousetrap-maker whom he had interviewed for the *Chronicle* in 1850 had made a bad marriage with a drunken bricklayer's laborer and "came ultimately to be an almost insensate and heartless woman."[21]

This special relationship was also reflected in the way he entitled his interviews in *London Labour*. By giving his subjects general titles which were nonetheless particularized—i.e., the Crippled Seller of Nutmeg-Grinders or the Blind Hurdy Gurdy Player, he demonstrated his respect for his informants by protecting their anonymity and asserting their individuality at the same time.

Despite Mayhew's empathy with his subjects, occasionally a bias, which had been subverted by the actual exchange between him and his subject, surfaced when he spoke in his own voice. The details surrounding the reported interviews sometimes show a condescension absent from the interviews themselves. While his reported conversations with the lower classes suggested an equality among men,

Mayhew held to a class separation, remarking at one point that skilled workers "may entertain exaggerated notions of their natural rank and position in the social scale" (XIX, 21 December 1849). In *London Labour* he noted that one of the informants with whom he had a very individualized exchange had nothing to distinguish his appearance from "the mass of mere laborers" (2:224).

Yet the failure of complete identification reflected sometimes in the narrative parts of the reports ultimately served as a control on Mayhew as an investigator. Even as his compassion in the interviewing prevented his picturing the lower classes as worse than they were, his distance enabled him to note their weaknesses without dehumanizing them. He recounted the stupidity of the street finders, who could not even understand the rudiments of buying and selling necessary for street trading, and the ignorant prejudices of the scavengers. He pointed out that many of the poor had gross appetites, and he criticized their excessive drinking.

This combination of sympathy and distance also meant that Mayhew avoided the most common distortion of the poor by well-meaning Victorian reformers—sentimentality. He was fully conscious of this important characteristic in his work, for he frequently castigated it in others: "This disposition to cant, and varnish matters over with a sickly sentimentality, angelizing or canonizing the whole body of operatives of this country, instead of speaking of them as possessing the ordinary vices and virtues of human nature . . . this tendency to put high and heroic motives on everyday conduct is the besetting sin of the age."[22] (Was he thinking of Dickens here, whose main weakness, he thought, was his "fatally-facile" sentimentality?)[23] The refusal to be sentimental is in the final analysis Mayhew's most impressive statement of respect for his subjects.

One of the disappointments for the reader of Mayhew's work is that he never interviewed the criminal classes in London. The kind of special relationship which he established with his informants would have been very productive in interviews with that frequently romanticized segment of Victorian society. The "extra volume" which was to accomplish this turned out to be an uneven production in the hands of others. Bracebridge Hemyng did the section on London prostitutes, and though conscientious did not have Mayhew's genius for detail or his ability to provoke self-revelation. Even John Binny's[24] interviews with thieves and swindlers, which were the liveliest in volume 4, suffered in comparison with Mayhew's conversations with the street folk.

If Mayhew's interviews were improved by his passion for detail, his statistics proliferated under the weight of that passion. Not only did his figures themselves tend to be magnified, but the figures and charts and other numerical data increased as the availability of official figures became greater, as is evident in the last fifty pages or so of volume 2 of *London Labour* (1851).

Even without the temptation of official figures, Mayhew's devotion to the "scientific" method in *London Labour* resulted in some astonishing elaborations. His method committed him to detailing how he arrived at a conclusion, and the subject of the street folk (unlike that of the wages of workers) gave him many unlikely topics for such enumerations. For example he drew out to nearly seven thousand words a discussion determining how much extra money people had to pay a year in various cleaning bills in consequence of bad scavengering of the streets (2:189–193). A more egregious example appears in the section on secondhand sellers.

> There are in round numbers 300,000 inhabited houses in the metropolis; and allowing the married people living in apartments to be equal in number to the unmarried "housekeepers," we may compute that the number of families in London is about the same as the inhabited houses. Assuming one young or old gentleman in every ten of these families to smoke one cigar per diem in the public thoroughfares, we have 30,000 cigar-ends daily, or 210,000 weekly cast away in the London streets. Now, reckoning 150 cigars to go to a pound, we may assume that each end so cast away weighs about the thousandth part of a pound; consequently the gross weight of the ends flung into the gutter will, in the course of the week, amount to about 2 cwt.; and calculating that only a sixth part of these are picked up by the finders, it follows that there is very nearly a ton of refuse tobacco collected annually in the metropolitan thoroughfares. (2:146)

However freakish Mayhew's extended statistics sometimes appear—and there are many examples like these—one should remember that he was in many cases only a little more elaborate than many of his fellow writers. He did not collect and calculate alone; in his days at the *Chronicle* and perhaps also in *London Labour*, he had helpers who provided some of the calculations.[25] He used official figures whenever they were available,[26] although often with reservations about their accuracy. Some of the more bizarre statistics in his work in fact had solid government status. The chart correlating the amount of food a horse ate with the amount of excrement it produced, which Peter Quennell and others have found an amusing example of Mayhew's statistics,[27] was actually not Mayhew's but, as he said, was taken by him from a French experiment which appeared in "Annales de Chimie et de Physique."

Many of the matters that Mayhew and others tried to calculate were simply not open to statistical analysis, and in his belief that they were he is at his most Victorian. In fact excessive tabulation of unlikely topics was common enough in the late 1830s for Dickens to satirize it repeatedly in the Mud Fog Papers. One of the best of these sketches ironically prefigured some of Mayhew's own calculations.

MR. SLUG then stated some curious calculations respecting the dogs'-meat barrows of London. He found that the total number of small carts and barrows engaged in dispensing provision to the cats and dogs of the metropolis was one thousand seven hundred and forty-three. The average number of skewers delivered daily with the provender, by each dogs'-meat cart or barrow, was thirty-six. Now, multiplying the number of skewers so delivered by the number of barrows, a total of sixty-two thousand seven hundred and forty-eight skewers daily would be obtained. Allowing that, of these sixty-two thousand seven hundred and forty-eight skewers, the odd two thousand seven hundred and forty-eight were accidentally devoured with the meat, by the most voracious of the animals supplied, it followed that sixty thousand skewers per day, or the enormous number of twenty-one millions nine hundred thousand skewers annually, were wasted in the kennels and dustholes of London; which, if collected and warehoused, would in ten years' time afford a mass of timber more than sufficient for the construction of a first-rate vessel of war for the use of her Majesty's navy, to be called 'The Royal Skewer,' and to become under that name the terror of all the enemies of this island.[28]

Dickens's satire here stressed precisely the formula followed by many amateur statisticians, including Mayhew: an unlikely subject, a carefully detailed calculation, the multiplication of numbers to their largest possibility, and a rhetorical comparison at the end. Part of the difficulty with these calculations was the assumption that anything could be quantified and that there was little difference in the methods to be used if the subject were food sold in the markets or cigar-butts collected from the gutters. Mayhew's figures are sometimes fantastic because he unquestioningly accepted this assumption. Though many of his quantifications of the details of waste, recycled foods, and sale of marginal goods are unreliable as figures, general impressions of the size of sale and exchange are at least indicative of the thriving business in these items. Moreover, in one case the development of figure after figure, whether accurate or not, resulted in a fascinating picture of the dependence and exploitation, the ingenuity and desperation of London's poor. A two-page table on "the quantity of refuse bought, collected, or found, in the streets of London" in the concluding pages of his survey of refuse collection (added in 1856) detailed the pathos, the grotesqueness, the enormity of the struggle of the poor for survival— all by means of statistics.

Mayhew also collected some original figures on street trading which could be used by others. J. R. McCulloch, for example, was convinced by his calculations as to the amount of poultry and game sold at Leadenhall market. (Mayhew accused him of stealing these statistics, but McCulloch gave Mayhew oblique credit.)[29] In many cases Mayhew's figures on street trading are the only ones we have, but their accuracy must always be in doubt. He seems never to have corrected the errors in his text. Information in an attack on low lodging-houses in *London Labour* was challenged by some correspondents, for example. Mayhew acknowledged the error and promised to correct the text in the future, but the mistake was never changed in any subsequent publication. Nor did he incorporate the typographical corrections, and the long list of errata to volume 1 was evidence that there were many mistakes. As Thompson has said: "Every single table and set of statistical data in Mayhew must be scrutinised, not for dishonesty or manipulation, but for sheer slipshod technique and haste in getting to press."[30]

Mayhew's methods of statistical calculation nonetheless were per-

fectly normal by Victorian standards. Few nineteenth-century statisticians, even the most professional, used any technique more
complicated than arithmetic. William Farr, the director of the census
(who lived on the same square as Joshua Mayhew and his family in
1833–1841) used the same kind of averaging and guesswork as Mayhew
did, although Farr was able to compile his results in a systematic fashion, while Mayhew, as a journalist, had to present his findings more in-
formally. In addition, because of the scope of the material he had at his
command, Farr could draw conclusions with more authority than
Mayhew, whose limited sources sometimes made the larger projections of his calculations uneven.

There is no doubt that Mayhew was acquainted with some
nineteenth-century theoretical statistics. In *London Labour* he mentioned one standard work, *Instructions populaires sur le calcul des
probabilités* (1828)—an English translation was published in 1839—by
Lambert Adolphe Jacques Quetelet (1796–1874), a Belgian astronomer
who helped found the statistical section of the British Association in
1833 and who sponsored the first International Statistical Congress in
Brussels in 1853 (wrapper 39, 6 September 1851). Mayhew may even
have derived some of his procedures and beliefs from Quetelet since
the Belgian insisted that every statistical work should give both the
sources of the data and the manner of their collection, a procedure
Mayhew followed rigorously. Also when he sought ways during his
first investigations to get ever-larger samples, Mayhew reflected
Quetelet's dictum that the number of sources must be large if general
causes were to emerge. Quetelet also believed that the regularity
found in statistical results could reveal the "laws" of the existing social
order. Though he never asserted it directly, Mayhew implied that he
shared this view, whether or not he derived it from the Belgian. We
have seen in his definition of his role as social scientist that Mayhew
planned to arrive "ultimately at the laws and circumstances affecting,
and controlling the operation and rewards of the labourer" (wrapper
10, 15 February 1851).

Mayhew himself considered his collection and enumeration of statistics the most important part of his work because it would lead to the
discovery of these social laws. Yet from our perspective the way he

sometimes used his figures for rhetorical purposes seems more interesting and more valid. For this journalistic effectiveness the exact accuracy of his numbers is less important, and the periodic ridiculous amplification of them served a strong creative purpose. Even his old enemy the *Economist* recognized this strength when it reviewed the early numbers of "The Great World of London": "The art shown in dealing with [statistics], so as to render them not merely perspicuous and interesting to the student of figures, but simple, intelligible, and entertaining to the mere lover of light reading, is equal to the diligence and ingenuity that must have been exerted in their compilation" (22 March 1856).

In his rhetorical use of his statistics Mayhew carefully maintained his disinterested stance by juxtaposing significant figures but leaving the reader to draw the obvious conclusion. In doing this he also found a way to reinvigorate the journalistic cliché of the contrasts of London. Before the interviews exposing the inhumanly low wages which tailors and seamstresses received for making by piece work the various parts of army officers' uniforms, Mayhew inserted an official report detailing the generous amount of money that army colonels were allowed for uniforms. The same kind of implied criticism by contrasting figures was made periodically in *London Labour*. "Were the street-orderly mode of scavaging to become general throughout this country," he wrote, "it is estimated that employment would be given to 100,000 labourers, so that, with the families of these men, not less than half a million of people would be supported in a state of independence by it. The total number of adult able-bodied paupers relieved—in-door and out-door—throughout England and Wales, on January 1, 1850, was 154,525" (2:259). The figures given in the first part of this calculation are highly suspect, but the point about government public works as an alternative to the work house was made with great force.

Not all Mayhew's rhetorical uses of figures eventuated in moral points. Some were simply for the literary effect though they grew out of the same expansiveness and meticulousness which gave amusing and doubtful numerical results. As did Mr. Slug in the Mud Fog papers, Mayhew liked to emphasize his figures either by spelling them out or by multiplying them out. Thus 100,000,000 tons of wet house-refuse was multiplied to become 6,603,110,400,000 cubic inches of sewage. After calculation to determine the area of London in square inches, Mayhew discovered that 10,686,132,230,400 cubic inches of rain fell on London per annum—and all that to show what an uncertain business street selling could be.

Finally even Mayhew's statistics could be affected by his tendency to humanize all the particulars about lower-class life. Late in volume 2, with a balance of rhetoric, method, and data which some modern readers might find absurd, he injected a human element into the "dry" figures.

> Three or four sheets of note paper, according to the stouter or thinner texture, and an envelope with a seal or a glutinous and stamped fastening, will not exceed half-an-ounce, and is conveyed to the Orkneys and the further isles of Shetland, the Hebrides, the Scilly and Channel Islands, the isles of Achill and Cape Clear, off the western and southern coasts of Ireland, or indeed to and from the most extreme points of the United Kingdom, and no matter what distance, provided the letter be posted within the United Kingdom, for a penny. The weight of waste or refuse paper annually disposed of to the street collectors, or rather buyers, is 1,397,760 lbs. Were this tonnage, as I may call it, for it comprises 12,480 tons yearly, to be distributed in half-ounce letters, it would supply material, as respects weight, for *forty-four millions, seven hundred and twenty-eight thousand, four hundred and thirty* letters on business, love or friendship. (2:464)

Though the exact numbers were unreliable, and excessively precise descriptions such as "a seal or a glutinous and stamped fastening" as well as the elaborate digression on geography, are amusing, the details do reassure the reader of Mayhew's care. Further, while the detailed numerical calculation based on the thickness of the paper reflect his compulsive inductive method, most of the effects in the passage—the juxtaposition of statistics, the spelling out of a large number—were rhetorical. In addition the last four words, turning the whole piece into an extended metaphor, removed calculation from the dreariness of waste-paper tonnage and humanized the figures in a way few statisticians ever did. In the cases where Mayhew achieved this kind of effect, his statistical calculations could contribute to the strong human dimension in his writing. In this element lies their main value for the modern reader.

Though Mayhew's failure to complete *London Labour and the Lon-*

don Poor did not significantly affect the interest we have in his interviews nor the value, albeit limited, of his statistics, it did make a final determination of his variations on established themes of political economy more difficult. His opinions developed as his investigations continued, never reaching a fully articulated form and even regressing to more conventional positions after the project was abandoned. At the height of his investigations, however, it is possible to see the direction of his thoughts.

His ideas on economic and social issues grew out of the general ideas of the time but were modified by his direct experience and a gradual shifting of perspective forced upon him through his personal contacts with the lower classes. This new vantage point was combined with some of the ideas of the major intellectual influence on him, John Stuart Mill. For example in making the distinction between the "honorable" and "dishonorable" branches of the skilled trades, he turned to Mill's distinction between wages determined by supply and demand and by custom. Workers in the "honorable" portion were "those whose wages are regulated by *custom*" while in the "dishonorable" portion were "those whose earnings are determined by competition" (LXV, 15 July 1850).

The importance of empirical method to Mayhew meant that in *London Labour* whatever economic ideas he had were muted and almost buried in his text. In the following passage for example, Mayhew's incipient radicalism is barely evident in a parenthetical remark. "If we take into consideration that in the immense suburbs of the metropolis, there are branching off from almost every street, labyrinths of courts and alleys, teeming with human beings, and that almost every room has its separate family—for it takes a multitude of poor to make one rich man—we may be able to arrive at the conclusion that by far the greater proportion of coals brought into London are consumed by the poorer classes" (2:82). The implications in the parenthetical "it takes a multitude of poor to make one rich man," are almost lost because of the understatement. Mayhew nowhere expands on this idea which could almost be called revolutionary, and yet the fact that it is in his text at all shows how close he was at times to significant dissent.

Toward the end of 1851, when Mayhew's method of investigation had established an identification between himself and his subjects, he finally abandoned the stance of the "disinterested" investigator although he chose another forum to do so. He first announced his intentions on a wrapper when he concluded that "a new Political Economy, one that will take *some little notice* of the claims of labour, doing justice as well to the workman as to the employer, stands foremost among the *desiderata*, or things wanted, in the present age" (wrapper 40, 13 September 1851). Though parts of this new political economy drifted into volume 2 of *London Labour*, Mayhew put most of his ideas into the wrappers and finally into a new weekly publication, *Low Wages*. Though the subject was more "philosophical" than his survey of poverty, he kept to the form that he knew, a popular periodical. Nine numbers of this publication were projected, but the four extant issues are probably all that were published.

Mayhew's willingness to enter the arena of theory at this point was the result of a gradual education. During 1851–1852 he read or reread some works on orthodox political economy; the wrappers refer to John Stuart Mill, David Ricardo, Adam Smith, the scientist Charles Babbage, author of *Economy of Machinery and Manufacturers* (1832); Dr. Andrew Ure, an early apologist for the industrial system and author of "Philosophy of Manufacturers" (1835), as well as obscure pamphleteers. What he derived from these works he tried to fit into the details of his own personal observation. While his fragmentary investigations meant that an original theory was unlikely to result, his penchant for particulars did enable him to make a significant commentary on prevailing ideas.

Although he respected both Ricardo and Mill, Mayhew recognized that he differed from the classical economists because of his use of empirical methods. Whatever conclusions he might come to were "perhaps based upon a greater number of phenomena than any economist has as yet personally obtained. . . . If he be open to the charge of generalising, before he has made himself acquainted with all the particulars, he at least has a greater right to do so than any economist of the present day—seeing that he is perhaps the first who has sought to evolve the truths of the Labour Question by personal investigation" (wrapper 16, 29 March 1851).

Among the English economists of the time there was little disposition to dismiss the importance of empirical data, as had Comte in
his contemptuous treatment of Quetelet's collecting of statistics.
Mayhew's emphasis on the personal knowledge of the data shows his
pride in his own accomplishments and his own particular turn of mind.
His compulsive interest in the manifold details of economic life put him
out of sympathy with what he called the "armchair science" of Adam
Smith. Moreover Mayhew now had reason to distrust untested
theories. His own investigations had forced him to reject the conventional notion of the regulation of wages by supply and demand and
the benefits of free trade to the working classes. His data had led him
to the conclusion that in some trades the cheapening of food prices
which followed the repeal of the corn laws had been followed by a low-
ering of wages. Stung once by theory, he sometimes went to the opposite extreme and refused to extend the conclusion of one survey to
another beyond what he had personally observed. Many workers and
street sellers felt that free trade had hurt them, but Mayhew "can-
didly" confessed he was "as yet without the means of coming to any
conclusion on this part of the subject" (2:229).

He was not always chary of generalization, and it became an absorb-
ing interest near the end of *London Labour* in 1851–1852. His main
contribution to the theoretical debate resulted from his shift in
perspective. Instead of looking at the working of the economy from the
point of view of the capitalist or considering the situation in abstract
terms, he based his argument on the way the economic situation
appeared to the individual workers. It was not the supply of available
workers but the supply of working hours made available under the
operation of the prevailing economic system which determined the
level of wages and the condition of the laboring classes. From above
one talked about increasing demand for labor, but from below one
saw that such an increase did not mean there were more jobs or
higher pay.

Mayhew began his analysis with a new definition of wages. The rate
of wages was not, as orthodox political economists had said, the ratio
between population and capital expended, but was instead "the *ratio*
of the remuneration of the labourer to the quantity of work performed

by him."[31] In other words compensation depended upon the hourly rate of pay or the rate of pay per unit of work. As Mayhew put it, wages were determined by the numbers of laborers, the hours of labor, the rate of laboring, the quantity of work, and the amount of the Wage Fund—i.e., "the gross sum expended upon the purchase of the labour" (wrapper 18, 12 April 1851).

Mayhew's analysis in some respects prefigures Marx's discussion of the effects of the length of the working day, but his reference to the wage fund points to a mingling of accepted theory with new insights. The wage fund theory was one of the fixed points of early nineteenth-century economic thinking. As originally formulated by Malthus it stated that the demand for labor was limited by the supply of available food. Ricardo and James Mill developed a less simplistic version of the principle, but in the public mind it was accepted doctrine that there was an absolute limit on the supply of money for wages. Much later John Stuart Mill abandoned the idea of the wage fund, and it gradually disappeared from economic theory.

Despite Mayhew's acceptance of this theory he was still able to attack the current explanation of the levels of wages. The idea that the supply of labor could be increased by altering the conditions of labor and not by an increase in population had come to him at the end of the *Morning Chronicle* series. In *London Labour* he developed this by dissecting and enumerating the ways that the workingman was robbed of his living by the alteration of his working conditions. In the *Morning Chronicle* he had laid the blame on the middleman system in which the work was contracted out in small sections and the worker was usually forced to enlist the help of his wife, children, or even to subcontract the work again in order to make a living. By the end of 1851 Mayhew had sorted out other means by which the same result was achieved. The men could be forced to work faster ("strapping"), and/or to "scamp" on workmanship; the working day could be lengthened, or the days of the week for labor increased. In addition in the mechanized industries the supply of labor had been further artificially expanded by the creation of six hundred millions of "steam men" and by the division of labor and "the large system of production," where "every increase of business would enable the whole to be carried on with a proportionally smaller amount of labour" (2:308). The net effect of such an expansion was to reduce the wages paid for a given quantity of labor.

Mayhew thus came to realize that the general tenet which was advanced by Adam Smith and the classical economists urging the capitalist to cut his costs so that more money could be saved for investment was a threat to the working classes. This precept resulted in *"the greatest possible good to the employer, and the greatest possible evil to the employed"* (wrapper 22, 10 May 1851). It is interesting in the light of Mayhew's shifting perspective that this statement echoed the cadences and the sentiments of the People's Charter of a decade earlier which had asked how much longer would the workers submit to watching "the greatest blessings of mechanical art converted into the greatest curses of social life." [32]

Faced with this recognition, Mayhew posited a new political economy which would be founded on the notion that production was a "partnership" between "the man of money and the man of skill" (LW, p. 35, and mentioned as early as wrapper 10). The word *partnership* was the key, for it meant equality, and hence responsibility of one side to the other. "A share," he said, "is a portion regulated by equity, and not by a scramble," a scramble being Mayhew's way of describing supply and demand (wrapper 14, 15 March 1851). If production was an equal partnership between employer and employed, then neither partner should be enriched at the expense of the other. The capitalist should receive just recompense for the use of his money for materials and for the risk involved. The laborer should also receive just recompense for turning raw materials into marketable goods. In all justice, Mayhew said, the worker should receive "a certain proportion" of the *"increased value that the workman, by the exercise of his skill, gives to the materials on which he operates"* (wrapper 42, 27 September 1851).

Mayhew seemed here on the brink of the assertion of labor's right to a share in profits. He stopped on the brink as usual. The words *a certain proportion* suggested that workers were to receive a definite percentage of the value added by their labor, not the subsistence wage which Ricardo and the other classical economists regarded as natural. Mayhew backed off the really thorny part of the argument, namely determination of what proportion would be just.

In this assertion Mayhew made a profound change in the nature of his argument. He shifted from a descriptive analysis to a normative statement. He had been led to this position by gradual steps—first an investigation of labor, then an inconsistent identification with its viewpoint. Having come that far, he next substituted a kind of natural right, such as the socialists of the period stressed, for the natural laws which the political economists claimed governed society. "Wages should be regulated by the increased value of materials upon which the labour is exercised, and . . . the property thus created is the labourer's absolute right, to which the employer can have no title in equity, unless by paying the labourer a full and sufficient consideration for it" (LW, p. 56). Though his assertion that workers had an "absolute right" to the value added by labor was again important, his failure to define "full and sufficient consideration" blurred the issue once more.

In his normative statement about wages he made the same point. "The only true and equitable system of wages," he said (perhaps echoing Mill's discussion of the subject), "is the 'tribute system'; or that which makes the remuneration of the workman depend on the value of the produce of his labour" (LW, p. 42). However, Mayhew did not make specific the precise manner in which such a wage could be determined.

In fact, having arrived at this analysis, Mayhew resisted entirely any "radical" suggestion about how the society could assure the working man a rightful share of the increased value that he contributed to production. He had witnessed how the government's use of pauper labor could lower the wages of nonpaupers; presumably the opposite effect could be achieved by government "interference," as the Victorians said. Mayhew did accept the idea in principle: in order to assure fair wages "it would appear that some kind of restrictive laws is required for the protection of the working man against the greed of the trader" (wrapper 34, 2 August 1851).[33]

Mayhew mainly wanted the workers to improve their condition by using the means at hand, to educate themselves and to inform the upper classes about their condition, and to rely on cooperative efforts. His experience had taught him to respect the trade unions although he tended to praise them in terms of their social services rather than any efforts to affect wages. He pointed out that the trade unions saved the parish money every year by supporting their own members when sick or too old to work. But he was against strikes and ambivalent about working class political actions, as can be seen in the prejudice against the Chartists in his work. By 1851 Chartism invoked images for many of violent methods, and Mayhew's casual bias reflected this common response.

To the modern reader Mayhew's suggestions are a disappointment after the brilliance of his social observation, the insight developed through his contact with the lower classes, and his appreciation of their point of view. Had he continued his work he might have developed further his modification of prevailing economic analysis. Unfortunately with the abandonment of his social surveys came an end to his interest in economic questions, leaving his "political economy" forever incomplete.

All Mayhew's projects—the survey of the street folk, the extra volume on the nonworkers, and *Low Wages*—came to an abrupt halt in late February 1852. When he returned to his project after four years, his main interest in *London Labour and the London Poor* was to complete the survey of the street folk. This time he managed to condense with a vengeance.

With his brother Augustus[34] he collected material to fill out volume 2 and to expand his *Chronicle* letters on street entertainers into a third volume. Apparently he had no plans to continue the extra volume at this time. Once more Mayhew started with great hopes unconnected with reality. An advertisement for *London Labour* in November 1856 stated that all of volume 2 and "so large a portion of the manuscript of the third volume" were in the printer's hands, "that he can confidently promise its entire completion at A VERY EARLY DATE."[35] But a number of interviews in volume 3 mention Guy Fawkes day of 1856 and so could not have been done at the time of Mayhew's optimistic announcement.

The completion of volume 2 was straightforward, but the book was apparently not released in 1856. The refuse-disposal discussion was finished, probably by a number ready for the press in 1852 but not published then. Following that came a survey of crossing-sweepers—men, women, and children who stood at curbside to sweep refuse away for pedestrians—probably written by Augustus. It was sharply condensed compared to the earlier portions of *London Labour*. The scope of the interviews was broad and the answers of the subjects faithfully reported in the biography form developed earlier. The subjects were interesting, and so their life stories have vitality. However there were none of the connecting remarks and none of the statistics and calculations which gave the special flavor to Mayhew's earlier surveys, and the overall effect of the section is one of thinness. This sense of incompleteness should make us wary of reading Mayhew only for the individual portraits. Without the context of statistical generalizations and commentary the interviews by themselves can seem bizarre and lacking general significance.

Volume 3 presents more problems of composition and intention. Strong evidence suggests that in its present form it was incomplete, possibly not in the order Mayhew wanted, and even that he had little to do with preparing it for the press in 1861.

The volume began with material unconnected to the street folk, some of it reprinted without change from the *Morning Chronicle*.[36] Then followed a section entitled "Our Street Folk" (the pronoun is odd and uncharacteristic of Mayhew) in which Mayhew's hand is clear in the interviewing although not in the organizing of the material as a whole. There were no discussions of the subclassifications of street entertainers, and as we have seen, such expansion of detail and categories was irresistible to Mayhew even when he wanted to condense. The first subcategory, Street Entertainers, simply followed the initial title with an interview reprinted from the *Chronicle* and some new material tacked on at the end. The abruptness and the failure to organize and generalize indicates either that Mayhew had not finished the manuscript or that he had lost interest in the project before it was published.

After the section on vermin destroyers, the next 177 pages of volume 3 integrated old interviews from *Chronicle* Letters LII–LVI and new ones conducted in 1855–1856. In a number of cases Mayhew returned to people he had seen in 1850 and updated his reports, but this was not usual, nor even frequently possible, given the transitory nature of the street folk. Illustrations were supplied only for the new material.[37] Some of the new interviews begin abruptly without the physical descriptions that Mayhew normally provided, and a number give abbreviated names of persons and streets, a procedure that Mayhew hardly ever followed.

The classification of the interviews followed roughly the same divisions of street entertainers Mayhew had developed in 1850—but without the more subtle subdivisions and without any further categorizing at all. The final section, Exhibitors of Trained Animals, had only three entries—two happy families (different animals living together), one from the *Morning Chronicle* and one new, and an exhibitor of birds and mice, which suggests that Mayhew was in the middle of this subsection when his work came to an end.

It seems likely from this evidence that in 1856 Mayhew put together in rough form the first 220 pages of volume 3, including twelve new illustrations. Since he wanted to publish volumes 1, 2, and 3 together as books rather than in parts, he decided to hold the first two back until volume 3 was finished. The material in that last volume probably remained in rough form after the death of his publisher stopped the project, and when it was revived again five years later the unrevised manuscript was converted into the finished volume.

The actual publication of the four volumes in 1861–1862 unfortunately adds even more confusion to the picture. Mayhew was probably out of England from at least the end of 1861 through the end of 1863, a period of time overlapping that in which *London Labour and the London Poor* was being readied for its final publication.[38] Several oddities about the four volumes undoubtedly resulted from his absence. With volumes 1 and 2 there were few problems, and they were published in an identical form to the 1851–1852 text, even to typographical errors. A puzzling outline of the contents was given in an advertisement for the first three volumes appearing in volume 4 of the 1862 edition. It made no mention of Mayhew's discussion of street buyers in volume 2 and included surveys of street artisans and street laborers which never appear in the four volumes.

Mayhew's probable inability to supervise the completion of volume 3 had a bad effect on the way in which his achievement was given to posterity. The last half of the volume is a hodge-podge. Apparently in order to make a book equal in length to the others without using any new material, a section entitled "Skilled and Unskilled Workers" was added. This long section consisted of selections from the *Chronicle*[39] plus a report of a meeting with some ticket-of-leave men which Mayhew held in 1856, all introduced in what seems a random manner. The criteria for the selection of the *Morning Chronicle* materials are not clear. One might have expected Mayhew to include the series on tailors and seamstresses on which his contemporary reputation was based. Or one might have expected a good sampling of skilled workers, since he had always claimed that was his main interest. But the only skilled workers who appear are a few cabinetmakers of the poorer sort, and there is not a word about the tailors.

The editor, whoever he was, did seem to try to render the *Morning Chronicle* material more coherent, but in actuality the whole section is very confusing in its organization. With no introduction or explanation the section "Skilled and Unskilled Workers" opened with a discussion of the honorable and dishonorable branches of the cabinetmaking trade, but no material on the honorable branch was reprinted. The section on cabinetmakers closed abruptly and was just as abruptly followed by the interview with the maker of dolls' eyes. Then followed most of seven letters on the dockworkers in the coal trade although no such general title was used. In this sequence two letters (pp. 258–265 and 245–258) were accidentally reversed, making nonsense out of the development of the survey because the letter on drunkenness among workers preceded that which gave the reasons that it was to be included.

Following the series on dockworkers handling coal and ballast came a late discussion of dock laborers who unloaded ships carrying wood; this was followed by three very early letters on dock laborers in general.[40] Perhaps Mayhew or the editor wanted to bring together all his letters on dockworkers in order to achieve his planned survey of "longshore workers," but chaos resulted rather than order.

The series on dockworkers was followed by five letters on the transit system of London which Mayhew regarded, so he said, as incomplete (wrapper 45, 18 October 1851). Letters on vagrants plus the ticket-of-leave meeting concluded volume 3. The letters on vagrants were additionally jumbled. Parts of one letter were glued onto parts of another.[41] If in reading this reordered material straight through one felt that the coherency of the series had been improved by the juggling, one might suspect that Mayhew was making a last effort to present his work in a viable form. Such was not the effect, however, although it might very well have been the intention. Because there were no connecting links, no attempt to do anything but change the order of great bits of material, the section on vagrants was much more disorganized in its presentation than it had been in the *Morning Chronicle* letters, where it had at least the internal logic of a chronologically consistent experience.

Whatever its confusions, the "editing" of volume 3 was the last of Mayhew's efforts on behalf of *London Labour and the London Poor* as a project. In its carelessness this last effort emphasized the paradox of Henry Mayhew—at once meticulous and obsessive about details in his investigations and apparently unconcerned for the coherence and accuracy of the final publication of his work.

The World of London Prisons

Six years before *London Labour and the London Poor* achieved its final four-volume form, Mayhew tried another version of his investigations in "The Great World of London." It was not to fare much better than his earlier work, and in later years he referred to *The Criminal Prisons of London*, as the new project was then known, as a "wretched fragment of a well-meant scheme."[1]

The change in title resulted from an unintentional curtailment of the original plan. The original advertisements, prospectus, and first eighty pages of *The Criminal Prisons of London* pointed to a grander survey. Mayhew now recognized that the expansion of particulars in *London Labour* had derailed his long-vaunted survey of labor, and his new project was designed to avoid this happening again. In "The Great World of London," he wrote, "the writer purposes being less minute and elaborate, so as to be able, within a reasonable compass, to deal with almost every type of Metropolitan Society."[2] To this end he devised yet another classification of labor, one more like the outlines in such popular semiliterary journalistic volumes as those of George Augustus Sala or Charles Manby Smith.

Mayhew proposed to survey twenty-one different types of life in London, such as Legal London, Criminal London, Fashionable and Serving London. Though this design was abortive, he did manage to survey with some thoroughness London penal institutions and the controversies over prison discipline.

To his modern readers this work does not have the interest of his earlier investigations, although it does provide a fitting conclusion to them for in it Mayhew finally achieved the form of reporting at which he had aimed from the very beginning. As we have seen, in both his contributions to the *Morning Chronicle* and in *London Labour*, he wanted to investigate the condition of labor and the poor "scientifically" or inductively and then to present the results of his observations in the deductive mode. In both his earlier works this plan was

THE WATER-CRESS MARKET

Here, in Farringdon, in the very early hours of the morning, some of the poorest of the street sellers bought "cresses" to sell in the streets for artisans' breakfasts. This illustration of the market by Hablot K. Browne ("Phiz") was for the novel *Paved with Gold* by Augustus Mayhew. The account of the watercress market in this novel came from *London* essentially destroyed by his increasing use of the long interview. Mayhew's loss of control over his projected form of investigations certainly contributed to his failure to complete the two previous works, although external events precipitated the end of each.

The Criminal Prisons of London was another effort on Mayhew's part to follow the "scientific" mode of reporting in his generalizations and observations. This time he was fairly successful in that goal but not because his obsession with detail had lessened. Had the author been given a chance, *The Criminal Prisons* would soon have become inundated by life histories of criminals; but Mayhew was not given the opportunity. Authorities sharply limited what he experienced in each prison. He could report what prison officials allowed him to see and what he felt about what he saw; he could also recount what the authorities told him. But he could not tell his readers what the inmates felt because he was not permitted to talk to them. Only in the juvenile section of Tothill Fields prison did he ask the prisoners a few simple questions in the presence of the guards.

The absence of the interviews, while it eliminated the elements of Mayhew's talent which were most productive, enabled him for once to be organized in his procedures and conclusive about his material. He wrote up the first numbers on each prison after he had collected his information, both official and personal. He might have made several visits to each prison before he sat down to write. He had also collected official documents from the prison officials, read books on the subject (Hepworth Dixon's *The London Prisons* [1850], which originally appeared in the *Daily News*, and George Chesterton's *Revelations of Prison Life* [1856] were the most frequently mentioned), and absorbed information from the prison commissioners and government committees. In addition the various arguments over prison discipline were long established. Mayhew knew in advance what to look for in his prison visits and what points to begin with in his reports.

If the obsession with detail did not distort the plan of *The Criminal Prisons of London*, it did result in a curtailment of the project "The Great World of London." Though London prisons were an odd place to begin such a broad survey, the subject evolved through his characteristic insistence on an ever-narrowing series of classifications and subclassifications similar to those in volume 1 of *London Labour*, which in their elaborateness betray the obsessive microscope still at work.

He first subdivided the Great World into "Professional London," a grouping which included all "those who obtain a living by talent rather than skill." His stated intention was to treat each subdivision of this category in turn, "estimating its population—marking out its boundaries and districts—and treating of the manners and customs of the people belonging to it, from the highest to the lowest" (p. 69). By beginning at this point Mayhew had apparently moved to the opposite pole of his concerns in the *Morning Chronicle* and *London Labour*, but the difference turned out to be more apparent than real.

After noting the various divisions of "Professional London," Mayhew picked up one subdivision, that of his father, the legal profession, which in turn was broken into criminal law and civil law, the first being further subdivided into four categories, one of which was "criminal prisons." Showing that his grand plans were expanding even as he wrote, this series of breakdowns of legal London departed from the initial one in the prospectus which had given a different list of topics under the same heading.

With this segment of a larger subdivision, Mayhew began his survey. The research and writing of this small piece of "The Great World of London" took close to a year, and it consumed nearly five hundred large, densely-packed pages. One thus sees that the possibility of his ever finishing the project of "The Great World of London" receded as he wrote.

Recognizing the peculiarity of beginning "Legal London" with a survey of prisons, Mayhew tried to justify it by referring to "scientific" methodology. One could either work down in a survey or begin at the bottom and work up, he said; and while "the first method is the one generally adopted by systematic writers," he proposed "taking the opposite course; and we do so, not from mere caprice, but because there happen to be such things as 'terms and returns' in Law, which give a periodical rather than a continuous character to legal proceedings, and so prevent attention to such matters at *all* times" (p. 79). By this awkward circumlocution Mayhew meant simply that the courts were not in session at the time he was writing. The opaqueness of the prose here might very well cover another reason for Mayhew beginning where he did. The only subject which ever motivated him to sustained and significant work was the lower classes. Although he started "The Great World of London" at the opposite end of the social scale, soon he instinctively turned his survey in a direction which brought him once again into contact with the elements of society outside his own class that could stimulate him to work.

The project proceeded in an orderly fashion from March 1856 through December, with a possible one-month break between monthly parts 7 and 8 owing to Mayhew's illness.[3] Accompanied some of the time by Henry Vizetelly,[4] who probably had taken over the role of Henry Wood as helper and note-taker, he visited the convict prisons for the serving of long sentences: Pentonville, the "model" prison built in 1840–1842; Brixton, the Surrey House of Detention which was replaced by Wandsworth in 1851 but was called back into use as a convict prison for women after the 1853 abolition of transportation for less than fourteen years; the foul Hulks, boats floating in the lower Thames which were now permanent prisons rather than depots for felons to be transported, and finally Millbank, built in 1812–1821. Next he toured the Middlesex County correctional prisons for short-term offenders— Coldbath Fields, Tothill Fields, and, finally, the new Surrey House of Correction at Wandsworth. Here his work stopped on the death of his publisher. (John Binny completed the survey of the Surrey prison in late 1861 and early 1862 and also the City of London correction prison built at Holloway in 1849–1852. Binny also surveyed the three detention prisons for those awaiting trial, Newgate in the city, Clerkenwell for the county of Middlesex, and Horsemonger Lane for Surrey.)

Before Mayhew began his investigations of London prisons, he had introduced a sixty-three-page section, "London considered as a Great World," which included earlier material from both the *Morning Chronicle* series and *London Labour*, a good deal of it statistical and none of it updated. The reader got a bird's-eye view of London, at one point literally, as Mayhew ascended from Vauxhall in a balloon with a Mr. Green.[5] What was not taken from earlier pieces in these opening pages was perfunctory and seemed a throwback to the style of the very first letter in the *Morning Chronicle* series. Mayhew was still un-inspired by the traditional London journalism of the sketch-writers. In trying to imitate them he wrote undistinguished descriptions and tended toward moralizing.

When the actual survey of the prisons began, he was once again back in form, detailing how things looked at a particular time and place and juggling his data with skill. Here as elsewhere in his work he combined his statistics and the disinterested descriptions of his empirical survey with journalistic liveliness. This led, as it had in the earlier works, to an informative survey. Obviously the form of his reports on the prisons had to differ considerably from his other investigations of the lower classes because much of his data was secondhand. He handled this statistical and documentary burden much more effectively in *The Criminal Prisons* than in *London Labour* by relegating many of his charts, prison documents, and other such material to footnotes, and allowing the reader, if he wished, to follow the narrative without the interruption of the specific proofs.

Mayhew also tried to maintain journalistic immediacy in his reports. After one or two sections on the history or special characteristics of a prison, he distilled his personal experiences from the several visits that he had made; and he built the survey on a single day at whatever prison was involved. The journalist put his account in the present tense, and he engrossed the reader with a step-by-step account of a typical but seemingly unique day in prison, which began as he walked out his own door. In the trip out to the prison he took in as much of "The Great World of London" as possible.

The advantages of the "day at" structure were mainly literary. In the first place it helped him overcome the repetitiveness of his experi-ences. The ingrained monotony of prison life appeared novel at every prison because Mayhew's immediate experience, distilled from a larger body of information, was itself different each time. More im-portant, by writing of his experience of each prison as it happened to him, Mayhew gave some sense of what it was like to be a prisoner, a sense lacking in Hepworth Dixon's account of London prisons, the source for much of the popular knowledge on the subject in the 1850s. Each "day at" a prison was severely limited because Mayhew had to

see it essentially as the warders did, but the degree to which the prisoners' experience of the regime finally emerges from *The Criminal
Prisons of London* is the measure of Mayhew's success as a reporter.

Mayhew looked insistently for different ways of increasing his and
his readers' understanding of the prisoners. For instance he tried to
project himself into the lives of the inmates as much as he could. He did
a stint on the treadmill, and spent an hour in a dark punishment cell.
He also developed the glimpses of individual life which he was permitted to see.

> One youth, with closely cut hair, and protruding ears, when asked
> whether he had ever been in prison before, without the least hesitation
> replied, "Never, s'elp me!" "I know better," replied the warder, looking
> earnestly at him. "I'm sure I haven't," continued the lad, with an inno-
> cent expression of face. "We'll see whether some of the officers will rec-
> ognize you," said the examiner. "But it wasn't for felony, sir," muttered
> the lad, who plainly saw that further concealment was of no avail. (p. 296)

Other means of giving the reader a sense of the individual per-
sonalities of the prisoners were less successful. Mayhew relied heavily
on descriptive passages, and though his eye for physical detail was as
sharp as ever in these passages, his range of vision had been reduced.
The drabness of the setting and the identical dress of all the inmates
robbed him of his usual source of differentiating material. The only
thing that distinguished prisoners was their faces, and the masks the
men wore at Pentonville made even this distinction impossible. In
prison scenes, then, Mayhew had to project individuality only through
analysing facial features.

Physiognomy was considered a fairly exact science by the Victorians, and reliance on it was especially evident in comments on
the lower classes. Carlyle saw the criminal character of a Chartist
prisoner in "his thick oily skin, his heavy dull-burning eyes, his greedy
mouth, the dusky potent insatiable *animalism* that looked out of every feature of him."[6] In the same year as Mayhew wrote *The Criminal Prisons of London* Dickens argued in *Household Words* that you
could always tell a man's character from his face.[7]

Mayhew seesawed back and forth between this assumption and what
he knew from experience was closer to the truth: "If one were to as-

semble a like number of individuals from the same ranks of society as those from which most of our criminals come . . . we should find that their cast of countenances differed so little from those seen at the Model Prison, that even the keenest eye for character would be unable to distinguish a photograph of the criminal from the non-criminal congregation" (p. 164). In a footnote to this remark he both denied that "brutal-violence" men "in general" had their characters "stamped on their faces" and asserted that "the generality" of this class were characterized by a "peculiar lascivious look . . . [and] that short and thick kind of neck which is termed 'bull,' and which is generally characteristic of strong passion" (pp. 164–165n).

Mayhew's uncertainty about the reliability of physiognomy suggests the uneven responses that he had to other broad questions about prison discipline and the causes of crime. Public debate over the organization of prison life and the ideal balance of punishment and rehabilitation in society's response to its lawbreakers is a perennial phenomenon. The nineteenth century was a good period for the ventilation of some of the different positions as well as for actual prison reform because there were numerous opportunities to try new schemes. Some old prisons were closed—in 1842, the two ancient debtors prisons, the Fleet and the Marshalsea, and in 1855, the City of London House of Correction, Giltspur Compter—and between 1842 and 1852 three new prisons were built. At each stage there was much discussion of the different regimes.

Though there was steady and slow progress toward uniform and decent prisons throughout the nineteenth century, at midcentury there were still many inequalities. Sentences for the same crime differed widely, as did discipline in individual prisons. Not until 1865 was there a fairly uniform standard of treatment, and not until 1877 did the country achieve a nationally administered penal system.

The ideas of the first great prison reformer, John Howard (1726?–1790), who exposed the brutal conditions of English prisons in the late eighteenth century, had a strong influence on public policy in the nineteenth century. Howard had been eager to prevent hardened criminals from corrupting the inexperienced ones while in prison, and this was one of the main goals of the two principal forms of prison

discipline in Victorian England: the separate system, in which prisoners lived and usually worked alone in their cells; and the silent system,
in which they slept and worked in groups but were prohibited from
speaking to one another. To prevent the idleness condemned by Howard and others, all versions of these two systems featured some form of
hard labor. This "labor" included the grueling ordeal of the treadmill
and the shot drill (moving a pile of cannon balls from one place to
another, usually for seventy-five minutes at a time). This latter torture
was so physically exhausting that men over forty-five years of age
were usually excused.

As far as rehabilitation went, the Victorian prisons were woefully
inadequate. Since conventional pieties generally prevented those responsible from really examining the psychology of crime, nearly all
efforts at rehabilitation were directed toward religious conversion. A
common justification for the separate system was that it induced a
self-examination which would lead to a religious conversion sufficient
to enable a prisoner to resist a life of crime in the future. Mayhew
himself was obsessed with self-communion in prisoners although he
was uneasy about its effectiveness as a deterrent for future crime.

Jeremy Bentham had favored the most rigorous separation of prisoners because he thought it best forced the criminal to reflect on his
way of life, and Pentonville was built on his model of separate cells.
Many other social observers opposed the separate system because it
seemed to them to coddle the criminal rather than punish him. The
belief that prisoners were better off than many of the honest poor was
a widely-held one. (J. J. Tobias has demonstrated that it also was
true.)[8] In "Pet Prisoners," published in *Household Words* in April
1850, Dickens argued that the separate system gave the prisoner an
inflated notion of his own worth. It was also very expensive. To prove
this, Dickens, in a manner much like Mayhew's, juxtaposed the statistics on food allowances at Pentonville prison and those at the St. Pancras workhouse. Unlike Mayhew he did not let the facts speak for
themselves but pointed the moral vigorously. In *The Criminal Prisons
of London* Mayhew remarked that for many persons prison held no
terrors once they had been incarcerated because it was more secure
than life outside the walls. Carlyle's attack on the separate system in

"Model Prisons" was the most scathing. He denounced the reformers and philanthropists who were anxious to see that the prisoner in a "model prison" was given the right amount of food and space but who were unwilling to do the same for the poor man who stayed out of prison.

Carlyle's attack was based in part on an assumption shared by many other Victorians—namely that prisons were to be mainly places of punishment. Mayhew certainly believed this. "Some people there are," he remarked, "who are of opinion that our prisons are being rendered so near akin to schools, as to hold out to the poor, by means of the comforts attainable within them, almost a premium to be a criminal. We incline partly to the same opinion, and have assuredly no desire to strip the prison of its character as a place of *'penitentiary amendment'*" (p. 375).

Despite the powerful voices of opposition, the forces of separation were to win, at least temporarily. The prison inspectors, created by an act of 1835, had consistently favored separation. The 1865 prison act said that all local prisons should have separate cells. In the 1860s, penal regimes seemed at their harshest, as did public opinion on these matters, perhaps in response to an outbreak of violent crimes in London. Carlyle and Dickens again reflect public sentiment. Both advocated flogging and life imprisonment for repeated offenders. Mayhew's attitude at that point was almost as stern. He argued in 1865 that first offenders should get light sentences and occupational training and that then the government should "insure" them to their future employers. Afterward any repeated offenders should get *"penal servitude for life."*[9]

When Mayhew began his survey of prisons in 1856, however, he had not made up his mind about the issue. He at first denied that the evidence irresistibly pointed to any conclusion. Invoking his usual excuse when uncertain about a social question, he hid behind the role of "collector of facts": "it forms no part of our present object to weigh the advantages and disadvantages of the altered mode of dealing with our convicts" (p. 95). He soon abandoned this position under the weight of his direct experience.

In the beginning Mayhew relegated his judgment on the merits of four different forms of prison discipline to a long appendix to the general descriptive section entitled "The London Convict Prisons and the Convict Population." There he devoted the least attention to the classification and the "mark" systems. In the classification mode of prison organization, designed to prevent corruption of new prisoners by old, criminals were incarcerated in cells and buildings according to their offenses. Mayhew was horrified by the looseness of this system, for habitual criminals were not always arrested for the same crime. In any case the expense of separate prisons for different crimes was prohibitive.

In the mark system, praised by Dixon and by Dickens, a man was "sentenced to perform a certain quantity of labour [which] . . . the convict would be bound to perform before he could regain his freedom, whether he chose to occupy one year or twenty about it" (pp. 105–106). Mayhew was also favorably disposed to this system of work sentences rather than time sentences because it seemed to induce a sense of personal responsibility and the proper attitude toward work. Since the process was not operating at any of the London prisons, however, he did not linger over its advantages.

That left the separate and silent systems. Mayhew's first judgment was unqualified: they were "as much *in extremis* as was the old plan of allowing indiscriminate intercourse to take place among all classes of prisoners" (p. 107). In addition, he said (though he later seemed to change his mind), both systems failed in rehabilitating the criminal because "they one and all make labour a *punishment*" (p. 108). At this point he appeared to recognize some conflict between the punitive and rehabilitative processes, but the idea later slipped away from him. Mayhew had no suggestions as to what to substitute for the unproductive labor of the treadmill and the shot drill. For example, he was against women prisoners sewing for tailors because such unfair competition drove down the wages of the women seamstresses outside the prison.

At this point in his discussion Mayhew was equally contemptuous about the only overt effort at rehabilitation in prison—religious conversion. "Can it be said that the merchant in the city honours his bills for the love of God? . . . It is worse than foolish to strive to give any such canting motives to criminals, and certainly *not* true, when it is asserted that people cannot be made honest by any other means than by special interpositions of Providence" (p. 111). Usually such an insistence simply forced the convict to add hypocrisy to his other sins, Mayhew concluded.

In this first evaluation of prison organization, Mayhew saw weaknesses in all the systems; but after he had investigated Pentonville and Coldbath Fields prisons he was in a position to make more specific criticisms. In Coldbath Fields most of the inmates slept alone in their cells but worked together in groups. At Pentonville most prisoners were on the separate system. Mayhew noted that the high rate of madness and suicide attempts indicated that both systems could exact a heavy psychological toll from the inmates. Nonetheless he felt the separate system was the best because it both punished and reformed. Still he could not ignore the fact that "the ratio of lunacy at Pentonville [is] still almost as high again as the normal rate deduced from the average of all other prisons" (p. 168).

Reformation under the separate system might occur, he said, because this system "seeks not only [to put an end to the contamination of prisoners by stopping all *inter*-communion among them], but at the same time to bring about the reformation of the prisoners by inducing *self*-communion" (p. 329), a contention Mayhew had earlier seemed to reject. Now he felt that solitude would lead the convict to see the error of his ways. He also believed that the system made labor "so agreeable a relief to the monotony of solitude, that it positively becomes a punishment to withhold it, and thus, by rendering idleness absolutely irksome to the prisoner, causes him to find a pleasure in industry" (p. 169).

He also thought the silent system was more inhumane. Mayhew came to this conclusion by projecting himself into the lives of the prisoners whom he saw at Coldbath Fields, but he offered a statistical "proof" of it. By bringing men together but preventing them from speaking, the silent system imposed a far greater strain on the convicts than did isolation. This was demonstrated by the very high number of extra punishments the officials at Coldbath Fields had to inflict in order to ensure silence. This actually proved nothing, of course, since the lack of opportunity at Pentonville to do anything to be punished for would naturally result in lower numbers. To help alleviate the strain of the silent system, Mayhew suggested the men be read to while they worked.

He remained uncertain enough about the value of any of these prison regimes to offer a completely different one. His suggestion was not very original, and he may have taken it from Dixon, who argued that prisons should surround "the offender in his state of expiation" with conditions "as near as is possible consistent with strict discipline, to those in which the new-made man will be placed on liberation."[10]

Mayhew was probably attracted to this idea because it brought together a number of aspects of his thought. Coupling his theory of man's natural reluctance to work with the definition of a good citizen implicit in the categories of those who will, can't, and won't work, he concluded that only by changing a criminal's attitude toward work could he be reformed. Instead of having food, clothing, and security given outright to him when he first arrived, Mayhew suggested: "We would have every man placed, on his entering a jail, upon the punishment diet, *i.e.* his eleemosynary allowance of food should be only a pound of bread and water *per diem*. We would *begin* at this point, and make all creature comforts beyond it purchasable, as it were, by the amount of labour done, instead of first leading the prisoner, as now, to believe that he is entitled to receive such creature comforts without work, and being *afterwards* obliged to resort to the punishment diet as a means of enforcing a certain amount of work from him" (pp. 302–303).

Yet Mayhew was not convinced of the value of even this system, for when in August 1856, the same period that he was posing this new system in *The Criminal Prisons of London*, he addressed the committee working to abolish capital punishment, he never mentioned the idea of convicts working for their board in prison. Instead he simply advocated that a modified separate system be used in place of capital punishment.

In this connection let us look at Mayhew's position on capital punishment. Basically he argued against the sentence on the ground that it failed as a deterrent. He believed that it hardened criminals rather than deterred them because it did not appeal to their better selves. More significant Mayhew advanced an important moral objection to capital punishment: the very act of the State taking a life seems to justify an individual's taking one.[11] In the midst of other irrelevant or unsubstantiated objections, this challenge of Mayhew's is still unanswered. That he could see that state or official violence can breed citizen violence is a tribute to his insight into the individual mind and to his recognition of society's share in the causes of crime. It would perhaps be too much to expect him also to see that this argument was far more significant than the necessity of punishment "rendering [the criminal] penitent" and "purifying his nature." Mayhew's paper on capital punishment was another example of his ability to expound popular sentiments and profound insights in the same breath.

Other uncertainties of opinion found voice in *The Criminal Prisons of London*. Mayhew's remarks on juvenile offenders were intelligent and sensitive if not original, but those on women criminals were plain silly. Both discussions grew out of a general survey of the causes of crime which in turn was part of a discussion of rehabilitation and crime prevention. Referring obliquely to the ragged-school controversy in the *Morning Chronicle*, Mayhew showed he was still unrepentant for his attacks on education as a deterrent to crime: "Some years back . . . we took the trouble of testing the greater number of the popular reasons for crime, by collating the statistics in connection with each theory, and thus found that none of the *received* explanations [i.e. ignorance, overcrowding, poverty, drunkenness, original sin, etc.] would bear the searching test of figures" (p. 381). Although earlier in his career he had been unwilling to give his explanations for men and women becoming criminals, in 1856 he was ready to do so. Hints of his position had appeared early in *The Criminal Prisons of London*, as well as in *London Labour and the London Poor*; but the experiences of Tothill Fields prison for boy and female offenders gave him the opportunity to formulate his thoughts on the issues of rehabilitation as they were linked to the causes of crime.

Mayhew had first visited Tothill Fields prison in the course of his investigations of the ragged schools in 1850, and perhaps his many years of thinking about the problem of juvenile crime enabled him to open the section on Tothill Fields prison with some ideas about the causes of it, a topic which itself immediately led him to a larger subject—the general nature of crime and of the criminal. The ambivalences of *London Labour* reappeared in this section. Mayhew reiterated the idea expressed in the first number of *London Labour*: the criminal and vagrant population of England were an inevitable subclass of the population, a kind of "wandering tribe" who were parasitic and lived off the industrious part of society. In this definition Mayhew reflected the Victorian belief in the existence of a criminal class "which lived a life of its own separate from the rest of the community."[12] Most Victorians believed that elimination of this class would eliminate crime.

Mayhew accepted the idea of a criminal class, but his passion for classification led him to recognize that the "professional" criminals were only a part of the problem. He had noted in the introductory section on "nonworkers" in the extra volume of *London Labour and the London Poor* (4:29) that most current theorists about crime erred because they did not distinguish between "habitual" criminals, who broke the law no matter what, and "casual" criminals, who were driven to break the law by reduced circumstances or economic conditions. In his view only the first constituted the criminal class.

Mayhew rightly saw that the crucial element as far as the state was concerned were the members of the criminal classes who were forced into crime. The prison system should direct its efforts toward preventing these "casual" criminals from repeating and becoming "habitual." Since most boys started as casual offenders, by rehabilitating them the "professional" criminal class could best be reduced.

The question was how. This subject had sparked a long discussion[13] which culminated two years before Mayhew's survey in an act of Parliament establishing reformatories for juvenile offenders. This had been preceded by the Select Committee on Juvenile Offenders in 1852 which in turn was the result of public pressure, much of it generated by Mary Carpenter and Matthew Davenport Hill. Mary Carpenter's influential book *Juvenile Delinquents—Their Condition and Treatment* appeared in 1853, and it is peculiar that Mayhew did not mention it in his discussion. She classified juvenile offenders even more

narrowly than he did and made a number of similar remarks. Her main
thrust was to substitute reformatories for prisons, and perhaps
Mayhew did not mention her work because he had chosen to limit his
subject to prisons and their relation to boy offenders.

Mayhew shared with Mary Carpenter the belief that little could be
done toward changing a boy's way of life in prisons as they were then
organized. The cursory instruction in reading and writing could not do
it, Mayhew asserted, reverting to his familiar sentiments: reading
and writing "are but the means of obtaining either *good* or *bad* knowledge, according to the cultivation and tendencies of the mind which
uses them" (p. 392). Nor did he think much of the job training available
because it was too limited in scope and uncertain in prospect.

If neither education nor job training by itself could rehabilitate boy
offenders, what could? Mayhew felt that the solution had to lie in steps
taken both before the boys reached prison and after they left it. The
crimes committed by children were due, he said in several places and
in several ways, "mainly to a want of proper parental control" (p. 386),
a common reason given for juvenile crime throughout the century.

Mayhew knew from personal experience that parents could not be
forced to accept their responsibilities, but this difficulty did not doom
the effort to eliminate juvenile offenders. Although he was not an advocate of state intervention in general, here, as in the regulation of low
wages, it seemed the only hope. If natural parents would not, then the
state much accept responsibility for its citizens, particularly for
juvenile delinquents. The state must become a foster parent, he said, a
sentiment Dickens would echo in "The Short-Timers" in *All the Year
Round*. Once again Mayhew's expression of this common idea was
more trenchant in its vision of social accountability when he repeated it
in his essay on capital punishment, perhaps because of the more identifiably sympathetic audience. "Society is only beginning to understand that it owes a duty even to its criminals, and that the moral
pestilence of crime is due almost to the same guilty neglect of those
laws for the social health of a State, as the physical pestilence of cholera is due to the violation of sanitary principles among the people" (p.
44). What "those laws" for social health were Mayhew did not say. He
did not make any practical suggestions as to how the state could take

over children from bad parents, nor did he note any of the difficulties of doing so. As in his remarks on the causes of low wages, he was wary of any concrete suggestions.

In one case, however—his attacks on magistrate courts and on the inequities of the law practiced there—his simply pointing out the problem was challenging. As with his feelings about religious conversion as a means of rehabilitation, Mayhew seemed to hold two different opinions about judges in the early and later parts of his work. Very early in "The Great World of London" part of the volume, in a general look at "Legal London," Mayhew gave fulsome praise to judges: "If there be one class in whose iron integrity every Englishman has the most steadfast faith—of whose Pilate-like righteousness he has the profoundest respect, and in the immaculateness of whose honour he feels a national pride—it is the class to whom the high privilege of dispensing justice among us has been intrusted, and who constitute at once the chiefs and the ornaments of the profession of which we are about to treat" (p. 77). This sounds like what his father might have said to him when he expounded the glories of the law to his young son.

Mayhew's iteration of these sentiments sounds the more strange because the only judges we catch a glimpse of in *The Criminal Prisons* turn out to be among the causes of juvenile crime. After the establishment of reformatories in England, fewer children found their way into prison, but there were still felons under ten years of age in some prisons. If the threat of prison was to be a deterrent to juvenile crime, boys should be kept out of jail as long as possible, since its threat lay in its unknown quality, Mayhew said. "The rule with the Middlesex magistrates, though, appears to be the very reverse, viz., to thrust a lad into prison on the most trifling occasion, and to familiarize him, even in his childhood, with scenes that he should be made acquainted with the very last of all in his manhood" (p. 409).

At this point he had even more devastating charges to make about justice in England. As he extended his attacks on the magistrates he came to the very brink of a recognition of class discrimination in justice. As far as trifling actions such as stealing a peach or breaking a window were concerned, there was definitely one law for the rich and one for the poor. In Tothill Fields, he said with barely concealed anger, "we find little creatures of six years of age branded with a felon's badge—boys, not even in their teens, clad in the prison dress, for the heinous offense of throwing stones, or obstructing highways, or unlawfully knocking at doors—crimes which the very magistrates themselves, who committed the youths, must have assuredly perpetrated in their boyhood, and which, if equally visited, would consign almost every child in the kingdom to a jail" (p. 406).

Mayhew was equally disturbed by the number of people he found in prison because they had defaulted on a debt or could not pay a fine levied by the magistrate. He was particularly moved when he learned that in Tothill Fields the women prisoners who were not prostitutes had nearly all been imprisoned for their inability to pay a fine. The use of jail as an alternative to paying a fine was another way in which the law discriminated against the poor. Some men "are incarcerated for their poverty, rather than their transgression" (p. 342). In his suggestion for an alternative way of meting out justice in matters of fines, he recognized class differences. The law should not always set the same fine for the same crime but should moderate it according to the means of the offender: "Assuredly the well-to-do and, therefore, the well-educated, have not one tithe of the excuse for their transgressions that can be fairly pleaded by those who have seldom been schooled by any kinder master than want and ignorance" (p. 344).

Mayhew at this point in his life's work was as close as he ever came to a significant social analysis which would break unreservedly with received opinion. It had taken him some seven years of erratic social investigation to reach a position where his antagonism to the Victorian attitudes endorsed by his father might become conscious. Though his past history did not indicate much chance that he could reconcile his uncertainties now at the age of forty-four, the uncompromising attack on the way class could determine justice in England, and his shrewd views on social accountability in his essay on capital punishment at least suggest that if he had had the chance to continue "The Great World of London" he might finally have achieved a new social vision. The abandonment of the subject of labor and the poor when "The Great World of London" failed—an event just weeks away when he wrote his remarks on justice—destroyed such a chance. Without that topic Mayhew never again rose above the commonplace.

His banality is painfully evident in the discussion on women criminals which followed that on boys. Victorian attitudes toward women
are notorious and have been the subject of an increasing number of
studies. Woman was idolized both as the source of the moral standards
of society and as the bulwark of peace and security. She was at the
same time considered inferior to man. Though her main role was as
mother, she was taught to reject her body, and to lace her thoughts as
tightly as she did her stays, hiding all "lower" notions as thoroughly
as her voluminous undergarments hid her shape. Though he certainly
did not subscribe to these notions, as intelligent a man as John Stuart
Mill idolized his wife in a manner that to us seems incredible; one
should not be dismayed perhaps that Mayhew, a man of far less intellectual powers, maintained the most thoroughly conventional ideas
about women.

In the novel *Whom to Marry* (1848), the kind of simple satire on the
foibles of the ladies which *Punch* published frequently, Henry and Augustus Mayhew had implicitly defined their ideal woman. Though
Mayhew's wife was certainly neither as silly nor as avaricious as the
"bad" woman in this novel, nor as sweetly empty-headed as the
"good" sister, the moral was clear: the way to a happy marriage if one
were a woman, was to be passive and docile, weak and weak-headed,
soft, and sweet-tempered—and, if a man, to find such a creature.

That Mayhew himself believed this is clear from his other remarks
on women. Explaining the devotion of some prostitutes to their fancy
men, he said "the admirable with woman would thus appear to be the
powerful rather than the sensuously beautiful; they seem to prefer
bravery to symmetry" (wrapper 61, 7 February 1852). Mayhew did
remark that in this if in nothing else the prostitute was like all women.

In *The Criminal Prisons of London*, Mayhew expressed his attitudes on women in their grossest form. His surrender to the conventions here as elsewhere weakened his prose style, which became
exaggerated in its metaphors:

> In a natural state of things, it has clearly been intended by the Great
> Architect of the universe that the labour of the man should be sufficient
> for the maintenance of the family—the frame of the woman being in itself
> evidence that she was never meant to do the hard work of society, whilst
> the fountains of life that she carries in her bosom, as well as the kindlier

and more affectionate qualities of her nature, all show that her duty was designed to be that of a mother and a nurse to the children, rather than a fellow-labourer with the man. (p. 387)

On such assumptions as this Mayhew based his analysis of female crime, which to him simply meant prostitution.

The sheer number of prostitutes in London in the 1850s was as distressing to the Victorians as it is astonishing to us. In 1859, 2,828 brothels and 8,600 prostitutes were known to the police,[14] and there must have been many more who were not. The Common Lodging House Act in 1851 had driven many of the worst "accommodation houses" out of business, but the number of prostitutes in London in 1856 seemed as high as ever. Although Mr. Podsnap might prefer not to see the problem, during the 1850s concern for some kind of understanding and control was widespread. Dickens was involved in the reformation of prostitutes with Miss Coutts from 1846 through 1858, and the most famous and intelligent study of the subject in the Victorian period, William Acton's *Prostitution, Considered in its Moral, Social, and Sanitary Aspects* appeared in 1857, the year after Mayhew's survey of prisons. Speculation about the reasons for the great numbers, estimated by the Victorians as high as 80,000 in London alone, was rife at this time and in the succeeding years. Acton, as well as Bracebridge Hemyng in the survey of prostitution for volume 4 of *London Labour* in 1861, thought prostitution was due in the main to poverty and hard conditions among the lower classes. Acton also felt that the Victorians' stress on propriety and their horror of imprudent marriages drove both married men and also those forced to be bachelors because of small incomes to brothels.

Mayhew did not intend to survey prostitution at this point, but he used the sections on women prisoners to make some points about it. Earlier he had recognized some difficulty in insisting that prostitution was a criminal act. As we have seen, he was trying to answer the question of whether or not there was an innate revulsion against prostitution. A few years later, in *The Upper Rhine*, he seemed to admit that the oldest profession might be inevitable. Society had only three choices, he said: illegitimate children, "public women," or that anathema "early marriages" (p. 263). He offered no judgment as to the best choice, although his society frowned on both illegitimate children and early and financially insecure marriages. By the time he wrote *The Criminal Prisons* this disinterested response had disappeared.

Mayhew's attempts to account for prostitution in *The Criminal Prisons of London* had little consistency except his abhorrence of the practice. Sometimes he inferred social causes, sometimes biological, sometimes psychological, both innate and learned. In this multiplicity of explanations he reflected his age. Ignoring his early attempt to deal with it historically, Mayhew turned to psychological explanations. Prostitution was a substitute for honest work; like thieving for males it was "an easy mode of living" and so was resorted to by those women who "are born to labour for their bread, but who find work inordinately irksome to their natures, and pleasure as inordinately agreeable to them." They were the female members of the roving tribes who "have only to trade upon their personal charms in order to secure the apparent luxury of an idle life" (p. 454).

Although Mayhew first introduced his explanation of prostitution as the avoidance of work in the extra volume, he did qualify it there by developing a four-part classification to distinguish types according to their motivations. As he saw it at that point, each social class had a different motive for turning to prostitution. "The prostitutes who proceed from the *poorer* classes of society become depraved because they perceive that greater creature-comforts can be obtained in our community by immoral practices than by regular industry; whereas those prostitutes who proceed from the *middle* classes are led to adopt a vicious life principally from the craving for admiration," he said, echoing one of the most common Victorian explanations of prostitution, namely the inordinate love of vanity.

In addition to these two types who took to it were those who were "*driven* to prostitution, either through want or seduction" or "those who are *bred* to a vicious course of life, being early depraved or allowed by their parents to associate with whomsoever and go whithersoever they please" (wrapper 49, 15 November 1851). Despite the important distinctions in this classification, Mayhew gave the name *prostitute* to all women with any sort of irregular arrangement. This inflexibility itself resulted in higher numbers of professional "public women," though Mayhew did not see it that way. As Kellow Chesney has pointed out, the tendency of the Victorians to consider any woman who had "slipped" on the level of the professional harlot all too often assured that prostitution did indeed become her actual fate (p. 315).

Mayhew nowhere in his work showed an awareness of what Mrs. Gaskell hinted cautiously in *Ruth* (1853), and what Acton insisted on strenuously: the middle- and upper-class men who used the prostitutes were equally "criminal." For his part Mayhew finally seemed to lay the blame on a psychological weakness in women. The mark of a civilized man or woman was the capacity to feel shame, he said in *The Criminal Prisons*, for the main counter to anarchy in a society was "love of approbation and dread of disapprobation" (p. 455). If this were true, a woman could turn prostitute only if she had no sense of shame, for then she was "left without any moral sense, as it were, to govern and restrain the animal propensities of her nature" (p. 467). Though Mayhew did not specify what the woman should be ashamed about, it was clearly her body and her sexuality. Like many people he thought shame the most important curb to licentiousness, stating the sentiment quite openly in *The Upper Rhine*: "Love, in its spiritual quality, is beautiful enough; but when it has the least animal taint with it, the exhibition of passion becomes—like the gratification of any inordinate appetite—grossly offensive for other persons to contemplate" (p. 235).

Still he did realize that the sense of shame was not innate but must be educated in girls just as industriousness must be taught to boys. This explanation of prostitution had the virtue of implying that the "crime" was largely the result of environmental factors. Mayhew could not leave this assertion alone, however; on the very page after he said that shame must be taught in order to curb prostitution, he posited a deterministic cause for the shamelessness which lay behind female crime. Female criminals, he said, were frequently given over to violent outbursts of temper, which were "perhaps referable to the same derangement of functions Esquirol, in his work on madness, has shown to be intimately connected with insanity among women" (p. 467).[15]

These mixed responses toward women in general and women criminals in particular led Mayhew down some curious paths. While visiting the prison nursery in Tothill Fields, he remarked how the mothers there did not have "the brazen looks and the apparent glorying in their shame that prevails among the more debased of the female prisoners." Indeed, he said, warming to the subject, "the very fact of their being mothers is sufficient to prove that these prisoners do not belong to the class of 'public women,' since it is a wondrous ordination of Benevolence that such creatures as are absolutely shameless and affectionless should be childless as well; so that the sight of these baby prisoners was at once a proof to us that the hearts of the women that bore them were not utterly withered and corrupt" (p. 475).

Despite the sentimentality in these remarks, they do demonstrate some enlightenment on Mayhew's part. Like Mrs. Gaskell, Mayhew here repudiated the time-honored notion that the child of a "fallen" woman was a badge of shame. To Mrs. Gaskell, in *Ruth*, a child could be the means of moral reformation of the mother; to Mayhew, in *The Criminal Prisons*, a child was the sign of a basically good heart. In a later recounting of his prison trip, moreover, Mayhew further modified the sentimentality of this remark by touching on social realities. In *Young Benjamin Franklin* the matron of the prison stated that even if the children touched their mothers' hearts, when the women left prison there was little for them to do, however good their intentions, but to return to their old ways. As a result the children of these mothers would grow up into "young devils" (pp. 383–389).

In Mayhew's attitude toward women prisoners we witness forcefully the important role his interviews played in his earlier works and the weakness their absence exposed in *The Criminal Prisons*. In the previous surveys Mayhew's long interviews controlled his own triteness and gave to the whole an air of sympathy, balance, and realism. Though in direct statements he seemed to have little charity for women forced into prostitution, in his report of the meeting of needlewomen who were also prostitutes, he seemed to be on their side because he gave each woman a chance to explain fully the details of her life. In addition, side by side with his own rigid moralizing about prostitutes, he faithfully repeated the opinions of the lower classes, who were invariably sympathetic toward the "women of the town." Much of Mayhew's own censoriousness was undermined by the tolerance expressed by his informants:

"Now, those poor things that walk down there," [a street seller tells Mayhew] (intimating, by a motion of the head, a thoroughfare frequented by girls of the town), "they're often customers, but not near so good as they was ten year ago; no, indeed, nor six or eight year. *They* like something that bites in the mouth, such as peppermint-rock, or ginger drops. . . . I've trusted them ha'pennies and pennies, sometimes. They always paid me. Some that held their head high like, might say: 'I really have no change; I'll pay you to-morrow.' She hadn't no change, poor lass, sure enough, and she hadn't nothing to change either, I'll go bail." (1:204)

By publishing nearly everything his informants said and by equating their opinions with his own in terms of the space and emphasis he gave them, Mayhew ensured a balance in his earlier works wherever the author's prejudices might distort the picture.

Mayhew wrote only ten more pages following his observations on women and boy prisoners. John Binny finished the survey (from page 498) with dispatch five years later.[16] He kept the statistical data to a minimum and limited himself to describing the regime of each remaining prison with few comments or interpolations. His part in *The Criminal Prisons of London* was very minor, and it is unfortunate for Mayhew's reputation that Binny is consistently listed as a coauthor. In its summary of prevailing controversies about the penal system and its evocation of prison life, *The Criminal Prisons of London* forms a solid part of Mayhew's achievement. It also sadly marks the end of his survey of London's poor and of London's workers.

Attitude as Style

Because of its more impersonal mode of investigation, *The Criminal Prisons of London* was closer in form and style to Victorian social inquiries written by other authors than were Mayhew's two earlier surveys. In these first works the conflict between his respect for Victorian values and his tendency to rebellion, which was activated by his personal contacts with the working poor, merged with his intentions for his work as both science and journalism to create a special mode of expressing his experience of London's lower classes. Both his duality of feeling and his double intention were essential, for when either dimension was absent, as in his books on Germany, his prose lost its vitality.

Mayhew's style in his books on the poor combined precise, neutral, rhetorically effective descriptions with personal commentary in a way that gave voice to the tension between empathy and distance in his response to his experience at the same time that it resolved an inherent contradiction in social science writing. His achievement of this style has the surprising result of rendering his work not only more lively than other "scientific" studies of the period but more "scientific" as well.

Mayhew's style in his work on London's poor grew out of the combination of his particular temperament and his journalistic mode of publication. Even though the result was unique, the development of it was part of a general Victorian attempt to absorb the techniques of the physical sciences and the goals of the social observers into the budding discipline of sociology, at that time frequently concerned with problems of poverty and crime. In early Victorian England, there were two types of nonfictional writing in the reports of social investigation. One was colored by the rhetoric of the pulpit, the most extreme example being the essays of Carlyle; the second was the unadorned plain style of reporting that was found in the new journals of statistical analysis and government investigations. Neither of these styles was adequate

THE ASYLUM FOR THE HOUSELESS

An illustration by Hablot K. Browne ("Phiz") done for *Paved with Gold* by
Augustus Mayhew. Henry Mayhew visited this asylum, in Cripplegate, in the
winter of 1849 as the metropolitan correspondent for the *Morning Chronicle*
"Labour and the Poor" series. His description was reprinted in *London
Labour and the London Poor* (3:428–429) and used again in an early number
of *Paved with Gold* in 1857. Courtesy of the British Library Board.

for meeting all the needs of social research. By engaging the emotions the first could move readers to do something about the situations revealed, but it could not convey the disinterestedness of the observer nor the inevitability of the results, which theoretically should be based on evidence as objective as that in the physical sciences. The second tried to express this objectivity but did so at the price of an effective expression which would involve the reader in the social problem revealed. The contradiction between the ultimate goal of sociology—the understanding and by implication the amelioration of the human situation—and methods of research modelled on the physical sciences is fundamental to the discipline and has not been resolved even today.

In 1953 Richard M. Weaver outlined problems of effective writing which resulted from this contradiction and which are as relevant to Mayhew's time as to ours. One reason social science writing is rhetorically weak is "a primary equivocation" between "positive and dialectical language." (Positive language designates "something existing simply in the objective world" while dialectical terms stand "for concepts, which are defined by their negatives.")[1]

In early Victorian sociology observers generally were not experienced enough to be conscious of the difficulties of expressing data and conclusions about human behavior in language that did not convey relative judgments. Mayhew had some sense of the problem, and although he did not discuss it in terms of his investigative works on poverty, he did touch on it in his remarks on descriptive writing in his preface to *The Upper Rhine*. The first method of descriptive writing was a rendering of the exact properties of a scene; the second a comparison of the object or scene to some known object, i.e. by simile or metaphor. The third, "the highest and most artistic of all," was a setting forth of "the effects or feelings produced" by the scene or person.[2]

The first style of describing objects or people or places exactly was the one Mayhew thought best for the kind of reporting he did. As usual when he turned to examine this category of writing he found it needed further division. There were two methods of exact descriptive writing: one was to list all the relevant aspects of the object under view, what Mayhew called the "cataloguing" style which he thought belonged to "the plainness of science." (The unqualified belief that this kind of exactness is possible when the subject is man and society leads to the equivocation in social science writing which Weaver notes.) Since Mayhew seemed to favor the scientific mode, it is a little surprising that he rejected this kind of writing. The literary artist in him overcame the scientist; he did not use the cataloguing style because including all the particulars in that way clouded "the idea with a mass of words." In order to communicate one's experience one should select rather the "*one* particular quality by which [the object being described] is immediately apprehended in the mind."

Mayhew repeated this assertion in 1861 when he attacked modern painters—both narrative and Pre-Raphaelite (he preferred Rembrandt)—for their failure to select: "The fact is, this 'truth' of detail is *no* truth at all, but downright pictorial *falsity*. . . . If a true picture of some one scene in Nature is to be painted, rather than a thousand and one portraits of the thousand and one minute and insignificant details that go to make up such a scene in the broad view of the landscape, then every collateral object must be toned down to the one on which the eye is meant to *rest*, and where, and where alone . . . the great intensity of light and shade, and consequently the distinct making out of particulars, will be visible."[3]

Mayhew's ideal mode of description by balancing scientific "objectivity" and artistic selectivity would not only create a more accurate impression in the reader's mind but would also have rhetorical effectiveness. The idea behind this combination was to make the reader "see" the object for himself. Mayhew could maintain the impression of his own detachment, and at the same time the reader would have a direct and thus potentially more powerful experience of the particulars. Mayhew was at one with the great social critics of his time. "For us in these days *Prophecy* (well understood) not Poetry is the thing wanted," Carlyle wrote his brother John in 1833; "how can we *sing* and *paint* when we do not yet *believe* and *see*?"[4] What was the major force behind *Modern Painters* if it was not Ruskin's intense desire to make his readers "see" the facts of their world and the world they were creating? The critic sees things as they really are, Arnold said; his definition brought himself, Carlyle, Ruskin, and Mayhew into the same relation.

Of all the talented social historians of the period Mayhew in his self-conscious dual role as scientist and journalist seemed one of the best equipped to resolve the dichotomy inherent in social science writing. By the time he wrote *London Labour* he had indeed evolved a style which seems to do so. In most of his descriptions of his subjects' physical appearances, for example, he picked details which brought the person into sharp focus for the reader without any implied judgment or interpretation by the author. He noted a girl selling walnuts lift "her brown-stained fingers to her mouth, as she screams, 'Fine warnuts! sixteen a penny, fine war-r-nuts'" (1:9); a policeman with clean gloves; and a turfcutter who wore "very strong unblacked boots" (1:157). He described a street seller of cigar lights as "literally drenched, for his skin, shining with the rain, could be seen about his arms and knees through the slits of his thin corduroy jacket and trousers, and he wore no shirt" (1:433).

In his long descriptions of various street scenes, his style was at its best. In these passages he combined relatively neutral language with carefully selected details and an artistic ordering of the particulars. The following paragraph, taken from a longer description in *London Labour and the London Poor*, provides a good example.

At Farringdon market for vegetables, on a November Monday, Mayhew watched the poorest of the poor buying ha'pennies' worth of watercress to sell in the streets for artisans' breakfasts. It was between five and six in the morning.

> As the morning twilight came on, the paved court was crowded with purchasers. The sheds and shops at the end of the market grew every moment more distinct, and a railway-van, laden with carrots, came rumbling into the yard. The pigeons, too, began to fly on the sheds, or walk about the paving-stones, and the gas-man came round with his ladder to turn out the lamps. Then every one was pushing about; the children crying, as their naked feet were trodden upon, and the women hurrying off, with their baskets or shawls filled with cresses, and the bunch of rushes in their hands. In one corner of the market, busily tying up their bunches, were three or four girls seated on the stones, with their legs curled up under them, and the ground near them was green with the leaves they had thrown away. . . .
>
> As it grew late, and the crowd had thinned; none but the very poorest

of the cress-sellers were left. Many of these had come without money, others had their halfpence tied up carefully in their shawl ends, as though they dreaded the loss. A sickly-looking boy, of about five, whose head just reached above the hampers, now crept forward, treading with his blue naked feet over the cold stones as a cat does over wet ground. (1:146)

Mayhew here conveyed his perceptions through a narrowing focus, much like the stereotyped opening shot of motion pictures. It was characteristic of his way of organizing his material. He started with an overview of the bustle of the market but then selected a single detail which was both evocative and "objective"—the railway van was "laden with carrots." We are then directed to consider the people milling about, but only one specific detail is introduced in the effort to convey the poverty and suffering inherent in the scene: the children cried "as their naked feet were trodden upon." Mayhew inserted no interpretive comment, content for the reader to see the scene and judge it for himself. A series of similarly described groups of street sellers followed until he selected one member of one group to examine closely. The picture of the five-year-old boy was given in restrained language but was startling nonetheless in its visual clarity. His physical appearance, his economic situation, his feeling about himself were all efficiently suggested by the five physical details Mayhew chose to report. The final one, given in a simile and left until the end of the sentence for maximum effect, was visually evocative but not emotionally provocative in an obvious way. The author seemed to remain "objective," but the reader is forced to visualize the boy's careful tiptoe walk across the cold pavement, and he must consequently feel strong pity. Thus the sense of scientific neutrality merged with a strong emotional impact through Mayhew's selection of details and construction of his description. He could maintain his dual role of recording eye—the microscope and the camera combined—and of concerned journalist.

Nearly all his set descriptions followed this general pattern. Some overviews were presented, for Mayhew felt a panoramic view would bring out the most significant particulars in a scene. For the *Morning Chronicle* he had climbed to the Golden Gallery of St. Paul's to look at the Port of London, and to the second story of the Asylum for the Homeless to gaze at the scene below; and as we have already noted, he

ascended in a balloon for a view of "The Great World of London."
After presenting his general view Mayhew focused on the people in the
scene, and as one would expect of him, he categorized them into ever
more specific segments. The descriptions usually ended on an extended
and detailed look at the most pathetic or bizarre figure or group. In
presenting this final image Mayhew frequently used a simile.

Mayhew's achievement in the fusing of this style of description is the
more impressive when compared to that used by both nineteenth-
century sociologists and journalists. Two descriptions of a kitchen of a
low lodginghouse, both part of longer passages, follow. The first, written by R. A. Valpry, is from Charles Booth's *Life and Labour of the
People of London*, the second, from Mayhew's "Labour and the Poor."

> In houses, such as we are concerned with, the kitchen is the common
> living room and provides the attraction of free social intercourse. A bright
> coke fire is kept burning day and night for cooking and general use. The
> furniture of this room, strong and of the roughest description, consists of
> a long table occupying the centre of the room, with wooden benches on
> either side, and perhaps a few common chairs in addition. The cooking
> apparatus provided is of the simplest kind. A few frying-pans or gridirons
> serve in turn to prepare for table, herring, saveloy, rashers, steak, or
> other form of food belonging to a succession of guests. The quality or
> quantity of such food betokens as often reckless extravagance as extreme
> poverty, while the limited number of cooking utensils is often a source of
> discord. Of crockery there is next to none; a few old jam pots will often be
> the only provision for tea or coffee. Tin teapots are usually provided, but
> smaller articles, such as cutlery, are too portable to be used in common,
> and clasp knives will be produced from the pocket; spoons are not always
> thought of, and we have ample illustration of the fact that fingers were
> made before forks, whilst an old newspaper will often supply the want of a
> plate. Seated on and around the tables are to be seen groups of men en-
> gaged in games of chance or skill with dice or cards of an ancient appear-
> ance, or in recounting anecdotes and experiences too often ill-fitted for
> polite ears, varied with song, dance, and discussion—political or
> theological—while beer, gin, and tobacco abound.[5]

Even though there were forty-odd years' difference in time and a different medium of reporting, Mayhew's corresponding piece showed a
surprising similarity and suggests that Valpry and Mayhew saw much
the same scene in their visits to a London lodginghouse.

The entrance was through a large pair of green gates, which gave it somewhat the appearance of a stable yard. Over the kitchen door there hung a clothes line, on which was a wet shirt and a pair of ragged canvas trousers brown with tar. Entering the kitchen, we found it so full of smoke that the sun's rays, which shot slanting down through a broken tile in the roof, looked like a shaft of light cut through the fog. The flue of the chimney stood out from the bare brick wall like a buttress, and was black all the way up with the smoke; the beams which hung down from the roof, and ran from wall to wall, were of the same colour; and in the centre, to light the room, was a rude iron gas pipe, such as are used at night when the streets are turned up. The floor was unboarded, and a wooden seat projected from the wall all around the room. In front of this was ranged a series of tables, on which lolled dozing men. A number of the inmates were grouped around the fire, some kneeling, toasting herrings, of which the place smelt strongly; others, without shirts, seated on the ground close beside it, for warmth; and others drying the ends of cigars they had picked up in the streets. (V, 2 November 1849)

Despite the similarity of the scene surveyed in these two passages, the investigators used opposing styles of reporting. Valpry's would probably be considered by most the more "scientifically" correct one, but the piece is not calculated to involve the reader in the scene. Like Mayhew, Valpry wanted to appear disinterested and uninvolved. What he did to achieve this was to destroy the effectiveness of his writing. First he put the passage into the passive voice and, like Mayhew in *The Criminal Prisons of London*, compiled a composite picture from visits to several different places at several different times. While this method had the advantage of a wider application, it also necessitated numerous qualifications (avoided by Mayhew's "day at" style in *The Criminal Prisons*) which diffused the immediacy and vividness of the picture.[6] The persistent qualifications also undermined the validity of the observation as a whole since it did not seem to be true of any one place. The only effort Valpry made to achieve immediacy was to use the present tense.

Mayhew found another way to convey his objectivity. He stuck to the particulars of a single experience: he had come to the lodginghouse to attend a "dinner." From the first word he tried to make the reader experience this particular event as he did—as it looked, as it smelled, even as it felt. He began with a long look at the place and followed this

with a categorizing of the inmates. The description itself thus combined the general characteristics of the lodginghouse and the specific
details of the men there at a unique moment. The selected details,
especially those of the inmates, were meant to be representative, but
the "green" of the gates and the precise nature of the clothes on the
line as well as other particulars made the presentation individualized.
While Valpry's generalized picture was meant to imply the specifics,
Mayhew's individualized account was supposed to suggest the general.
Because readers are more likely to be convinced as well as interested
by specific details rather than by generalized narration, it is arguable
that Mayhew was more successful in his method than Valpry in his.

The most important difference in the two pieces is the one between
the inherent value judgments in Valpry's language and the relative
lack of this language in Mayhew's description. Because he kept a single
place in mind, Mayhew could report what he experienced without any
interpretation, or in Weaver's sense, he could keep to "positive
terms." This method of reporting helped Mayhew control his potential
sense of superiority. Valpry on the other hand collapsed the particulars into one observation, and so was forced to use language which
conveyed judgment in his effort to generalize the findings. The reader
as a result learns of the author's reactions to the scene rather than
experiencing the lodginghouse for himself; he feels what Valpry felt
rather than seeing what Valpry saw. And Valpry's feelings about his
experience were clearly negative. His condescension was betrayed by
the elaborate circumlocutions he used in his generalized description
("we have ample illustration of the fact that fingers were made before
forks"). By reporting no particularized data, he did not enable the
reader to check whether the social investigator's feelings were justified. Mayhew's report, because it eschewed overt generalization,
seems more accurate, more "objective," and more interesting.

Because it avoided generalization, however, Mayhew's work ultimately lacks the scope of Booth's; as Weaver says "every formula of
expression incurs its penalty" (p. 208). Mayhew's reports as a whole
would seem to remain in the province of journalism. Yet when we turn
to other journalists' treatments of London, Mayhew is as different
from his fellow reporters of low life in his style as he is from the early

sociologists. By being more "artistic" Mayhew's sociology seems, on the level of specific description at least, more "scientific"; by being more "scientific" his journalism turns out to be more artistically successful. His work is truly *sui generis*.

Many journalists contemporary with Mayhew also attempted to describe the London slums and slum-dwellers and to inform their audience about lower-class lives and occupations. The difficulty that all these writers for a popular audience faced was how to render the more brutal aspects without overstepping conventional Victorian proprieties. One of the greatest of them, Charles Dickens, found a method in symbolism. But the normal journalistic mode of respectably rendering reports of slum conditions for a popular audience was to make the scene a representative one in which either the particulars could be blurred or the most unpalatable details ignored. Because such generalization tends to enervate prose, however, many of these journalists strove to bring life to their pictures by the use of figures of speech which frequently were whimsical enough to lighten the tone of the whole piece.

To the modern reader this humorous tone is one of the more disconcerting aspects of much Victorian journalism of low life. At its worst the whimsy displayed a class voyeurism. At its best, as in Dickens's sketches, the whimsy and humor were really protective devices, a way in which the reporter separated himself and his readers from details which might be too strong if confronted directly. As Dickens said in "Gin Shops" in *Sketches by Boz*: "We have sketched this subject very slightly, not only because our limits compel us to do so, but because, if it were pursued farther, it would be painful and repulsive" (p. 186). Although Mayhew too sometimes used humor to separate himself from his subject, basically he liked being close to the working poor. His sensitivity to potentially humorous situations frequently helped him bring his subjects to life by giving his reports a balance between the dry facts he was seeking and the individuality of the people who were the source for the details. In many of his interviews, for example, Mayhew's pleasure in odd combinations of details led him to ask questions revealing incongruities which, while they amused, also insisted on the human quality of the informant. Thus he led an exhibitor of happy families ("assemblages of animals of diverse habits and propen-

sities living amicably, or at least quietly, in one cage" [3:214]) to explain how he and his collection shared the same bedroom at night—
cats, dogs, monkeys, rats, and owner. The interview with the dolls-eye
maker, first written for the *Chronicle* survey on toymakers, was one
of Mayhew's favorites exactly because it was a kind of apotheosis of
humorous oddity. His interview exploited all the whimsical possibilities. "Where we make one pair of eyes for home consumption,
we make ten for exportation," the maker told Mayhew, who interrupted to ask if the country would not be overpopulated with dolls if a
great number of them were not to emigrate every year? "Yes, I sup-
pose," the man answered, "the increase of dolls goes on at an alarming
rate every year." Mayhew inquired if the yearly rate of mortality were
not very high? "As you say, sir," was the reply, "but still it's nothing
to the rate at which they are brought into existence" (XXXIX, 28 February 1850). In both these cases, though Mayhew and the reader
laugh, the individual subject was not belittled by the humor; the seriousness with which the dolls-eye maker considered his work even gave
him a kind of dignity.

Although he selected many of these examples because they aroused
his sense of humor, Mayhew's commitment to giving expression to the
lives and ideas of the working poor prevented his humor from under-
cutting his presentation of the brutalities of lower-class life. The
reader was not given much protection from these "facts." In this honesty lay the major difference between him and many other London
journalists, including Dickens. Mayhew never lightened the exploitation of workers and the imprisonment of small children for trivial
offenses by humor, nor did he sentimentalize their condition by rhetorical exaggeration. Thus the tone of the *Chronicle* letters, which dealt
in the main with cruelly underpaid and mistreated workers, was grim-
mer than that of *London Labour* in which the subjects were poor by
and large but certainly not helpless.

Just as Mayhew's sense of humor could play a different role in his
work from that usual in London journalism, so did his marshalling of
the "facts" when no humor was involved. Charles Knight's *London* is
a useful juxtaposition. When Knight and his contributors issued *London* from 1841 to 1844, they combined engravings with a short history
of different regions of the city, its monuments and institutions, written

in a clear and simple prose for their mainly lower-middle- and working-class audience. Some of the pieces were whimsical in treatment, but many pieces were intended to be simply informative. In the chapter "St. Giles's Past and Present," for example, the writer, W. Weir, described the current Rookery thus:

> The stagnant gutters in the middle of the lanes, the accumulated piles of garbage, the pools accumulated in the hollows of the disjointed pavement, the filth chocking up the dark passages which open like rat-holes upon the highway—all these, with their indescribable sights and smells, leave scarcely so dispiriting an impression on the passenger as the condition of the houses. Walls of the colour of bleached soot—doors falling from their hinges—door-posts worm-eaten and greasily polished from being long the supports of the shoulders of ragged loungers—windows where shivered panes of dirty glass alternate with wisps of straw, old hats, and lumps of bed-ticken or brown paper—bespeak the last and frailest shelter that can be interposed between man and the elements. It is a land of utter idleness. Groups of women, with dirty rags hung round them, not put on, cower round the doors—the old with wrinkled parchment skins, the young with flushed swollen faces and heavy eyes. The men lean against the wall or lounge listlessly about, sometimes with pipes in their mouths.[7]

A sensitive observer wrote this; his eye had picked up the most important element of the slum, namely the listlessness of the inhabitants with nothing to do, nowhere to go, nothing to spend, little to say. Yet in describing this "indescribable" scene, the reporter introduced no new images. From Dickens onward, and even before, most journalistic observers noted broken windows and idle inhabitants, and asserted bad smells and shabby clothes. In Mayhew's description of the same "familiar" scene, the reader is led into a particular alley which has startling "new" details but which still encompasses the general traits of slum life as suggested by Weir and others. General hints in Weir's piece Mayhew rendered specifically. He went to St. Giles to find a street seller of salt whom he wanted to interview, and in the course of trying to find the place where the man lived, he observed the following scene:

> Stretching across the narrow street, from all the upper windows, might be seen lines crossing and recrossing each other, on which hung yellow-looking shirts, stockings, women's caps, and handkerchiefs looking like

soiled and torn paper, and throwing the whole lane into shade. Beneath this ragged canopy, the street literally swarmed with human beings— young and old, men and women, boys and girls, wandering about amidst all kinds of discordant sounds. The footpaths on both sides of the narrow street were occupied here and there by groups of men and boys, some sitting on the flags and others leaning against the wall, while their feet, in most instances bare, dabbled in the black channel alongside the kerb, which being disturbed sent up a sickening stench. Some of these groups were playing cards for money, which lay on the ground near them. Men and women at intervals lay stretched out in sleep on the pathway; over these the passengers were obliged to jump; in some instances they stood on their backs as they stepped over them, and then the sleeper languidly raised his head, growled out a drowsy oath, and slept again. (2:89–90)

Here Weir's "land of utter idleness" was visualized in the card-playing and the sleeping derelicts. His "indescribable smells" were sharply evoked by the details of the boys' bare feet stirring the ditch. While the one simile describing the drying handkerchiefs as looking "like soiled and torn paper" suggested a personal response on the part of the narrator, the most shocking detail, and the one likely to remain with the reader, was given with remarkable understatement. While one would not be surprised at the idleness, the bad-smelling drains, or the gambling, the vision of a number of sleeping bodies blocking the path was startling, all the more so because the narrator was apparently concerned only to point out the situation without commenting on it. Mayhew's genius for description is evident in the expansion of this scene. Rather than emphasizing it by exclamation or narrative comment, he drew out the details: not only were there sleeping bodies on the sidewalks over which some pedestrians stepped, but in the general disregard of these slum dwellers for each other some pedestrians actually stood on the sleeping derelicts. Such an act had to be deliberate, for it was an easy matter to step over the sleepers as some walkers did. Mayhew did not draw this conclusion or moralize about it. He seemed content if we "saw" the events for ourselves.

Most of the time in his descriptions Mayhew relied on selected details like these to paint his picture. He avoided the use of the figures of speech which other London journalists tended to depend upon, but he did not avoid them completely as sociologists normally do. Mayhew seemed to recognize that carefully controlled figurative language could add as much to the scientific accuracy of his work as to its effectiveness in moving the reader's emotions. When he used figurative language, almost always in the form of similes, he did so to portray a physical reality more clearly as in the description of the boy in Farringdon market. Mayhew usually first tried to describe the object without figurative expressions, and when he used a simile he usually placed it at the end of a long passage. This placement, like the structure of his descriptions in general, combined two goals. It meant that the observation would seem "scientifically" objective because the figure came last, and at the same time would be effective rhetorically.

Mayhew's attempt to find similes for description which would not connote judgment was deliberate, for in other works he frequently used figures of speech for direct, and usually ironic, comment. In "The Great World of London" part of *The Criminal Prisons*, for example, he complained that "the gentlemen who fabricate books on London, from Mr. M'Culloch downwards, do not hesitate to dig their scissors into [my statistics], taking care to do with them the same as is done with the stolen handkerchiefs in Petticoat Lane—viz., pick out the name of the owner" (p. 37n.). The structure of this passage was the same as that in his more "scientific" descriptions, but the purpose of the final comparison was quite different. He wanted to elicit his reader's sympathy by comparing himself to a man who had had his pocket picked, an act of thievery all the worse for being petty and clandestine.

One of the best demonstrations of all of the characteristics of Mayhew's descriptions—his selection of particulars, his fusion of the general and the specific, his use of specific detail to suggest general applications, and his introduction of similes—appeared late in volume 3 of *London Labour*. Though related to the early *Chronicle* series, it did not appear in the newspaper. It seems to be an expansion for a few sentences in Letter XXV which described the Asylum for the Houseless Poor at Cripplegate, the oldest and largest of the metropolitan asylums. The initial description in the *Morning Chronicle* was general in its categories and vague in its details.

> The crowd gathers in Playhouse-yard, and many among them look sad and weary enough. Many of the women carry infants at the breast, and

have children by their sides holding by their gowns. The cries of these, and the wrangling of the hungry crowds for their places, is indeed disheartening to hear. The only sounds of merriment come from the boys,— the "errand boys"—as they call themselves, whom even starvation cannot make sorrowful for two hours together. (11 January 1850)

Even in this picture Mayhew did not exaggerate, but the words had been used too many times in the same way to make a strong impression. The emotions, both of the waiting indigent and the social observer, were rendered imprecisely: the former looked "sad and weary," the latter was "disheartened."

When Mayhew combined selected details with the general picture in order to describe the same place, perhaps the same experience, he achieved a very different result. Since each sentence in the first piece was expanded, I have chosen only a small part of the longer piece to analyze here. The differences were consistent throughout the longer piece, and my remarks are relevant to the whole passage.

In the first place Mayhew was now at the asylum at a definite time—deep winter when the temperature was below freezing. It was dusk. He stood at a window on an upper floor of the asylum, looking down on the crowd of homeless men and women waiting for the doors to open.

There they stand shivering in the snow, with their thin, cobwebby garments hanging in tatters about them. Many are without shirts; with their bare skin showing through the rents and gaps of their clothes, like the hide of a dog with the mange. Some have their greasy coats and trousers tied round their wrists and ankles with string, to prevent the piercing wind from blowing up them. A few are without shoes; and these keep one foot only to the ground, while the bare flesh that has had to tramp through the snow is blue and livid-looking as half-cooked meat. (3:428)

The crowd, earlier described only as "sad and weary," here are individualized by being classified according to their clothing or lack of it. Each subgroup had an equally distressed state of dress, but in the order of presentation Mayhew gave a hierarchy of misery by selecting details which would focus on the increasingly harsh effect of the cold. As Mayhew said, "nearly every shade and grade of misery, misfortune, vice, and even guilt, are to be found in the place."

He began with a general picture—beggars shivering in the snow, forcing the reader to visualize their garments through the metaphor "cobwebby." Next he began to classify by selecting details. These specifics were easily extendable not only to the scene at large but to all similar places in London. The men and women were without shirts, good coats, and even shoes. Yet these general details were particularized by unusual analogies and the one precise detail of the string around the wrists and ankles. The two similes, bare skin showing through clothes like the "hide of a dog with the mange" and bare feet "blue and livid-looking as half-cooked meat," provided the means by which Mayhew fused the specific and the general. The groups remained generalized, but the similes in their visual sharpness also made them specific. The suddenness with which each simile evoked a singular picture turned a general, and even stereotyped, scene into a powerfully felt one. The startling effect of these similes was the stronger because they seemed to strive only for visual clarity. Actually the similes have emotional associations as well. They both suggest, though in a far more subtle way than did the pickpocket metaphor, that the beggars have been reduced to an animalistic level.

Descriptions of this sort were an important part of Mayhew's presentation of the facts, but set passages of scenic detail did not form the bulk of his volumes. The weight of his surveys was achieved first in the interviews and then in the series of general comments and arithmetical calculations by the author. In generalization and presentation of statistical data lies the real challenge in creating an effective style for the social sciences. The results of the equivocation between objective and relativistic language, and the "pedantic empiricism" or hedging which is introduced to counteract this uncertainty, which Weaver noted, are particularly evident in this kind of sociological writing. Yet Mayhew was able to avoid diffuseness, verbosity, and hedging phrases because of the strong identification he had with his subjects. Just as in the form of his interviews he amalgamated himself and his subjects through the merging of his questions and their answers, so he enlivened the style of the generalized part of his survey by infusing direct quotations from his informants into his own prose at every opportunity. The strength of Mayhew's prose then comes in

large part from the vitality of the language of his informants. Even if
he as scientist had to be "objective" and his language sober and uncol-
orful, that of his informants did not. His use of quotation moreover fit
neatly with his goals of "scientific" method, for he could fuse his own
generalizing with the "proof" in a single sentence. The result was not
just a concise, lively, and seemingly accurate narrative, but also his
strongest assertion of the importance of his subjects as citizens and as
human beings.

The language of the working poor was highly effective in its figura-
tiveness and concreteness although Mayhew may have leaned toward
the more vivid examples in his reports. One street seller of secondhand
glass and old shoes told him that he "made both ends meet that way, a
leather end and a glass end" (2:15). A coster said of others who had
risen in the world: "Some marry the better kind of servants,—such as
servant-maids as wouldn't marry a rag and bottle shop, but doesn't
object to a coal shed" (1:47). Even their descriptions of misery could
be vividly metaphoric: "I've stood up to the ankles in snow till after
midnight," a sandwich seller told Mayhew, "and till I've wished I was
snow myself, and could melt like it and have an end" (1:178).

Before enumerating the ways in which Mayhew fused the words of
his informants with his own prose, it is important to consider his mode
of rendering Cockney dialect. In his preface to volume 1 of *London
Labour*, he claimed that in his volumes the lower classes of London
gave a "literal" description of their lives "in their own 'unvarnished'
language." Despite this assurance Mayhew, like all his contemporaries, not only varnished but sometimes painted over the words of
his informants. P. J. Keating has isolated two traditions in the representation of Cockney speech in Victorian writing, one characterized by
Dickens and the other by Thackeray. The first was "Standard English
with occasional pronunciation differences noted. . . . The form of these
variants is rarely consistent."[8] While this method was the one mainly
used by Mayhew in his surveys of London, he could also report
Cockney in the other style with its aspirates and phonetic spellings.
This second tradition of Thackeray and Surtees was primarily used,
according to Keating, to make fun of the vulgarity of working-class
speech. Mayhew used this style in reporting the conversation with Bil-

berry the English clown in *German Life and Manners* exactly because
he wanted to mock him. When a few pages later in that work he reported the speech of an illiterate circus-player toward whom he felt
more sympathy, he dropped the comic Cockney and returned to the
first mode of rendering lower-class speech, the one he used in *London
Labour.*

The real problem in representing Cockney speech was the obscenity
inevitable in any faithful report. No writer of the period went so far as
to give realistic speech of that kind. Mayhew was careful, however, to
let his readers know he was omitting it. "Some details, given by coarse
men and boys in the grossest language, are too gross to be more than
alluded to" (1:254). Yet, he added, "the full truth must be manifested
if not detailed," and so he tried to give the general drift without the
specific obscenities.

Mayhew had no such reservations with other aspects of his subjects'
speech. He deliberately used sentences, phrases, sometimes single
words of his informants to make his work seem more reliable as social
science. He used the words of the workers to express their opinions or
to explain their trades. Thus, defining the term *small masters*—those
who made goods for the "slaughterhouses" or stores selling cheap
ready-made furniture—he said: "These are 'small masters,' who make
or (as one man said to me, 'No sir, I don't make these drawers, I put
them together, it can't be called making; it's not workmanship') who
'put together' in the hastiest manner, and in any way not positively
offensive to the eye, articles of household furniture" (1:333). In his
discussion of the psychology of the patterers he quoted them about
themselves: "'We are the haristocracy of the streets,' was said to me
by one of the street folks, who told penny fortunes with a bottle. 'People don't pay us for what we gives 'em, but only to hear us talk. We
live like yourself, sir, by the hexercise of our hintellects—we by talking, and you by writing'" (1:213).

Yet Mayhew could also use direct quotation to achieve the opposite
effect—that of social criticism. He did not draw the moral himself but
let the informants do it for him, thus maintaining his stance as disinterested observer at the same time as he conveyed a judgment. Speaking of the variation of prices for spectacles, he said: "Then there is the
chance of which street-sellers are not slow to avail themselves—('no

more nor is shopkeepers,' one man said)—I mean, the chance of obtaining an enhanced price for an article, with whose precise value the buyer is unacquainted" (1:444). He quoted a long-song seller to criticize implicitly the thoughtlessness of others: "Very few [long songs, ballads printed on long sheets of paper] were sold in the public-houses, as the vendors scrupled to expose them there, 'for drunken fellows would snatch them, and make belts of them for a lark'" (1:221). And he also satirized the pretensions in all classes through the same device. He repeated a dog seller's remark that "he hardly knew what made many gentlemen so fond of bull-dogs, and they were 'the fonder on 'em the more blackguarder and varmint-looking the creatures was'" (2:55). In a report of a conversation with another seller he wrote: "Along with each glass of hot elder wine is given a small piece of toasted bread. Some buyers steep this bread in the wine, and so imbibe the flavour. 'It ain't no good as I know on,' said an elder-wine seller, 'but it's the fashion, and so people must have it'" (1:190).

Mayhew also used the language of the poor to expose the tricks some of them resorted to in order to "earn a crust." Correspondents sometimes complained that he did a disservice by exposing them in this way, but in this case as in the others he had protected himself. It was not he who made the charges but his informants. "Many of the [fish] friers are good, but some, I was told, 'in anything like muggy or close weather were very queer fish, very queer indeed,' and they are consequently fried with a most liberal allowance of oil, 'which will conceal anything'" (1:166).

These reported conversations not only supported Mayhew in his role as scientist, but they also made his reports lively and readable. A good number of the direct quotations seemed to be included for no other reason. On umbrella sales: "In so desultory and—as one intelligent street seller with whom I conversed on the subject described it—so *weathery* a trade, it is difficult to arrive at exact statistics" (1:304). A benefit society of patterers "'sprung up accidental,' as it was expressed to me" (1:242); "on the second Sunday in February [1851]—as well as my informant could recollect, for almost all street-traders will tell you, if not in the same words as one patterer used, that their recollections are 'not worth an old button without a neck'—the police 'put down' the sale of these Exhibition cards in the Park" (1:266). Here it is also important to note how Mayhew, by putting quotation marks around words which really did not need to be distinguished that way ("put down"), tried to remind his readers that he was not doing anything in his survey except reporting other men's language and emphasis.

Mayhew's use of direct quotation developed more slowly than did his techniques of description, which were present from the start. The subject of the *Morning Chronicle* letters hindered the use of his informants' words as a part of his own. From the skilled workers he wanted the figures on wages and living costs for the most part. This kind of information was fairly easy to generalize and to represent statistically. Even so, about midway in "Labour and the Poor," he did begin to use quoted phrases not just as data but also as descriptions of working processes and conditions among the skilled trades. The kind of information he wanted about the street folk was different: he hoped to elucidate their minds and hearts as well as the details of their incomes. Such material was much more difficult to generalize in a neutral way and Mayhew relied more on their words to justify his picture. The integration of his language and that of his subjects became a habit, however, and by the time he came to write the sections on street cleaning at the end of volume 2 of *London Labour*, Mayhew seemed naturally to treat any subject, however unlikely, in this style.

> The sewer-rat is the common brown or Hanoverian rat, said by the Jacobites to have come in with the first George, and established itself after the fashion of his royal family; and undoubtedly such was about the era of their appearance. One man, who had worked twelve years in the sewers before flushing was general, told me he had never seen but *two* black (or old English) rats; another man, of ten years' experience, had seen but one; others had noted no difference in the rats. I may observe that in my inquiries as to the sale of rats (as part of the live animals dealt in by a class in the metropolis), I ascertained that in the older granaries, where there were series of floors, there were black as well as brown rats. "Great black fellows," said one man who managed a Bermondsey granary, "as would frighten a lady into asterisks to see of a sudden." (2:431)

The structure of this paragraph was typical. In the process of a parenthetical discussion on the prevalence of brown versus black sewer rats, Mayhew referred to no less than four experts, including himself, about the predominance of one over the other, and he compulsively detailed the evidence which his sources provided. His sense of humor lightened the effect of this "statistical" weight by his direct reference to the joke about George I and by the kind of quotation he chose to repeat at the end of the passage. By putting this quotation at the end he achieved a rhetorical effect; the structure moving from the general to the specific also mimicked the deductive mode of writing that the scientist in him strove for.

All the best of Mayhew's writing had in it this subtle tautness between art and science, the general and the specific, engagement and distance. The loss of any of these dualities, particularly the last, had bad effects on his style. We have already noted in *The Criminal Prisons of London* the flabby clichés in some of his observations on prostitutes, a group he never interviewed and with whom he never achieved a sympathy. The most sustained examples of how the loss of his facility for identification affected his prose style were in his books on Germany. Mayhew's German works displayed conventional platitudes and outright uninformed prejudice. *The Rhine* was a travel narrative with the emphasis on scenic description. *The Upper Rhine* alternated scenes with commentary, most of it ill-natured, unsupported by evidence, and all in all quite far from the openness with which Dickens, for example, reported on his travels abroad. The longest of these diatribes against Germany and the Germans was *German Life and Manners in Old Saxony*, written in the early 1860s when Mayhew was doing research for a book on Martin Luther. But "our Luther tourbook ultimately merged into one mainly descriptive of the wretchedness of the life of the people in Saxony at the present time" (1: vii). The purpose of his resulting book was "to let our countrymen know how much better housed, better fed, better paid, better cared-for, and better treated, were English work-people than the labouring population abroad" (1: vi).

Mayhew's presence was far more evident in *German Life and Manners* than in his work on London; the reader was treated to stories of his wife's trips to the butcher, his son's search for a camera, his daughter's experiences at a ball. This greater degree of personal involvement, however, did not make the book more lively nor interesting.

Mayhew's work was best when he struggled to hide himself because that forced him to allow his subjects full play at self-revelation.

Despite their wretchedness Mayhew could not see the Germans as human beings. His ability to respect the human in even the coarsest of his London informants was missing in his response to the Germans because he felt himself alien to them in a way that he never felt separated from the lower classes in London. Without his sense of sympathetic identification, this passage became typical of Mayhew's writing about the Germans:

> Hence the miserliness, which is the cause of the national poverty—and the national squalor—as well as the national pigmy race (for that to stint is to stunt, is but an ordinary physiological law)—is likewise the cause of that national meanness which is so strongly marked a characteristic of the German tribe. Such is the jaundice of avarice that it stains and pollutes every part of the system with the taint of gold; the eyes are dyed with gall, so that nothing is seen in its natural colour; the finger-ends sullied by it, till they are like the talons of a kite, rather than human digits; the heart is turned to a lump of ochre, and the life-blood flows like so much mud in the veins. The loathsome yellow tinge extends even to the soul itself, till the living creature is like a corpse, with the eyes closed with pieces of money; and every natural tie and affection—every principle of honour and duty—is absorbed in the raging hunger of the passion; as thoroughly as with cast-aways upon a raft gambling which shall eat the other. (2:625–626)

Mayhew was describing the physical appearance of the Germans here, but he submerged every detail in judgmental adjectives and verbs—"stains," "pollutes," "loathsome." The three similes conveyed no picture, only his disgust. The hysterical exaggerations were banal, the images visually meaningless. The only people quoted in the book were English residents, for Mayhew apparently conducted no interviews with Germans. He hated the German language, referring to it five times in two pages as "absurd" and in the same space also calling it "folly," "silly," and "nonsense" (1:554–556). This is what could become of his combination of neutral description, respect for the words and thoughts of his informants, and personal delight in oddity and incongruity without a tension between sympathy and distance.

Only once in *German Life and Manners*, in a seventy-five-page account of the visit of an English circus to Eisenach where he was living, did Mayhew rise above this style. With his old gusto he began to interview the circus folk, although he still used these interviews as a stick with which to beat the wantonness and filth of the Germans. His characteristic style returned in his recounting of his conversations with Bilberry the English clown. Even the descriptions in this part of his book improved, for Mayhew also seemed to need to identify himself with the people in a place in order to realize the scene.

Such identification was possible for him only with the English lower classes, particularly the street folk.

> The boys who ply their callings in the street, or are much in the open air, are very fond of these puddings, and to witness the way in which they throw the pudding, when very hot, from hand to hand, eyeing it with an expression that shows an eagerness to eat with a fear of burning the mouth, is sometimes laughable and sometimes painful, because not unfrequently there is a look of keen hunger about the—probably outcast—lad. The currant puddings are, I believe, sold only at Billingsgate and Petticoat Lane. (1:197)

How different was such a passage from *German Life and Manners*! Mayhew coupled matter-of-fact information about the customers who bought hot puddings sold in the streets and the qualified assertion of the location of the sales with a personal experience in which he combined the outside view of the social scientist with a quick empathy, even as he united amusement and pity in his report. Out of this unity sprang the implied moral of his work: "Might not 'the finest gentleman in Europe' have been the greatest blackguard in Billingsgate, had he been born to carry a fish-basket on his head instead of a crown?" (1:320).

THE CONVICT SLOP-WORKER

From the *Penny Illustrated News*, 9 February 1850, illustrating a reprint of another of Mayhew's *Morning Chronicle* letters of November 1849. Courtesy of the British Library Board.

Mayhew & the Literature of His Time

Thus far I have concentrated on the development and characteristics of Mayhew's three major investigations of London's lower classes. Throughout his life he wrote many works in other genres—farces, novels, travel books, comic and miscellaneous journalism, and educational works for children. Yet most of his efforts in these areas were undistinguished. Neither the form nor the subject of any of his other books activated the tensions in him which were crucial to the achievement of his investigative reporting. In his plays and novels he usually needed a collaborator to initiate or continue a project, and friends reported that in many cases Mayhew did little more than suggest the idea.[1]

Because Mayhew on some level was not really motivated by the challenges of his other works, they tended to be standard in treatment and theme. Without the control of his role as scientist, for example, his boys' books were conventionally moralistic, and the "scientific" aspect of them confused their direction and tone. Mayhew believed in teaching children to love knowledge for its own sake through learning by experiment and through discovering things for themselves. His boys' books thus detail the way a specific child—Humphry Davy or Benjamin Franklin—learned by experience. But he also seemed to want to instruct the young reader in the complexities of science, and so he often included tedious footnotes to his sources, to statistics, and to scholarly treatises which were inappropriate in a children's book.

As a second example Mayhew's novels with Augustus depended almost solely on Victorian commonplaces of humor. They satirized women in time-honored terms, poking fun at their love of finery, their susceptibility to flattery, and so on. In *The Greatest Plague in Life*, the author satirized both wives whose ill-temper, ignorance, and selfish love of display made them bad mistresses of households and servants for their drunkenness, thieving, attraction to soldiers, etc. The novels were sometimes uncertain in their conception. In two of them the brothers seemed to want to preach the simple morality of "The Magic of Kindness" and the wisdom of the Golden Mean to grown-up men and women through a children's fairy tale.[2] In others the simple-minded satire could be abruptly abandoned for serious social criticism. *Fear of the World* was built on the broad character types and farcical situations of a *Punch*-like satire, yet at times the subject of the step-by-step process by which a barrister and his wife sink into bankruptcy evokes more serious responses from the reader. The humor as a result frequently seems misplaced. The whole narrative, despite one or two well-realized scenes, never achieved coherence.

Even Mayhew's comic journalism seldom rose to the level of trenchant social analysis as could the comic pieces of Douglas Jerrold or Dickens. Most of the targets were typical in those issues of the *Comic Almanac* which were under Mayhew's direct editorship. Some did display his special concerns: one piece attacked the theory of overpopulation by systematically listing the groups who could stand to be depopulated—namely lawyers, policemen, the underpaid, and the poor. A satire on the census of 1851, a favorite target of Mayhew's, mixed humor and social comment as it recounted the adventures of several citizens who slept nowhere on the night the census was taken.

In their very conventionality, however, Mayhew's less important books can sometimes illuminate various trends of the period. For example, his plays were basically stock farces. Yet Bradley has analysed one of them, *The Wandering Minstrel*, in terms of the way it displays two representative trends of the light drama of the 1830s and 1840s. Because Drury Lane and Covent Garden had a monopoly on theatrical rights until 1843, minor theaters (such as those Mayhew and his friends wrote for) staged mainly ephemera—farces, burlettas, burlesques. *The Wandering Minstrel* defines the low taste in humor popular in these pieces at this time, but, Bradley pointed out, a subplot hinted at a more realistic view, looking forward to the "realistic plays of Robertson and others which were to shape Victorian drama in subsequent decades."[3]

One can examine one of Mayhew's novels in a similar way. *Whom to Marry* shares some common satirical sources with *Vanity Fair*, published a year before the Mayhew work. In its use of humorous clichés, the novel by the Brothers Mayhew can help define Thackeray's use of, and triumph over, conventional humor. Thackeray and Mayhew knew each other and shared the same immersion in the world of humor, farce, and journalism. Thackeray's early insouciance, carelessness with money, and bohemianism would have made him a sympathetic friend for Henry Mayhew, although the lack of reference to Mayhew in personal terms in Thackeray's letters may indicate that they were not intimate. By the late 1840s Mayhew probably felt a certain bitterness over his ouster from *Punch*, and his personal problems might have also contributed to his apparent withdrawal from his earlier crowd of friends. Nonetheless Thackeray read Mayhew's *Morning Chronicle* articles with enthusiastic pleasure and reported on the first of Herbert's Female Emigration Society embarkations for *Punch*. There is no indication that he knew *London Labour and the London Poor*.

In both the Mayhews' *Whom to Marry* and Thackeray's *Vanity Fair* the satirical thrusts were aimed at targets also favored by *Punch*, which is not surprising in the light of the men's association with the journal around the same period. Both mock the social pretensions of the middle classes, money as the basis for human relations, and the discrepancy between words and actions among all classes. Although the tone of *Whom to Marry* is closer to *Punch* in its exaggeration, Thackeray also reflected the genial criticism of that journal, deepening its significance by his broad tolerance and the wistfulness of his authorial stance. The balance with which Thackeray viewed his characters, especially Becky, might compare with Mayhew's sympathetic treatment of the working poor of London, but in Mayhew's novel with his brother, there is no such rounded view because the form of the novel did not force balance on Mayhew as did the form of the social survey.

Nonetheless several parallels exist in the two novels beyond the general level of satire. These include some specific incidents, such as a scene of old friends coming to pick over the goods at a bankruptcy sale and a few parallel adventures of Charlotte de Roos (the "heroine" of *Whom to Marry*) and Becky Sharp. The Brothers Mayhew criticize through laughter the ladies' school Charlotte attended, particularly its snobbery, its bad education, and the hunting for husbands among the brothers of schoolmates. Thackeray of course opened his novel with a

similar satire. Since Charlotte accepted the school's values unquestioningly, the Mayhew version of the story remained a humorous but
stereotyped situation. The presence of Becky in *Vanity Fair*, however, made of the same situation, the same satire, even some of the
same characters (the schoolmistress) something far more disturbing.
Through Becky, the unexpected element in the stock situation here as
elsewhere in the novel, we see snobbery as a brutality which is not
comic, though the seriousness is lightened by her rout of her oppres-
sors at the end of the chapter.

Despite their different roles Becky and Charlotte have several aspects in common. Both are contrasted to a "model" woman whose for-
tune inversely follows theirs. Charlotte's foil is her sister Fanny who,
even as Amelia is juxtaposed to Becky, is everything Charlotte is not:
gentle, retiring, docile, and dependent; loving, suffering, pure, and ultimately rewarded.

The most extensive parallel in the two works is that between Charlotte's last adventure and Becky's second. The details of both are similar enough to suggest a common source, perhaps in the convivial
discussions of projects for *Punch*. Both girls become governesses in
the household of a dirty, miserly, selfish, and foolish baronet. Both of
them rout their female competitors for the baronets' favors—in Charlotte's case the housekeeper, in Becky's the present Lady Crawley—
by pandering to the baronets' weaknesses, doing their accounts, cater-
ing to their appetites, and making them generally comfortable. Both
girls leave their households and are pursued by the baronets and
finally proposed to in the same way. In *Whom to Marry* Sir Luke
finally grumblingly goes down on his knees, even as does Sir Pitt.

Up to this point the parallels are almost exact, and they are based on
conventional comic sequences. Yet the events following Sir Pitt Crawley's proposal to Becky, when compared to the corresponding sequence of events in the Mayhew novel, introduce an important
complication into Thackeray's story. Charlotte marries her baronet.
Having achieved her goal she subsequently behaves in a totally
predictable manner: she neglects Sir Luke's papers and his food;
she becomes a victim of his penuriousness now that he is sure of her,
and ultimately—and inevitably—finds herself estranged and in

straitened circumstances. The expected reversal of her victory and the moral it teaches were part of the stock situation.

The reader of *Vanity Fair*, recognizing the convention in Sir Pitt's courtship of Becky, might expect a similar outcome, even though Becky is a more complex character than Charlotte. It is not just that Thackeray betrays this expectation by having Becky announce that she is already married and so adds surprise to the suspense with which he ended the monthly number. He achieved a far more cunning reversal of the reader's expectations.

In *Whom to Marry* because of the stock situation we know the marriage will turn out badly even before it is achieved; in *Vanity Fair* we have the same sense to the moment that Sir Pitt proposes. At that point Sir Pitt, against all expectation, becomes a more rounded character because of the manner in which he speaks to Becky. His plainness of speech, his honest admission of his need of her, and his recognition of her worth give him a depth and complexity that are inconsistent with the conventional figure in whose form he, like Sir Luke, had appeared before. Furthermore Becky, because of the "genuine tears" she sheds, has our good will. Though little in the preceding scenes between her and Sir Pitt justifies it, at this point we believe that if Becky accepted him they could have lived happily together. This is not the last time in this novel that Becky's behavior reverses convention. In fact the betrayal of our expectations is part of the ironic vision of the novel.

Mayhew could achieve a similar startling effect in his social surveys by reversing the expectations that his readers had of the lower classes, but in all of his other works he surrendered to convention rather than challenging it. For most of his life he blended in with his background. Nonetheless one might expect that his truly innovative contributions in the development of sociology and investigative reporting might have exerted some influence on his contemporaries. The fact is that they did not.

The reasons were ones of both the time in which he wrote and the form he used. Despite his "scientific" conception of his work he did not really advance beyond the state of knowledge at a particular time. The rapid advance of sociological investigative techniques in the second half of the nineteenth century outstripped his usefulness as a model almost at once. His method of collecting statistics through personal interviews was demonstrably inadequate and improvements in the kind, scope, and reliability of the dicennial census alone soon made this procedure obsolete. Growing sophistication in the methods of research also made his interviewing techniques seem idiosyncratic and unscientific, although he did have some influence on a few journalists in the following decades. John Binny followed Mayhew's model in some of his descriptive passages in his section on thieves and swindlers in volume 4 of *London Labour*. James Greenwood's journalistic surveys of poverty (*A Night in the Workhouse*, 1866; *The Seven Curses of London*, 1869; *The Wilds of London*, 1874) as well as those of another journalistic investigator, George R. Sims (*How the Poor Live*, 1883), were in the tradition of Mayhew but "lacked the profound social understanding of the best of their predecessors in this field."[4] Greenwood, following Mayhew's mode of personal investigation, outdid his source by disguising himself and spending a night in the workhouse.

Furthermore, though modern readers know Mayhew through the four-volume version of *London Labour and the London Poor* and were until recently mostly ignorant of his work for the *Morning Chronicle*, in his own time the situation was reversed. His contemporaries respected him for his investigations into the skilled and unskilled trades in London in 1849–1850 for the "Labour and the Poor" series and knew less and cared less about the early publication on the street folk. Mayhew's social surveys were essentially forgotten after the 1860s moreover because of the form in which they were published. His contributions as the "metropolitan correspondent," released as they were in an ephemeral newspaper format, have even yet not become generally available in complete form; and in his own time, except for the handful reprinted in *London Labour* some eleven years after the fact, they were inaccessible. Thus after 1850, when his contributions to the *Morning Chronicle* ceased, people would remember that he exposed bad conditions in London trades but they would be unlikely to recall many details. His influence then was probably only very general. The only exception, discussed in detail below, was Charles Kingsley, who wrote two works during and just after Mayhew's *Morning Chronicle* letters which were specifically influenced by the journalist.

Mrs. Gaskell is a more characteristic example. Her novel *Ruth* (1853) may have been indirectly influenced by Mayhew. As I noted in chapter 4, in this novel Mrs. Gaskell wanted to criticize the hard line Victorian society took toward girls who had "slipped" by having an illegitimate child but who were not professional prostitutes. For her heroine she chose a young dressmaker who was seduced by an upper-class cad. In the beginning the novel briefly presented the long hours, the cramped and alternately too hot and too cold workrooms of the dressmakers' shop as well as the loneliness of the apprentices and the severity of the rule against "followers," all of which contributed to Ruth's downfall. Aina Rubenius, tracing Mrs. Gaskell's attitude toward dressmakers from *Mary Barton* through *Ruth*, attributed her increased rage at conditions in the latter novel to Mayhew's surveys.[5] (His *Chronicle* articles were known in her circle although she did not refer to them.) In *Mary Barton*, written before Mayhew's investigations, Mrs. Gaskell demonstrated knowledge of the conditions in dressmakers' shops but she displayed little indignation about them. When she wrote *Ruth* she was more acid in her comments.[6]

Mayhew's 1851–1852 investigations of the street folk had an influence even more problematic for the same reason. It is possible that Dickens used them, but the transient form of *London Labour and the London Poor* when it was first published limited its effect. The two penny numbers had a good circulation for such a periodical, but they did not reach the same readers nor have the prestige of the *Morning Chronicle* series. Also the distribution was probably erratic (at one point a street seller was hawking them) and limited to certain areas.

Even those who read the first version were told periodically on the wrappers that the survey of the street folk was only a preface to Mayhew's continuation of the investigations into his—and their—primary interest, the skilled and unskilled workers in London. Hence *London Labour* in the 1850s was likely to seem even more unfinished to its readers than to us. The abrupt cessation of the parts in early 1852 and the fact that for ten years volume 1 and part of volume 2, though available, were scarce, meant that *London Labour* was as generally inaccessible to Mayhew's contemporaries as the *Morning Chronicle* articles. By the time the four volumes (through which modern readers have discovered his work) finally appeared in 1861–1862, the "revelations" were out of date and irrelevant to contemporary concerns. For this reason the four-volume publication had practically no influence on either the sociology or the literature of the late Victorian period. It was mid-twentieth-century historians and literary scholars who ultimately were to be most impressed by Mayhew's surveys of the working poor.

The case of Charles Kingsley and Mayhew is another matter, for Kingsley did borrow directly from Mayhew's *Chronicle* series both in his famous Christian Socialist pamphlet *Cheap Clothes and Nasty* and in his novel *Alton Locke* (1850). Although in some ways Mayhew's influence on Kingsley is obvious, especially if one turns to the parallel passages pointed out by Bradley, the work of the two men is revealed in interesting fashion by a more detailed look at the variety of ways in which Kingsley used Mayhew's work. *Cheap Clothes and Nasty* was mainly a matter of Kingsley quoting Mayhew's material; to compare the pamphlet to its source indicates the strengths and weaknesses of both Kingsley's polemic and Mayhew's journalistic inquiry. *Alton Locke*, on the other hand, showed Mayhew's influence more subtly. In some ways the journalist prepared Kingsley for what he was to see; Mayhew's powerful reports schooled the clergyman's eye in his personal encounters with London's poor. Thus, when Kingsley came to write his novel about a Chartist tailor, his own experiences, those experiences given to him by the working men whom he knew, and Mayhew's revelations blended to make what all readers of *Alton Locke*, from the earliest reviewers on, have agreed is the best part of the novel: the detailed scenes in sweat shops and in the hovels of Jacob's Island.

Kingsley's first direct contacts with the lower classes in England were with the farm workers in Hampshire where he was first a popular curate and then rector, and their experiences provided the basis for his first novel. Most important in his development as polemicist and social novelist, however, was his friendship with Frederick Denison Maurice, which began in 1844. Under Maurice's influence Kingsley became increasingly concerned to involve the clergy and the church in some effort toward ameliorating the social ills of the day. In 1848 although his responsibilities as rector kept him from full participation in the day-to-day activities of the group who were later to be known as Christian Socialists, he went up to London a number of times, particularly during the period immediately prior to the mammoth Chartist demonstration on April 10. Convinced that the Chartists' grievances had some validity and afraid that if the grievances were not assuaged England would have a revolution, Kingsley, Maurice, and their associates met some radical workingmen, including the shoemaker and poet Thomas Cooper, who wrote *The Purgatory of Suicides* (1845) while he was in prison.

The year 1848 also saw Kingsley's first literary publication, the novel *Yeast*, which he began in April in the heat of agitation over the failure of the Chartist petition. It appeared serially July through December in *Fraser's Magazine*, but the hostile reaction to the novel caused the editors to curtail its publication sharply. *Yeast* brought together many of the forces and ideas that were contributing to the social unrest of the period—the Oxford movement, Chartism, Social Toryism, Carlylean hero-worship—and the author endeavored to distinguish and to reconcile them.[7] In fact Carlyle was the major influence; he was the model for one of the characters, Trevegara, and his sentiments on work were one of the main themes.

Yeast was set in the agricultural districts and was concerned mainly with the spiritual regeneration of the young hero rather than with the condition of the poor, although their distress and resulting brutalization played their part in turning Lancelot Smith from egotism to service. Despite Kinsley's personal knowledge of these conditions, he did not convey to his reader a clear impression of the agricultural poor. There were few concrete details and those were heavily colored with moralism. Two descriptive passages in *Yeast*—one of a workhouse and the other of a country fair—were given to expose the living and working conditions which had resulted in the degradation of the agricultural worker. "As he [a Puseyite pastor] came up to [the twenty men and women and children refused lodging in the workhouse] coarse jests, and snatches of low drinking-songs, ghastly as the laughter of lost spirits in the pit, mingled with the feeble wailing of some child of shame."[8] The distaste for the "lost spirits of the pit" and the crying of a child (who inevitably was illegitimate) are the main concern of this narrator. This workhouse scene was unlike that of Mayhew, in which the observer tried to project what it felt like to be destitute, ill-clad, cold, and waiting for the doors of the shelter to open. One of the techniques that Kingsley later learned from Mayhew was to combine his moral exhortations with specific descriptions.

During his recuperation from nervous exhaustion in late 1848, Kingsley was apparently mulling over an idea for another novel to be called the "Autobiography of a Cockney Poet." Kingsley was working on this new novel in the fall of 1849 when, during a series of late summer and early autumn meetings in London, Maurice and other Christian Socialists began to lay plans for concerted action to improve the London working men's condition. At that moment their attention was directed toward cooperative organizations such as they saw in France, and in connection with this idea they decided to bring out a series of polemical pamphlets to be called "Politics for the People," that were actually directed toward the middle classes. In October, before they could get started on this, the group was deflected by Mayhew's account of housing in Bermondsey into working on sanitary reform in that slum.[9] Kingsley's letters show that this project absorbed him until late in 1849, when Mayhew began to reveal the conditions of the east end or badly-paid part of the tailor trade. At this point Kingsley and the rest turned their full attention toward setting up a tailors' cooperative association to combat the ills of sweating. It was finally established in February 1850. In the interests of this association Kingsley made his first use of Mayhew's material.

Kingsley apparently wrote *Cheap Clothes and Nasty* to drum up support for the Working Tailors' Association, the general aims of which were listed at the end of the pamphlet in an address to the public by Walter Cooper. *Cheap Clothes* has long been famous as a brilliant polemic. Some readers have preferred it to the novel *Alton Locke*. W. E. Aytoun, for example, who reviewed the novel for *Blackwood's*, compared *Alton Locke* to the pamphlet *Cheap Clothes*, although he said he did not know whether they were written by the same author or not. (*Alton Locke* was first published anonymously; *Cheap Clothes*, under Kingsley's pseudonym *Parson Lot*.) Aytoun preferred *Cheap Clothes* because in it one saw "the actual condition of the working classes." The pamphlet was "clear, specific, and apparently well-vouched."[10]

Such praise for Kingsley's pamphlet was not accompanied by any recognition of the manner in which its strength depended on Mayhew. Even Bradley, who first detailed Kingsley's nearly total reliance on Mayhew's letters of December, did not go beyond calling *Cheap Clothes* "little more than a series of acknowledged excerpts from Mayhew's *Chronicle* articles."[11] There is more to it than this. The way Kingsley used Mayhew's material taught him lessons of precision, particularity, and detailed description with the result that *Alton Locke* was a much better social commentary than was the confused *Yeast* that was written before Kingsley read Mayhew.

Kingsley's pamphlet mainly used, as he admitted, information made public in Mayhew's reports of two large meetings of tailors in December 1849. Since *Cheap Clothes and Nasty* was published in January 1850, probably less than six weeks lapsed between Mayhew's articles and Kingsley's pamphlet. Mayhew's first gathering in Shadwell of east end tailors was recounted in his 14 December letter (XVII); the second, of many west end tailors crowded into a room in Hanover Square, was reported on four days later. Kingsley himself probably was not present at either meeting.[12]

Although Kingsley quoted heavily from Mayhew in his pamphlet, he had different ends in mind, and therefore his finished product was quite unlike its source. Mayhew reported the raw data with an almost tedious inclusiveness while Kingsley selected the facts and shaped their presentation. Moreover Kingsley was primarily interested in using the material he gleaned from the reports of these meetings for its shock value and dramatic effect; he was less interested in objective presentation and in at least one place he was careless even as to factual accuracy. For him the effect the material had on the reader was all that mattered. For example, he at no time in his pamphlet distinguished the exact source of any individual piece of information. He did not tell who said what, or whether the man speaking was part of the well-paid or exploited branch of tailoring, nor why we should trust the accuracy of his remarks. There were, in fact, no distinctions in Kingsley's use of the material from the meetings, either as to the trade itself or the men who worked for it. On the other hand Mayhew's letters were obsessed with distinctions between the honorable and dishonorable side of the trade, the west end responsible masters and the east end sweaters, the reliable and the unreliable informants. For Kingsley's polemical purposes, such distinctions were beside the point; for Mayhew, they were the whole purpose.

This difference between the two is demonstrated in Kingsley's use of one of Mayhew's experiences to point a moral, one which, incidentally, had also been made by Carlyle in *Past and Present* and which would later be made in the same way by Dickens in *Bleak House*. Mayhew recounted in Letter XVII (14 December) a visit to a sick tailor in the east end:

> I expressed my surprise that the bed of the sick man should be covered with the new garment, and was informed that such in the winter time was a common practice among the workpeople. When the weather was very cold, and their blankets had gone to the pawnshop, the slop-workers often went to bed, I was told, with the sleeves of the coat they were making drawn over their arms, or else they would cover themselves with the trowsers or paletôts, according to the description of garment they had in hand. The ladies' riding habits in particular, I was assured, were used as counterpanes to the poor people's beds, on account of the quantity of cloth in the skirts.

Kingsley in *Cheap Clothes* did not quote Mayhew's quietly understated description; he translated it into the polemics of the pulpit and leaped to a conclusion that Mayhew had resisted.

> The Rev. D—— finds himself suddenly unpresentable from a cutaneous disease, which it is not polite to mention on the south of the Tweed, little dreaming that the shivering dirty being who made his coat has been sitting with his arms in the sleeves for warmth while he stitched at the tails. The charming Miss C—— is swept off by typhus or scarlatina, and her parents talk about "God's heavy judgment and visitation"—had they tracked the girl's new riding-habit back to the stifling undrained hovel where it served as a blanket to the fever-stricken slopworker, they would have seen *why* God had visited them.[13]

The tone in this short paragraph clashed with the factual understatement in the passage which Kingsley quoted from Mayhew, though, as we shall see, the ironic moralism was characteristic of him when he

treated the material in his own voice. It shows what a weak performance *Cheap Clothes and Nasty* might have been stylistically without
Mayhew's reports.

Cheap Clothes and Nasty started with two paragraphs of introduction, fulsomely decked out with literary and biblical references. The
rest of the pamphlet was an amalgam of passages from Mayhew's letters very freely cut and pasted together to create a strong picture of
exploitation and distress. Kingsley added very little to the snippings
from Mayhew's longer reports other than frequent strings of exclamation marks and a free use of italics to make sure the reader got the
point. His careless regard for the manner in which he used the material
resulted in a confusion at one point where his direct quotation, un-
changed for the new context, gave the impression that the interviews
were done by Parson Lot rather than quoted from the papers: "'On
this you see the price is marked at 12s.,' continued my informant" (p.
15), meaning of course Mayhew's, not Kingsley's, informant.

Since he was writing the pamphlet to propagandize the Working
Tailors' Association, most of the examples Kingsley culled out of
Mayhew's two letters concerned the way prices were cheapened by the
sweaters at the expense of the workers. After giving Mayhew's statistics on the established well-paid branch of the tailor trade, Kingsley
took some paragraphs from scattered interviews mostly from the December 18 meeting and gave a fairly coherent account of the method of
sweaters. His lack of concern for distinctions is again seen in the way
that he fused part of a statement made by a sweater with someone
else's description of the "kidnapping" of inexperienced tailors. Kingsley's next group of quotations came from the letter of December 14,
among which are attacks on the customers who patronized shops which
depended on sweated labor. He concluded his exposé with a statement
from the December 18th letter, which revealed that even the government supported sweated labor by the way it commissioned uniforms.
At the very end Kingsley, returning to his own voice, asked what was
to be done, and he continued with three suggestions, two of them dealing with associations among workers.

One of the first things one notices in comparing Kingsley's pamphlet
and its source is that Kingsley reversed the order in which he used the

material from Mayhew's articles. He began with almost exclusive quotation from Letter XVIII (December 18) and only at the end took most of his material from Letter XVII (December 14). While Kingsley was influenced by Mayhew's data, his methods of organizing it were his own. Mayhew's first letter told of a meeting which grew out of his earliest investigations of the tailor trade; only after this first meeting did he come to understand certain subtleties in the trade and see the need for the larger meeting of west end tailors which occurred four days later. At the conclusion of this second meeting Mayhew clarified definitions and the organization of the trade. Mayhew's letters unfolded the experience as it happened to him, in the inductive and experimental method he was usually forced to use in the *Morning Chronicle* series. Kingsley, on the other hand, argued deductively by example from the general situation to the suggested solutions. He brought together different statements dealing with the same topic. He organized the topics in an ascending order of importance, from general descriptions to an attack on the customers. Kingsley had the advantage of hindsight in writing his pamphlet. He could select, focus, generalize, and order the experiences Mayhew had elicited, something Mayhew intended to do but which as we know he never did.

Kingsley's *Cheap Clothes* thus shows up the inherent weakness in Mayhew's articles, which had none of the pamphlet's direction, selection, and organization and which, in comparison, seem a sprawling, disorganized, repetitious, and at times confusing set of startling specific revelations. Nonetheless Kingsley's pamphlet is not really superior to Mayhew's letters in its effect on the reader. As Kingsley's response indicates, Mayhew's two letters were powerful reading despite their fragmentary form and the disorganization of important general information. Their force came from Mayhew's obsession with details. As the many individual workers recounted the different facts about themselves and their work, the reader came to see each informant as a distinct human being. The workers do not assume life and identity in Kingsley's pamphlet, for he made no effort to differentiate them. Instead he used a single interview in three different places, making it appear to come from three different men. The reader consequently received no impression of the individuality of this worker. Ironically it is Kingsley who turns out to be dedicated to the bare "facts" rather than Mayhew, who, in his larger projection of the human element, had a much broader scope than Kingsley in his use of the specific material.

Even though Mayhew's letters played an important role in Kingsley's thoughts about the Working Tailors' Association, there appears to have been no attempt to involve the journalist in the project itself.[14] Mayhew seemed never to attend any meeting of the Tailors' Association although he knew some of the members, for one of the founders of the group, Walter Cooper, represented the working men at an organization meeting of one of Mayhew's abortive associations, the Friendly Association of Costermongers.

Mayhew's absence from the Kingsley project might have been due to his desire to set up his own "Tailors' Guild." An informative essay in the *British Quarterly Review* for May 1850, which reviewed the development of socialism in France and in England, gave some insight into the theoretical positions of both Mayhew and Kingsley at this time. Mayhew's Tailors' Guild never went beyond the paper prospectus printed by the *British Quarterly Review*, but his outline of goals for the organization, when compared with the intentions of Kingsley's Working Tailors' Association, sharply emphasizes the disparity between Mayhew's commitment to the working-class view in his interviews and the middle-class caution of his directly stated opinions in his earliest letters.

As against the innovative principles of the Christian Socialists' Working Tailors' Association, Mayhew's suggestions for a Tailors' Guild were traditional, as the anachronistic word *guild* indicates. He eschewed any political or economic action by the group, yet asserted that the mere fact of association would solve all problems.

> All that is needed is association. The suffering, the squalor, and the abasement of the single victim are to be met and overcome by union. And by such union, be it distinctly understood, no combination is meant or intended that shall in any way interfere with either the social or commercial freedom of the individual. . . . The object of the TAILORS' GUILD is, then, unequivocally, neither political nor communistic.[15]

Mayhew then listed seven "vital principles" of such association. The most important of these were the institution of "an office for the insurance of an uniform rate of income to the workman throughout the 'brisk' and 'slack' seasons of the year" and also of a poor fund; but as later in his remedies for low wages, he gave no details how the "insurance" or fund were to work. He further suggested that the unemployed be found employment, "at a less rate than the ordinary wages of the trade," upon making the clothes of the members and their families, a suggestion that few knowledgeable artisans would have accepted since it would have undermined regular wages. Mayhew also wanted the guild to collect statistics on "the past and present condition of the trade" and finally to provide a savings and loan bank, a club for refreshment, assemblies for the recreation of all its members, a library, and lectures and evening classes.

Mayhew might not have been serious about the Tailors' Guild; he may have been forced by public opinion into offering some sort of solution for the ills that he so movingly documented before he was ready to do so. Yet the paucity of innovation in his projected guild shows Mayhew's reluctance to move outside established patterns.

The Working Tailors' Association, on the other hand, was a fairly concrete endeavor. Cooperation was as frequently advanced a solution for working conditions in the 1840s as was emigration. There were many such efforts, beginning with those of Robert Owen. The Working Tailors' Association was not the only such organization which the Christian Socialists themselves began; others included workshops for shoemakers and printers. None of these endeavors lasted very long, however; by 1854 the experiment was over.[16]

While it continued, the Working Tailors' Association opened a shop in Castle Street "to which the publication of *Cheap Clothes* took many customers."[17] The master tailor (Walter Cooper) managed the shop; one-third of the profits were used to pay the wages of new members, and the rest was divided among the workmen in proportion to their work. Such a practical effort to help tailors in London makes the vagueness of Mayhew's suggestions even more apparent. Whatever his strengths of observation Mayhew was at this time unaware of the underlying system which supported sweating. In a few months, however, he was, and this juxtaposition provides one of the clearest examples of the way that he was educated by his experiences.

In addition to his efforts on behalf of the Working Tailors' Association and the writing of *Cheap Clothes and Nasty*, Kingsley was also working on *Alton Locke* in the winter of 1849–1850. The writing of the pamphlet had sharpened his understanding of Mayhew's materials and enabled him to use them in his novel in a more integrated and imaginative way. *Alton Locke* was published in August 1850. Kingsley and his wife both insisted that the reviews were adverse, and the reviewers were hard indeed on the improbable love story, the strong sentiments expressed by Crosswaite, and the nature of his and Alton's conversion as well as on Kingsley's attack on the University, which he modified in the editions after 1861. The critics were almost equally laudatory, however, about "the episodes which are carefully constructed from ascertained and unquestionable facts, and in which the proprieties of nature and circumstance are not exaggerated or forsaken, whilst the pictorial power of the author is shown to the greatest advantage."[18] These were the passages related to *Cheap Clothes* and to Mayhew's letters.

Kingsley emphatically denied Mayhew's influence on *Alton Locke* in the second edition of *Yeast* in 1851: "Hopeless and bewildered, [Lancelot Smith] left the books, and wandered day after day from farm to market, and from field to tramper's tent. . . . What he saw, of course I must not say; for if I did the reviewers would declare, as usual, one and all, that I copied out of the *Morning Chronicle*."[19] He always spoke of the *Chronicle* letters in the highest terms, however, including in all editions of *Alton Locke* this footnote: "Facts still worse than those which Mr. Locke's story contains have been made public by the *Morning Chronicle* in a series of noble letters on 'Labour and the Poor.'"[20]

The influence was there nonetheless, though it was not at all a question of simple copying. Bradley has noted with some thoroughness the parts of *Alton Locke* written under the direct influence of Mayhew. Kingsley looked to the letters, Bradley said, "for urban descriptions, for means of advancing the narrative, and for certain specific incidents." He gave seven examples, beginning with a juxtaposition of the two passages on Jacob's Island in which the "parallels in diction and phraseology are too obvious to escape notice."[21] Other comparisons Bradley listed included the details of Irishmen "kidnapped" by sweaters' wives (from Letters XVII and XVIII; in *Alton Locke*, chapter 21); the sweaters' appropriation of their workers' clothes in order to prevent them running away (from XVIII; in *Alton Locke*, chapter 21); an interview with a distressed gentlewoman, daughter of an army officer (from IX; in chapter 8); illegal profiteering of army officers in buying uniforms (in VIII and throughout *Alton Locke*), and finally the situation of needlewomen forced into prostitution because of low wages (from VIII; in chapter 8). There is not much to add to this list of parallels, except to reiterate mention of the analogous passages in Letter XVII and in the death of Alton's cousin.[22]

Let me make some distinctions about the ways in which Mayhew influenced the novel. Direct verbal echoes were few, perhaps only in the passages on Jacob's Island that are quoted in part by Bradley. Yet even when Kingsley used Mayhew's words, he did not do so in the same way as in *Cheap Clothes and Nasty*. The description of Jacob's Island, compared with Mayhew's description as a whole, convinces one that Kingsley saw the place that he described with his own eyes. It is true that Mayhew's piece helped Kingsley in his choice of language: a ditch "the color of strong green tea" in Mayhew became an "olive-green hell-broth" in Kingsley; the "heaps of indescribable filth, the phosphoretted smell from which tells you of the rotting fish there" was rendered by Kingsley as "phosphorescent scraps of rotten fish." Mayhew's vision of "swollen carcases of dead animals almost bursting with the gases of putrefaction" became "bloated carcasses of dogs, and lumps of offal" in Kingsley. Through Mayhew Kingsley also learned that this ditch was the only water the people in Jacob's Island had to drink. But when Kingsley visited Jacob's Island in the October before he began to write his novel, he saw something that Mayhew had not described. Characteristically, when he reported this experience of his own in *Alton Locke*, Kingsley pointed the moral with heavy-handed irony. His own experience was thus sharply separated in tone and treatment from the parts of his description which he owed to Mayhew: "The neighborhood was undergoing, as it seemed, 'improvements' of that peculiar metropolitan species which consists in pulling down the dwellings of the poor, and building up rich men's houses instead. . . . There they loomed up, the tall bullies, against the dreary sky, looking down with their grim, proud, stony visages, on the misery they were driving out of one corner, only to accumulate and intensify it in another" (8:203). The difference between this passage and those that corresponded to Mayhew's report rests in an ironic and moralized use of particulars and an objective but detailed description. Kingsley's blunt use of quotation marks and personification made the passage his, not Mayhew's.

Another type of influence is seen in the plot. Kingsley took a disclosed fact from Mayhew and split it up among his characters in order to achieve maximum effect from all the particulars. For example the details about the kidnapping of the Irish tailors by sweaters' wives came from several accounts given by different tailors at the December 18 meeting. In the novel Kingsley used the information skillfully and efficiently by giving some of the facts to Alton (the enticement by Jemmy Downes's Irish wife), part to the wild Irishman Mike Kelly, and part to his friend Billy Porter (son of a prosperous farmer near Cambridge). Again, however, Kingsley was not content to let the material stand alone as Mayhew had. He attached his own direct lesson: Kelly and Porter came to the end they did because when their firm changed hands they refused to sign a pledge not to accept piece or sweated work.

Another detail taken from Mayhew and scattered throughout *Alton Locke* was the government's collusion with the sweaters. "Government contract work is the worst work of all, and the starved-out and sweated-out tailor's last resource," Mayhew quoted an informant in Letter XVIII. This information angered Kingsley more perhaps than any single fact uncovered by Mayhew. Diatribes by Crosswaite and Alton against the government's support of low wages occur throughout the novel until by repetition the culpability of the government became one of the main objects under attack.

One other example of Mayhew's influence on *Alton Locke* cited by Bradley seems to me problematic. There is little similarity between the whining old woman in chapter 8 and the dignified distressed gentlewoman in Letter IX even though they were both daughters of army officers. Kingsley did not need Mayhew to provide that detail, although he may indeed have taken the pathetic situation of the sisters, one of whom has become a prostitute to support the other who is dying, from his revelations about needlewomen turned prostitutes. Another similarity in this chapter Bradley does not mention. The way in which Mackaye and Alton traverse the streets and climb to the garret of the tailor is reminiscent of a number of scenes in the early letters.

If Kingsley did gain inspiration from Mayhew to construct the scene in chapter 8 in the way that he did, the novelist nonetheless had his own experiences to draw upon as well, for the important description of the decrepit building did not come from Mayhew's letters. Kingsley's particulars about this slum dwelling, once a rich man's abode, were too precise to be imaginary; yet without Mayhew's detailed report to control him, the novelist shifted the tone into one more blunt and direct:

> We went on through a back street or two, and then into a huge, miserable house, which, a hundred years ago, perhaps had witnessed the luxury, and rung to the laughter of some one great fashionable family, alone there in their glory. Now every room of it held its family, or its group of families—a phalanstery of all the fiends;—its grand staircase, with the carved balustrades rotting and crumbling away piecemeal, converted into a common sewer for the inmates. (7:202)

The evident distaste for the experience, the moralizing, the irony, and the manner in which the ugly details were insinuated into a larger picture—all mark Kingsley's response when not moderated by Mayhew's. Kingsley was justified in his anger when reviewers complained that his novel was a collection of details from the *Morning Chronicle*, but nonetheless the social investigator directed Kingsley's eye and provided a model for objective description. As *Yeast* showed, without such control Kingsley could be an inferior social novelist.

While Mayhew's influence on Kingsley is obvious, the influence on Charles Dickens is more complicated and difficult to analyze. Not only was Dickens a more original artist than Kingsley, but he also maintained a silence on his relationship with Mayhew. Nonetheless the names of Mayhew and Dickens have been linked since the very beginning, even by those who do not know their personal connection. Early reviewers drew the parallel frequently. A writer in the *Literary*

Gazette in 1851 saw the two writers as similar in their study of London characters; reporters for the *Christian Watchman and Reflector* and the *New York Evening Post* (both American journals) made the same observation in the same year. In this century reviewers of Peter Quennell's selections from *London Labour* frequently drew parallels between the two, as did W. H. Auden in his review of the first complete reissue of *London Labour and the London Poor* in 1967, and Francis Sheppard began the last chapter of his history of nineteenth-century London with a comparison of the two writers.[23]

The recurrence of this association suggests that even though they wrote their major works in different media, there is something profoundly similar between the two men. Though the similarities go beyond the question of direct influence, some internal evidence does suggest that Dickens might have drawn on Mayhew's work for his own. They certainly were friendly before Mayhew began his social surveys. This makes Dickens's knowledge of the journalist's investigations more than likely.

Like Thackeray and Mayhew, Dickens partook of the lively camaraderie and vague liberalism of Fleet Street and Drury Lane in his younger days. The concerns and attitudes of the *Sketches by Boz* generally agreed with those of Mayhew. In regard to education both writers condemned the curriculum of Greek and Latin and the practice of corporal punishment.[24] Their attitudes on philanthropy, sanitation reform, or the hypocrisy and corruptness of some elements of officialdom were also similar. In one case, pointed out by Philip Collins in *Dickens and Crime*, their very subject of attack was identical.[25] This target was a notorious magistrate, one Laing, pilloried by Dickens as Fang in *Oliver Twist*. Under Mayhew's editorship *Figaro in London* also criticized Laing and claimed full credit when he was removed from the bench in January 1838.[26] Mayhew's association with *Figaro in London* was responsible for another connection in their lives, for Robert Seymour, who did some of the cartoons for the journal, apparently first considered Mayhew as a collaborator for the project which eventually became *Pickwick Papers*.[27] In 1845 Dickens and Mayhew were close enough for the latter to take part in the novelist's amateur theatrical *Every Man in His Humour*: Mayhew played Knowell.[28]

Despite all this evidence of early connections, after 1845 there is no indication of a continuing association between the two men. It appears that they almost became strangers to one another. In 1851 in *London Labour* Mayhew spoke highly of Dickens's *Sketches* but in terms which indicated no personal friendship between them. Dickens apparently did not mention Mayhew in his letters or works.[29]

Even if their friendship suffered from his general withdrawal from old ties that appeared to follow Mayhew's troubles, it seems strange that Dickens did not at least mention the famous *Morning Chronicle* articles. Perhaps he ignored them because, however erroneously, he saw them as a kind of rival for public acclaim. He was launching *Household Words* at the same time as the *Morning Chronicle*'s "Labour and the Poor" hit its stride. Or a quarrel over some issue—such as the difference between Dickens and Jerrold over the novelist's change of heart about capital punishment—might have resulted in a coolness which led to silence on Dickens's part.

On the other hand the failure to refer to *London Labour and the London Poor*, whose subject would have delighted Dickens, was perhaps an effort to hide the fact that he used details from it in a few instances, if in fact he did. He always insisted on his personal knowledge of the facts of his novels and thus might not have wanted to acknowledge Mayhew's investigations as a source.

On some issues Mayhew and Dickens did diverge sharply after 1850. Dickens's journalism, as Collins has demonstrated, tended to follow the shift of Victorian public opinion to more conservative attitudes about social questions, particularly crime, after midcentury. The novelist also periodically displayed strong hostility to the law-abiding lower classes, the group Mayhew found so fascinating. Dickens could be intelligently sensitive with the prostitutes whom he and Miss Coutts set about to reform at Urania Cottage, but when he met an ordinary eighteen-year-old lower-class Irish girl in Hyde Park and the girl swore at him, he tried to have her sent to prison in spite of the resistance of the police and the magistrate. "Do you really wish this girl to be sent to prison?" the incredulous magistrate asked Dickens, who reported himself "grimly" answering, "If I didn't, why should I take the trouble to come here?"[30]

Though Mayhew's intensity about social matters also lessened after 1856, he never completely abandoned his earlier social concerns. During the years in which Dickens was apparently reversing his position on the abolition of capital punishment, Mayhew still addressed the committee which advocated an end to the penalty. Dickens, perhaps following Carlyle, called for the reinstitution of flogging in prison and perpetual imprisonment of "ruffians," while Mayhew denied that making prison more repellent would reduce crime. In fact Dickens's increased respect for Carlyle and Mayhew's reiterated disgust with the author of "Model Prisons" might in itself reflect growing differences which made a continued intimacy impossible.

Whatever the reason for Dickens's silence about Mayhew's investigations of the working poor, there are a few close parallels between his novels and Mayhew's surveys which strongly suggest that he did know them. Harland Nelson first pointed some of these out in 1965.[31] He found possible sources for Betty Higden, Gaffer Hexam, and Jenny Wren in *London Labour and the London Poor* and in the *Morning Chronicle* articles. Other parallels exist. A scavenger, like Gaffer Hexam, insisted it was not right for a child to know more than his father (2:226), and Mayhew's description of one of the best-known "pinners-up" of ballads resembles Silas Wegg. He had old books as well as ballads for sale and he had a reputation for being argumentative about politics and literature even when he knew nothing about them (1:272). Recently Richard Dunn has pointed out parallels between Krook in *Bleak House* and details of a rag-and-bottle shop owner in volume 2 of *London Labour*.[32]

In all these cases, if Dickens did indeed use Mayhew's work, he did so by picking out one or two salient details to add to a picture already formed in his own mind rather than by borrowing wholesale as Kingsley did. If he read *London Labour and the London Poor*, Dickens ignored information which contradicted his own ideas, for Mayhew denied the "popular notion" that any dustman ever got rich from his collection of dust (2:137).

Whatever the truth about Dickens's use of Mayhew's work, direct influence is not the factor to account for our sense of their profound similarity. Instead, among all the many evocations of the Victorian metropolis, their visions of London strike us as the most powerfully particularized and encompassing. This is true despite the overt narrowness of each of their Londons. In *London Labour* the metropolis was essentially a city of the streets—the same was true for Dickens—and both writers limited their view to that of the lower-middle and lower classes. Yet a sense of inclusiveness comes from the work of both authors because, despite this narrow scope, each managed to suggest a larger abundance of life. In Dickens's novels as well as his sketches, neighborhoods, courtyards, houses were filled with a seemingly inexhaustible supply of individuals.

> It is growing late, and the throng of men, women, and children, who have been constantly going in and out, dwindles down to two or three occasional stragglers—cold, wretched-looking creatures, in the last stage of emaciation and disease. The knot of Irish labourers at the lower end of the place, who have been alternately shaking hands with, and threatening the life of each other, for the last hour, become furious in their disputes, and finding it impossible to silence one man, who is particularly anxious to adjust the difference, they resort to the expedient of knocking him down and jumping on him afterwards. The man in the fur cap, and the potboy rush out; a scene of riot and confusion ensues; half the Irishmen get shut out, and the other half get shut in; the potboy is knocked among the tubs in no time; the landlord hits everybody, and everybody hits the landlord; the barmaids scream; the police come in; the rest is a confused mixture of arms, legs, staves, torn coats, shouting, and struggling. Some of the party are borne off to the station-house, and the remainder slink home to beat their wives for complaining, and kick the children for daring to be hungry.[33]

The sense of movement, of crowded streets and rooms that occurs in passages like these was also frequently reinforced in Dickens's novels and sketches by the many names of specific places which he gave in his work.[34] Furthermore, as Dorothy Van Ghent first demonstrated, even inanimate objects in Dickens's world could take on life and motion.[35] Dickens also paralleled Mayhew's techniques when he included in his journalistic reports seemingly irrelevant details.

The sense of teeming life in Mayhew comes from another source. His compulsion for subdivision in his surveys as well as for detail in his interviews resulted in what seems an equally large canvas, although this sense of scope is largely unjustified. A more legitimate sense of multiplicity and quantity, particularly in *London Labour and the London Poor*, lay in the stress Mayhew placed on the individuality of all his subjects, who were forced by privation, by harassment, by handicaps or by temperament to devise seemingly endless ingenious methods to keep body and soul together. Caught by competition, they had to stretch their wits to the utmost in order to differentiate themselves from one another. Inevitably, as Mayhew's microscope magnified each branch of the street trade further, the adaptations became increasingly more unusual and the sense of variety stronger. Thus Mayhew like Dickens also made London seem a place where the recognizable and familiar were romantic and unusual, and where the variety of life seemed inexhaustible.

Dickens and Mayhew were not alone in their projection of the variety and multiplicity of London life of course. As P. J. Keating has stated, the nineteenth-century London novel, whose prototype was Pierce Egan's *Life in London* (1821), always focused on "the variety and mystery of the London streets" (p. 11) and tried to open the readers' eyes to the strange in the familiar. Mayhew and Dickens, however, managed to communicate the multiplicity of life in London and the energy with which the population lived it in modes which triumphed over the inherent chaos—a chaos that Wordsworth, for one, felt put the whole creative powers of man asleep.

> Oh, blank confusion! true epitome
> Of what the mighty City is herself,
> To thousands upon thousands of her sons,
> Living amid the same perpetual whirl
> Of trivial objects, melted and reduced
> To one identity, by differences
> That have no law, no meaning, and no end—
> Oppression, under which even highest minds
> Must labour, whence the strongest are not free.[36]

The means by which Mayhew and Dickens overcame this paralysing sense of formlessness were different, though the effect was the same. Intentions and modes would vary in different media, of course; but even in their journalism Mayhew and Dickens had opposite modes of controlling the varieties of urban life. It is also important to note that the separation between fiction and journalism in their work was never absolute. As we have seen, Mayhew's sociological journalism could partake of the selectivity and rhetorical organization of fiction. Dickens's novels frequently had a journalistic base in contemporary events, and he insisted on the factual nature of his novels.[37]

The factual base of Dickens's journalism and the artistic shape of Mayhew's nonetheless reflected two quite different responses to the experiences of London lower-class life. Dickens, son of a ne'er-do-well father of the lower middle class, forced by his own unconscious needs and his early circumstances into proximity to the chaos of lower-class urban life, controlled his conflicting responses (his "attraction of repulsion" for the slums, as Forster said)[38] through a variety of distancing devices which never completely isolated him. Mayhew, son of a successful upper-middle-class father, did the opposite, as we have seen; he tried to destroy his separation from the teeming life of the city without losing his sense of difference. Because both of these men felt ambivalent about their responses, Mayhew using almost the same phrase as Forster in referring to the "attractively-repulsive" details of street art in *London Labour* (1:215), neither of them was completely successful in establishing his special relationships with the urban population. Both men's work was subject to distortions—Dickens's by whimsy and sentimentality, Mayhew's by a substitution of a part for the whole.

The need to achieve a distance and the need to identify oneself with his subject made Dickens and Mayhew different kinds of reporters. Mayhew said in his second article for the *Morning Chronicle* series: "My vocation is to collect facts and register opinions"; to do this he tried to minimize his own role. He tried to detail the way that the labor situation looked to the poor; he consistently tried to find ways to experience their lives vicariously. As we have seen, in an escorted tour of a prison, he did his stint on the treadmill; he conducted an interview with a blind man in the dark.[39] He also visited an illegal gambling game, and described the watch set for the police (1:17–18). In fact he avoided the police while interviewing the inhabitants of slums. When he held a meeting of ticket-of-leave men, he prohibited a constable from attending, although he did take one with him when he toured the Ratcliff Highway, a notorious and dangerous criminal neighborhood.[40]

In general Dickens had a different sense of his role as a reporter. He interpreted the social facts rather than "collecting" them. As Harry Stone has said, he "illuminated" them, filtering them "through a sensibility that has organized and 'understood' them for us."[41] The process of interpreting the facts could separate him from his subjects. In "Gin Palaces" in the *Sketches*, for example, Dickens quite intentionally distanced himself by treating the unpleasant realities of the scene humorously. When he did become involved with those whom he observed, he did so not by ferreting out the details of their lives but by fictionalizing them.[42] In *Household Words* and *All the Year Round* he repeated these distanced stances in his role as reporter and added another. As the uncommercial traveller his tendency in his walks through the east end was "to regard my walk as my beat, and myself as a higher sort of police-constable doing duty on the same."[43] Such a policeman by definition was separated from the people he saw, for his purpose was to "investigate" the poor in terms of various deviations from the norm as opposed to the role Mayhew assumed in giving a voice to the poor and thereby establishing their view as the norm. As a result Dickens's reports did not present, as did Mayhew's, a combination of himself and his subjects but instead a personal and essentially middle-class response to the details of London's slums. Because his responses were so deeply realized and so fundamentally humanistic, his reports of conventional scenes move us, but we are affected mainly because the narrator himself is touched. Nor does he really tell us much that we did not know before.

Yet Dickens's reporting was not always a matter of interpretation or illumination. In his interview with "the king of the bill-stickers," an encounter very reminiscent of Mayhew in its delight in incongruity and the abounding curiosity of the reporter (if not in his whimsical condescension and exaggerated description), Dickens called himself by Mayhew's label: "I am a sort of collector," he told the bill sticker, "a collector of facts."[44]

Dickens's understanding of what were "facts" was not the same as that of Mayhew, however. Mayhew meant by "facts" statistics and the faithful repetition of the words of others. Dickens disliked Mayhew's kind of facts, finding *Household Words* a failure when it lapsed "too much into a dreary, arithmetical, cocker-cum-walkingame dustyness that is powerfully depressing."[45] Mayhew of course planned eventually to get to the stage of interpreting the facts, but his belief in induction and his scientific method prevented him from expressing as he went along the kind of intuitive illumination of the "facts" which Dickens did. It also kept him from making some of Dickens's misjudgments and engaging in some of his inconsistencies. Mayhew, for example, through the slow accumulation of personal experiences, came to support the trade unions. Even in the 1860s, when he echoed some standard platitudes about commerce, he apparently did not change his mind about this. Dickens's view of trade unions, because it was not rooted in the same kind of personal experience, was not consistently maintained. While he supported the workers' right to organize, he was distrustful of labor leaders.

In Dickens's reporting the presence of a strongly individualized narrator (who was thus identifiably different from his subjects) was necessary before he could use Mayhew's sort of "facts." In *Sketches by Boz* the narrator was a conventional bland and smiling essayist familiar to all readers of the London periodical press,[46] and the "facts" in these sketches were strongly fictionalized. In *Household Words* the narrator was more clearly a special person, one who admired the police, was famous enough to be annoyed by begging-letter writers, and who loved to travel. This individualized narrator reported some of Dickens's most Mayhewian articles, such as "Bill-Sticking," "Down with the Tide," and "A Plated Article" (the latter may have been mainly written by Wills, the managing editor of *Household Words*).[47] Finally, in the "Uncommercial Traveller" series for *All the Year Round*, Mr. Uncommercial was even more fully rounded as a character and though the tone in these pieces was darker the reporting itself was the most consistently factual, in Mayhew's sense, in Dickens's three collections.

Dickens's separation from, and Mayhew's attempts to get closer to, the working poor in London also resulted in two quite different relationships between the reporter and the poor. As we know, Mayhew, trying to lose parts of himself and his background, identified himself with them—that is, he assumed their attitudes and thoughts, although the tie was never complete. Dickens on the other hand, in his attempt to deal with his conflicting responses to the urban scene, projected himself into his subjects, made them feel as he did. However different the ultimate source, both responses had the effect of controlling the multitudinousness of the urban scene, and both resulted in a vision of a multilayered world. We have seen many examples of Mayhew's identification in the preceding pages, and examples of Dickens's projection are recurrent throughout his journalism. For example in the *Sketches* he imagined a "true" life-history of loneliness and devotion for a man whom he saw in St. James Park and whom he described in close detail; in a visit to Newgate he posited a sentimental life for a hardened criminal; in the "Hospital Patient," while claiming to report an affecting scene between a brute and his beaten wife, he actually told a conventional story of suffering and love. J. Hillis Miller has noted further that when Dickens gave these "true" stories to the people he observed in the *Sketches*, he inevitably presented a stock fictional convention (p. 118).

Dickens's projections sometimes created disturbing effects in his reports of lower-class life. Unlike Mayhew he liked to tour the slums with the police; in his journalistic accounts of his adventures, he tended to give to the lower classes his own feelings about the police officers rather than to try to imagine what the lower classes actually felt. Thus he showed little concern while watching Inspector Field disturbing the sleep of people in asylums for the homeless and bullying the inhabitants of low lodginghouses and in general running through his job with condescending efficiency. (Inspector Bucket in *Bleak House* acts with the same brutality toward Jo. The effect is disconcerting since Dickens wanted us to admire Bucket, whose attitude toward Jo seems violently at odds with our own.)[48]

In one tour with Field, for example, Dickens described the inspector at work in a cellar which the reporter called Rats' Castle:

> Inspector Field's hand is the well-known hand that has collared half the people here, and motioned their brothers, sisters, fathers, mothers, male and female friends, inexorably to New South Wales. Yet Inspector Field stands in this den, the Sultan of the place. Every thief here cowers before him, like a schoolboy before his schoolmaster. All watch him, all answer when addressed, all laugh at his jokes, all seek to propitiate him.[49]

The reader might be forgiven if he missed the condescension in this piece because Dickens was not complacent or smug in his attitude.

Although he gave no sense of what was really going on in the minds of these men and women and presented them as an undifferentiated mass, his symbolic generalization which saw them as blood relations with the whole criminal class made a strong moral point about the interconnectedness of poverty and crime. The effect is all the more impressive when compared to the clumsy effects that Mayhew achieved when he tried to do the same thing later in *Young Benjamin Franklin*:

> Few, indeed, know what it is to see crime in the mass—wickedness in the lump, as it were; to look upon some hundred heads, and feel as if they were fused into one monster brain, instinct with a hundred devil-power, and quickened with a hundredfold more than ordinary human cunning and cheatery. . . . It is no longer one wayward human heart we contemplate, but hundreds of such hearts; every one of them pulsing, like a hundred clocks, in terrible unison, throbbing with one universal rancour and hatred of all that is good and grand; and never a generous passion nor a noble sentiment, and hardly a kindly feeling stirring within them. (p. 366)

In their reports of interviews Dickens and Mayhew repeated their characteristic responses of projection and identification. Dickens in *Household Words* and *All the Year Round* recounted a number of interviews with people very much like Mayhew's informants. In "Down with the Tide" he accompanied a police launch at night and had a long conversation with a toll-taker on Waterloo Bridge. He reported on this interview whimsically, and as a result, though we learn a little of what it would be like to be a toll-taker and a great deal about what the narrator thinks of this particular toll-taker, we learn less about the individual man as he saw himself. Most important in this piece is the general dark vision of London at night, a city teeming with life engaged in dubious and desperate enterprises.

As the uncommercial traveller Dickens also interviewed a number of residents of the slums of the east end of London. In each case he "interpreted" their words in his reports. One method of doing this was to repeat not only his questions but also his feelings about the answers. "'God bless you, sir, and thank you!' were the parting words from these people,—gratefully spoken too,—with which I left this place."[50] The quoted dialogue rings true and does not differ from that found in Mayhew's interviews; the parenthetical reflection on its sincerity however was Dickens's way of projecting himself into the scene.

Another way Dickens made his interviews as much about himself as about his informants was to shift them from direct dialogue into indirect discourse, thus giving his responses to the scene rather than realizing those of his subjects. Nonetheless the individual dialogue in the following passage, while ironically indirect, does succeed in presenting the woman interviewed as an effective representative of the whole class of exploited workers. She becomes important because her experience is that of all distressed needlewomen in London, and her suffering is increased in dimension because it includes theirs.

> But, you see, it come to her through two hands, and of course it didn't come through the second hand for nothing. Why did it come through the second hand at all? Why, this way. The second hand took the risk of the given-out work, you see. If she had money enough to pay the security deposit,—call it two pound,—she could get the work from the first hand, and so the second would not have to be deducted for.[51]

Mayhew's interviews on the other hand subjugated the interviewer to his subjects by trying to eliminate the observer's responses and to melt his questions into the answers. The result was sharply defined individuals but limited general application.

> "Ah, its wonderful how a poor person lives—but they don't live. My clear gains are about 1s. 6d. a week. In the summer time it's better, because I don't want no candle light. I work second-handed for the piece master. I don't know what he makes. I've done the basting of the Sappers at 3d. a coat; the pockets are fully made, and the shoulder straps fully made, and for the basting of the trowsers I get 1d., and two button-holes worked in the waistband. Why they baste up only I don't know. Them I work for doesn't know." (VII, 9 November 1849)

Mayhew's role as interviewer is deducible. We can determine his questions—i.e. how do you live, how much do you make, whom do you work for, what does he make, etc. In reading the interview, however, we have the sense that the subject speaks by herself as well as of herself.

Both Dickens's and Mayhew's modes of realizing lower-class life had limitations. Dickens's tendency to distance lower-class life by projection at times resulted not only in the failure of sympathy we saw in his tour with Field but also in what George Gissing labelled a "misrepresentation of social facts"[52] about the lower classes through inappropriate whimsy and sentimentality. On the other hand, the more precise and detailed Mayhew's picture was, the less significant each example became. Finally the overall picture of slum conditions and the causes of poverty was lost. This characteristic of his work got worse as he got more involved in his investigations, for the very element which liberated his energies—the possibility of looking close while standing distant—forced him to be more and more particular and less and less coherent.

Although he never fully understood why his own work failed of fulfillment, Mayhew's experiences did enable him to see the weaknesses in Dickens's fiction, but at the same time to keep them in perspective. In 1851 he described the novelist as "one of the most minute and truthful of observers" (2:24), but years after he had abandoned his own survey of the poor, he was more discriminating about Dickens's achievement. Not only did Mayhew not care for the style of *A Tale of Two Cities*, he also had come to think that Dickens distorted the nature of the lower classes by sentimentality. "If Mr. Dickens had been but wise enough to eschew the fatally-facile trick of sentiment . . . he would beyond doubt have been as great a literary genius after his kind—as fine a painter of the broadly marked characteristics of human life and out of the way places—as England has seen for centuries" (*Young Benjamin Franklin*, p. 250n).

Before the *Morning Chronicle* articles the Mayhew brothers had tended toward similar kinds of distortion. The street sellers in *The Greatest Plague in Life* were humorously patronized, and in *Whom to Marry*, when the heroine visited a poor seamstress, the woman was not even one of the "deserving poor" but a distressed gentlewoman with a sentimental tale. Early in the *Morning Chronicle* series Mayhew seemed to believe such tales since he was embarrassingly deferential in his interview with a distressed needlewoman who had been an army officer's daughter (IX, 16 November 1849). Later he came to distrust this response, for experience taught him that reduced gentlefolk were frequently the least "deserving" of the poor (wrapper 29, 28 June 1851).

When Henry and Augustus wrote a novel after the surveys of 1849–1852, moreover, the humor and the sentiment disappeared, and the lower classes were particularized in a manner consistent with Mayhew's nonfictional surveys. In *Paved with Gold*, the picture of the lower classes was deliberately antisentimental as well as objectively precise in the description of low-life neighborhoods and activities. In the scenes depicting the antics of the crossing sweepers the tone was carefully controlled to prevent the reader from laughing at the boys. Several of the passages were reprinted verbatim from *London Labour* without interrupting the dramatic narrative of the novel. Other scenes, such as that of the market at Farringdon, were repetitions with some dialogue of Mayhew's descriptions in *London Labour*.

Though Mayhew was not able to overcome the fragmentation of his picture, we have seen how Dickens could control the potential distortions of whimsy and sentimentality through his use of symbolic extension of detail. In his report of his tour with Field, for example, though the men and women were not particularized, they achieve life by Dickens's symbolic reference to the interconnectedness of society.

Dickens also undermined his oversimplifications of lower-class life in his journalism by the literary means of personification. This was particularly evident in his descriptions. A famous one has obvious parallels with both Mayhew and Kingsley, and though it comes from a novel rather than from his reporting, its relevance to a comparison with Mayhew is clear. In *Oliver Twist* Dickens described the notorious Jacob's Island thus:

> Crazy wooden galleries common to the backs of half-a-dozen houses, with holes from which to look upon the slime beneath; windows, broken and patched, with poles thrust out, on which to dry the linen that is never there; rooms so small, so filthy, so confined, that the air would seem too tainted even for the dirt and squalor which they shelter; wooden chambers thrusting themselves out above the mud, and threatening to fall into it—as some have done; dirt-besmeared walls and decaying foundations; every repulsive lineament of poverty, every loathsome indication of filth, rot and garbage. (p. 382)

This powerful description has been frequently pointed out as an example of Dickens's realistic portrayal of the details of the slums. Dickens himself insisted on its accuracy in his preface to the novel. Its realism, however, is quite different from that in Mayhew's corresponding descriptions which we have already seen influenced the language of Kingsley in *Alton Locke*. Mayhew saw a place little changed in the ten years since Dickens had written of it.

> In [the ditch] float large masses of green rotting weed, and against the posts of the bridges are swollen carcasses of dead animals, almost bursting with the gases of putrefaction. . . . The striking peculiarity of Jacob's Island consists in the wooden galleries and sleeping-rooms at the back of the houses which overhang the dark flood. . . . Across some parts of the stream whole rooms have been built, so that house adjoins house; and here, with the very stench of death rising through the boards, human beings sleep night after night, until the last sleep of all comes upon them years before its time. Scarce a house but yellow linen is hanging to dry over the balustrade of staves, or else run out on a long oar where the sulphur-coloured clothes hang over the waters, and you are almost wonderstruck to see their form and colour unreflected in the putrid ditch beneath.[53]

Mayhew's and Dickens's descriptions begin in a similar fashion with a generalized look at the way in which the galleries hang over the ditch. After the opening clause, however, their methods diverge. While Dickens's description remains general, Mayhew's becomes increasingly more particular, especially in regard to colors: the yellow linen and the green ditch. In Mayhew's description one responds to the repulsiveness of the details of the scene which are conveyed not only through precise adjectives but through unrelentingly visual figures such as the metaphoric "sulphur-coloured clothes" (which also suggests hell) and the oyster shells "like pieces of slate."

Dickens's description stimulates a similar negative response, not, however, solely through a direct visualization of Jacob's Island. Partly the effect is achieved by the rhythms of his rhetoric. The pounding repetition of sound patterns in the last sentence build up to a climax that does as much to move the reader and convince him of the vileness of the place as do any of the details, which themselves—by the simple device of removing the definite articles from "crazy wooden galleries," "windows," "rooms," and "dirt-besmeared walls"—are transformed by a form of personification into representative elements of all slums everywhere in London. The adjective *crazy*, moreover, does not attempt solely to render a visual image, as did Mayhew's adjectives.

Instead, though suggesting both position and shape, the word *crazy* gives the slum itself the connotation of insanity.

Dickens, in both novels and journalism, used different kinds of personification as a means of extending the significance of the particulars. At its most extreme, as in "Meditations on Monmouth Street" in the *Sketches*, he could inject a general life into the most unlikely inanimate objects. In this piece the narrator, strolling by an old-clothes shop, suddenly asserts that different sets of clothes could have belonged to a single person, and he projects various fictional histories which summarize the characteristic sad lives of the lower classes. In "A Nightly Scene in London" in *Household Words* for 26 January 1856, he took the life from a group waiting for the doors of the asylum to open ("five dead bodies taken out of graves") and gave it to their clothes. The specific scene is vague, but the moral point about the condition of the poor is unmistakable. The same kind of point is made in Dickens's description of Covent Garden market. Mayhew's description of the scene at Farringdon (discussed in chapter 5) also focused on the children lurking about the vegetable market, but he described them as objectively as possible. Dickens, by taking a little life from the children and giving it to some vegetables, made of the scene an allegorical statement about official neglect: "A painful and unnatural result comes of the comparison one is forced to institute between the growth of corruption as displayed in the so much improved and cared for fruits of the earth, and the growth of corruption as displayed in these all uncared for (except inasmuch as ever-hunted) savages."[54]

As we have seen Mayhew seldom used either personification or metaphor in his own descriptions. Nonetheless the overall structure of description in the journalism of both writers was the same. Miller has remarked of *Sketches by Boz* that "the literary strategy" was "first the scene, with its inanimate objects, then the people of whose lives these objects are the signs, and finally the continuous narrative of their lives, which may be inferred from the traces of themselves they have left behind" (p. 96). Mayhew's descriptions were organized exactly the same way though with one difference: in Dickens's case the "continuous narrative" was a projection of a fictional story; in Mayhew's case it was the fused voice of the reporter and his subject.

Symbolic extension and personification were the main methods Dickens used to overcome the limitations of whimsy and sentimentality in his journalism, but in his novels after *Oliver Twist* he undermined his own distortions in other ways as well. He came to imply the "true" facts of lower-class life through an attack on the middle classes. In the early Christmas story *The Chimes* (1844), for example, Trotty Veck, an impoverished porter, and his daughter Meg, a slop seamstress, are both sentimentalized, and Trotty was additionally degraded through humor. Though Trotty and Meg may have brought tears to the eyes of Dickens's readers, the picture of lower-class life was, as Mayhew said, "profound rubbish" (*Young Benjamin Franklin* p. 250n); nothing brought forward the complicated details of vacant squalor and violence which Mayhew discovered in his interviews with unskilled laborers for the *Chronicle* series. *The Chimes* does legitimately engage our concern for Meg and Trotty, though, through Dickens's bitter attack on the impeccable representative of middle-class morality, Alderman Cute (modelled on an actual magistrate, Sir Peter Laurie).[55] In *Bleak House*, when we first meet the brickmakers, who are among the most realistic lower-class characters Dickens ever drew, we are mainly concerned with the ugliness of Mrs. Pardiggle's middle-class philanthropy. We come to sympathize with the rough and hard brickmakers through their wives, whose maternal feelings are stressed to assert their symbolic connection with humanity.

Although Mayhew unconsciously controlled and often denied his own biases through his use of multiple extended interviews, he never achieved Dickens's kind of "moral" extension of his experiences. Yet Mayhew filled in much of what Dickens left out, and he reinforced and proved much that Dickens asserted. When taken together, their works provide a picture of sharp detail and extraordinary scope. Mayhew's contribution remains a very important corollary to all the best social observations of the period as well as an impressive achievement in its own right.

Afterword

One night, after I had been working on the manuscript of this book for a long time, I had a dream in which I met Henry Mayhew, looking very much like his picture in the frontispiece of *London Labour and the London Poor*. He was sitting on a park bench. Seeing him there in the flesh, I suddenly lost the confidence of my argument in the foregoing pages and felt that Mayhew as a person remained as much a mystery to me as when I had first encountered his work. "I am so glad to see you," I said to him. "There are so many questions I want to ask you." He was cordial and communicative, but in the way of dreams the answers that he gave me have disappeared. Only my questions remain vivid.

Such is the fate of any investigator who would try to explain the many contradictions, blank spaces, and obscurities that make up the record of Mayhew's life and work. Any theory, including mine, must remain tentative. Mayhew himself in the only explanatory remarks that he made later in his life about his social surveys provided little help to those of us who have come after him. Three decades after his work on poverty in London, while justifying his witnessing a hanging he summed up his feelings about his past career. He began with a matter-of-fact description of his earliest investigations and ended with a reference to his survey of *The Criminal Prisons of London*. One might think that, looking back on his hey-day, Mayhew would express some pride in his accomplishments or on the other hand some bitterness at the barriers that had been put in the way of its accomplishment. Yet neither attitude informed the tone of these remarks.

> It had fallen to my lot to be *obliged* to see some of the lowest forms of London life. I had been to a "friendly lead" at a low tavern in that most unfashionable of all quarters called *Fashion* Street (Brick Lane) and seen the garotters' women in rags dancing with swell-mobsmen got in diamond rings and Albert chains as magnificently as Whitechapel Jews on a Saturday. I had dined at a Thieves' Kitchen off a plate of "block ornaments." I

Henry Mayhew in later life.
From the frontispiece to *A Jorum of Punch* by Athol Mayhew (1895).
Courtesy of the General Research and Humanities Division,
the New York Public Library; Astor, Lenox,
and Tilden Foundations.

had seen the wretched herd of mudlarks, sewer hunters, rag-pickers, match vendors, and the like huddled together of a night at a "two penny rope" in the neighborhood of the Docks. I had been threatened with having a kettle of boiling water poured into my boots if ever I went down Wentworth Street again. . . . I had passed half an hour in the dark cell of a convict prison, in order to understand the real rigour of the punishment. In fine, I had been everywhere—seen everything which maybe a gentleman should not. (*London Characters*, pp. 348–349)

Saying that seeing this sort of life to the bitter end was fitting since he had witnessed all the rest, he concluded: "But why was I obliged to see all this? . . . Frankly, I had made the study of poverty and crime a profession, and it had consequently become a duty on my part to scan every form of human wretchedness and villainy. In as few words as possible, I had been forced to examine the ugly sores of society for the same reason a medical man requires to attend to the several ghastly phases of physical and mental disease: simply because I had made it my business to do so" (p. 350).

The circularity of Mayhew's thought in this passage is striking, as is his almost exclusive emphasis on the more bizarre elements in his research. At this point he seemed to agree with the popular opinion that his achievement had been mainly to chronicle the more obscure corners of London low life rather than to attempt "to apply the laws of the inductive philosophy for the first time, I believe, in the world to the abstract questions of political economy," as he had said in his letter to the editors of the *Morning Chronicle* in 1850. Was it only because this latter part of his work remained unfinished that he ignored it in his summary, or were there other reasons? The verbs he used to justify his taking up the subject at all are also unusual. He was "obliged" to do this, a word so important that he italicized it and repeated it later in the passage in the verb *forced*. Both words make the passage sound defensive, and certainly do not indicate that Mayhew was proud of his work.

On the other hand, at the end of the passage, Mayhew calls his investigations a "profession," a term which gives dignified expression to the serious intentions he had had. Yet he does not follow through the implications of that term, choosing instead to end on a weak tautology that he had seen all this because he had been in a position to see all this. Mayhew's implied comparison of himself to a doctor does throw some light, perhaps, on the murky sentiments that lie behind this obscure explanation. Of all the professional practitioners in the community the doctor is the only one who combines the position of an objective, disinterested observer (something a clergyman does not have) and an intimate involvement with the private misery and joy of the lower classes. A medical man is able to come nearest the lower classes of any middle-class philanthropist without losing caste. Mayhew, even at this late point in his life, was still anxious about the "unrespectable" nature of his investigations: "I had been everywhere—seen everything which maybe a gentleman should not." This uncertainty perhaps is the reason that he was unable even at this point to assert with confidence the value of his surveys.

His hesitancy has been repeated by later historians and social scientists. The judgment of his work has only recently been very high. Biographers of Charles Booth, for example, dismissed Mayhew's books as impressionistic.[1] Even so sympathetic a reader as E. P. Thompson seems to me unnecessarily defensive about Mayhew at one point. Thompson was disturbed by a remark Sutherland Edwards made about Mayhew's days at the *Chronicle*: "London labourers of special interest, with picturesque specimens of the London poor, were brought to the *Chronicle* office, where they told their tales to Mayhew, who redictated them, with an added colour of his own, to the shorthand writer in waiting" (p. 60). The detail here which Thompson felt damaging was the "added colour," which he thought meant that Mayhew altered the interviews somehow.[2] Edwards's remark is certainly vague, and parts of it are at variance with the evidence in the *Chronicle* letters themselves. Mayhew seldom mentioned interviews in the newspaper office, but instead reported frequently on visits to homes and workrooms as well as large meetings. Furthermore Edwards, writing many years after the event, seems to have muddled the subjects of the *Chronicle* series and those of *London Labour*, for "picturesque specimens of the London poor" certainly does not describe the exploited workers who make up most of the *Chronicle* letters, though it does cover many of the subjects in *London Labour*. The suggestion that Mayhew doctored the interviews is also in direct conflict with all of his own assertions of his process at the time. It seems to me there is another explanation of Edwards's remark: the "added colour," rather than being any alteration of the interviews or the "facts," refers to Mayhew's descriptions of the places and the people he saw, as well as the circumstances of each interview, which he did indeed consistently add to his reports.

Partly because of this nervousness about the "accuracy" of Mayhew's work, very few sociologists have claimed that it is important. On the surface it would seem Mayhew's surveys are ideal social surveys as defined by A. H. Wells: "A fact-finding study correlating the results of numerous aspects of social life. It has reference to a limited geographical area. Its aim is the description of the social conditions under which workers live, and often also an attempt to arouse interest and action directed by the inhabitants of the locality studied towards their own social problems." Yet because Wells knew nothing about Mayhew in depth and because in the last analysis he, like so many social scientists, trusted statistics more than anything else, he cited Booth as the originator of the social survey and noted Mayhew only as an example of the "concrete descriptive method of a journalist or novelist."[3]

Yet such a narrow approach to the subject of sociology ignores completely what is special in Mayhew and what a challenge he presents. For there is a picture of London's working-class life at midcentury in his volumes, and there is a sociological overview—the humanity of his subjects, a theoretical framework that can be all too often absent in more "sociologically reliable" surveys. As a minor character in an even more minor social novel of the 1840s remarked, "You see, the facts are brought up before Parliament, by having witnesses up to be examined on oath before the committee; these reports . . . are printed and sold, too: but . . . I don't think one lady in a thousand ever looks into them, to say nothing of other classes. . . . What we chiefly want is to have some public information given about it, such as will be read, and may stir up the hearts of God's servants to succour us."[4] Mayhew's work shows us only too strongly the price one can pay for eliminating the human dimension in the search for a more "scientific" sociology. Inherent in many of his solutions to the more difficult scientific problems of his project seemed to be his sense that the facts, once known, should lead to the betterment of the situation, and the best way of moving of men to action was by art.

Mayhew's work at its best moved on the two fronts of art and science, and it was no little part of his achievement that he maintained the balance as well as he did. Early in the *Morning Chronicle* series he developed the long interview as a means of collecting raw data scientifically; but his instincts for the narrative human drama helped him encourage his subjects in self-revelation. While he tried to eliminate his own personal control as observer in his reports, a sound "scientific" desire, he developed the artistic process of using selected details to give a general picture, and neutral similes to give clearer perceptions. The artistic qualities of selection, order, and direction not only gave Mayhew's work force and effectiveness, but they also rendered it more precise, more accurate—more scientific. Mayhew's investigations were successful as social science, in other words, because they were artistic. Though his categories were usually crude, his techniques sometimes amateurish, and his data often sketchy, his eye and his talent and temperament combined to override these disadvantages.

Without even intending to do so, a modern critic put Mayhew in his proper place, demonstrating his importance to the period. Richard Altick in *The English Common Reader* tried to account for the difficulty the Victorian reading public had in confronting the realities of poverty.

It is hard, perhaps impossible, to recreate the spirit of so large and inarticulate a community as the English working classes in the nineteenth century. If we attempt to do so by examining only the immense body of sociological data assembled by parliamentary committees and statistical societies, we must believe that men and women were so brutalized out of any semblance to normal mortals that they were physical organisms and economic units alone, without any of the emotional life and the intellectual and spiritual aspirations which mark the man from the animal. But this is an incomplete view, springing from the limited nature of the age's humanitarianism. Reformers like Chadwick, Kay-Shuttleworth, and Shaftesbury were concerned simply with ameliorating the common man's physical existence, and parliamentary inquiries never showed the slightest curiosity, except where it was a question of religious observance or ordinary morality, about the inner lives of the workers—a subject which in any case hardly lends itself to investigative treatment.[5]

However true such an observation might be of Chadwick, the blue books, and so on, it was patently not applicable to Mayhew, whatever else one might charge him with. In spite of all the inadequacies in his surveys, Mayhew was able to approach success in what Altick said was perhaps impossible. He tried to give the inarticulate community a voice—one of their own moreover, not his; he tried to make his readers see the human element in the statistics; in his interviews he strove to help his subjects express the intellectual and spiritual aspirations of the lower classes. In so doing, he came as close as anyone in the period to revealing the inner lives of the working classes to his readers. He did for both his contemporaries and for us what no social survey had done before. He enabled us all, for one brief moment, to make some contact with the spirit of the lower classes in Victorian England at midcentury.

Henry Mayhew: A Chronology

1812   Mayhew born on 25 November, the fourth surviving son of Joshua Dorset Joseph Mayhew and Mary Ann Fenn.

1827   Henry runs away from Westminster School and is sent to India as a midshipman.

1831   *Figaro in London* is founded; Mayhew is editor 1835–1839.

1831–1839   Mayhew is involved in various theatrical and journalistic schemes and projects.

1834   Mayhew's play *The Wandering Minstrel* is produced.

1835   Mayhew probably meets Douglas Jerrold and W. M. Thackeray in Paris.

1841   The first issue of *Punch* appears 17 July; Mayhew edits it until 1842; he maintains some connection until 1845.

1842   *What to Teach and How to Teach It* is published.

1844   *The Prince of Wales's Library* is published; Mayhew marries Jane Jerrold.

1846   Mayhew declares bankruptcy.

1847   Bankruptcy suit. The publication by the Brothers Mayhew of *The Greatest Plague in Life* and *The Good Genius Who Turned Everything into Gold*.

1848   *Whom to Marry and How to Get Married!* and *The Image of His Father* by the Brothers Mayhew.

1849   *The Magic of Kindness* by the Brothers Mayhew. On 19 October the first letter from the metropolitan correspondent is published in the *Morning Chronicle*.

1850   *Fear of the World* and *Acting Charades* by the Brothers Mayhew. Henry Mayhew edits the *Comic Almanac*. On 12 December the *Morning Chronicle* publishes its last letter from the metropolitan correspondent. Probably on 14 December the first weekly number of *London Labour and the London Poor* appears.

1851   *London Labour and the London Poor* is published serially in three volumes. *1851; or the Adventures of Mr. and Mrs. Sandboys* (with George Cruikshank). Mayhew edits the *Comic Almanac*. Articles on the Great Exhibition by Mayhew are published in the *Edinburgh News* (November-December). *Low Wages*.

1852   The last number of *London Labour and the London Poor* is published on 21 February. In March his suit with the publisher George Woodfall is heard in Chancery.

1853   Mayhew speaks in favor of opening the Crystal Palace on Sunday.

1854   Mayhew is in Germany; *The Story of the Peasant-Boy Philosopher* is published.

1855   *The Wonders of Science, or Young Humphry Davy*.

1856   "The Great World of London" (March–December). "On Capital Punishments." *The Rhine and Its Picturesque Scenery*.

1857   Henry Mayhew begins *Paved with Gold* with his brother Augustus in April; leaves project after the fifth number.

1858   Joshua Mayhew dies; Henry Mayhew publishes *The Upper Rhine and Its Picturesque Scenery*.

1859   Mayhew edits *Morning News* for month of January after which newspaper folds.

1861   *Young Benjamin Franklin*. Mayhew goes to Germany to do research for a book on Martin Luther. *London Labour and the London Poor*, volumes 1–3.

1862   Volume 4 of *London Labour and the London Poor* is published. *The Criminal Prisons of London*.

1863   *The Boyhood of Martin Luther*.

1864   *German Life and Manners as Seen in Saxony at the Present Day*.

1865   Mayhew edits *The Shops and Companies of London*. A second printing of the 4 volumes of *London Labour and the London Poor*.

1870   Mayhew edits *Only Once a Year* and also serves as a correspondent in Metz with his son Athol.

1871   Report on Working Men's Clubs for the Licensed Victuallers.

1874   Mayhew's name appears on the second edition of *London*

Characters; his play *Mont Blanc*, written in collaboration with his son, fails.

1880   Jane Jerrold Mayhew dies on 26 February.
1887   Henry Mayhew dies of bronchitis on 25 July.

Notes

Chapter 1 · The Making of a Social Historian

1. Mrs. L. M. Coumbe, a descendant of Alfred Mayhew. I am grateful to Patrick Mayhew of London for allowing me to see this manuscript. The first published biography of Henry Mayhew was written by John L. Bradley in his introduction to *Selections from London Labour and the London Poor* (London: Oxford University Press, 1965), pp. vii–xl; the second, by E. P. Thompson, "Mayhew and the *Morning Chronicle*," appeared in Thompson and Eileen Yeo, *The Unknown Mayhew* (New York: Pantheon, 1971), pp. 11–50. Bradley gives a summary of most of the facts known about Mayhew; Thompson enriches this picture with a study of the context of the *Morning Chronicle* series. Although I read his work after I had finished mine, Alan Thomas, in "Henry Mayhew's Rhetoric: A Study of His Presentation of 'Social Facts'" (Ph.D. diss., Univ. of Toronto, 1970), has some observations similar to mine. His treatment of Mayhew's approach to his material provides a different perspective on this matter.

2. The exact number of children in the Mayhew family is in doubt. The *DNB* entry states that there were seventeen children; a family tree I saw through the courtesy of Patrick Mayhew notes fifteen children. A footnote in *The Shops and Companies of London*, a journal edited by Henry Mayhew in 1865 (p. 142), states that the author came from a family of ten, six of whom were sons. All accounts seem to agree that the number of sons who survived childhood was seven. Mayhew's count in 1865 ("six sons") probably resulted from the suicide of his brother Thomas.

3. Sutherland Edwards, *Personal Recollections* (London: Cassell, 1900), pp. 56–57.

4. This information and the following stories of Joshua's relations with his sons come from Mrs. Coumbe's manuscript.

5. Henry Mayhew, *German Life and Manners as Seen in Saxony at the Present Day*, 2 vols. (London: William Allen, 1864), 2:553.

6. See Thompson, *The Unknown Mayhew*, pp. 13–14, for a discussion of Thomas's career.

7. *Men of the Time* (London: David Bogue, 1856), p. 543.

8. Horace Mayhew, ed., *The Comic Almanac* (London: David Bogue, 1848), p. 47.

9. Thompson, *The Unknown Mayhew*, p. 12. The original account is in Frederic H. Forshall, *Westminster School, Past and Present* (London: Weyman, 1884), pp. 329–330.

10. Edwards, pp. 55–57. Athol Mayhew, Henry's son, said the scene occurred the next morning. See *A Jorum of "Punch"* (London: Downey, 1895),
pp. 7–9.

11. Athol Mayhew, p. 51.

12. Herbert Clayton, "The Henry Mayhew Centenary," *Notes and
Queries*, 11th ser., 6 (1912): 71–72.

13. Mayhew claimed to have helped Lemon with *Gwynneth Vaughan*,
Grandfather Whitehead, and others, including *The Gentleman in Black* (Brad-
ley, Introduction, p. xxiii). Mayhew wrote *The Wandering Minstrel* (1834) and
The Barbers at the Court (1835) on his own, and *But However* (1838) with
Henry Baylis. Other Mayhew dramatic works named by Bradley include *A
Troublesome Lodger* (1839) and *The Young Sculptor* (1839). See Bradley, In-
troduction, pp. x–xiii, for a discussion of these theatrical works. According to
Arthur à Beckett, Mayhew wrote some of his works under the name *Ralph
Rigamarole* in order to prevent his father finding out what he was doing. See
The à Becketts of Punch (London: Archibald Constable, 1903), p. 50.

14. See Thompson, *The Unknown Mayhew*, p. 16, and also F. David
Roberts, "More Early Victorian Newspaper Editors," *Victorian Periodical
Newsletter* 16 (June 1972): 15–28, for discussions of these journalists.

15. See Bradley, Introduction, pp. xiv–xvii, for a discussion of *Figaro in
London*. Bradley says Gilbert à Beckett was editor of *Figaro* from 1831 to
1834, and Mayhew from 1835 to 1839. Athol Mayhew claimed his father had
left the editorship of *Figaro in London* by 1838, and his "connection with it"
lasted "one or two years." See *A Jorum of "Punch,"* p. 40.

16. Mayhew's connection with *Punch*, probably more than any other issue
in his biography, has been the subject of argument and acrimony. R.G.G.
Price, in *A History of Punch* (London: William Collins, 1957), tries to sort out
all the claims in an appendix (pp. 353–355). The major early source is M. H.
Spielmann, *A History of "Punch"* (New York: Cassell, 1895). Both Price and
Spielmann credit Mayhew with a strong influence in the early days of the journal.

17. The joke, according to Spielmann, appeared in the almanac for 1845, and
was based on an "ingenious wording of an advertisement widely used by
Eamonson & Co., well-known house furnishers of the day" (p. 141). The poem
is quoted by Edwards, p. 61.

18. Information about Mayhew's location and activities in the 1830s is contradictory. He was connected with journals and the drama in London during
most of the decade; and therefore if, after the debacle with his father's papers,
he went to Paris in 1835, as Athol said (*Men of the Time* said he went to
Wales), his stay must have been short. Bradley is not sure about the story of
the Paris trip (Introduction, xviii).

19. The source for this story is Athol Mayhew, pp. 17–20. It is also mentioned by Walter Jerrold, *Douglas Jerrold*, 2 vols. (London: Hodder and
Stoughton, 1914), 1:247.

20. Walter Jerrold, 2:478.

21. Bradley, Introduction, p. xxii.

22. All Mayhew's fiction (except *1851* with George Cruikshank) was published under the authorship of the Brothers Mayhew and was written with Augustus. These works included moralistic fables, *The Good Genius that Turned Everything into Gold* (1847) and *The Magic of Kindness* (1849), and novels, *The Greatest Plague in Life* (1847), which *Men of the Time* (1856) said sold more copies than any other serial since the days of *Pickwick Papers; Whom to Marry and How to Get Married!* (1848); *The Image of his Father* (1848); and *Fear of the World* (1850). The Brothers Mayhew also published *Acting Charades* in 1850. A Bogue catalogue for 1854 listed a novel by the Brothers Mayhew, *The Magic of Industry: or, the Good Genius* as appearing that year, but I have found no copy of this volume, which was probably a reissue of *The Magic of Kindness. Fear of the World* was reissued in 1855 as *Living for Appearances*.

23. Herbert Clayton, "The Henry Mayhew Centenary," *Notes and Queries*, 11th ser. 5 (1912):433.

24. The story is told in Thomas Willert Beale, *The Light of Other Days*, 2 vols. (London: Richard Bentley, 1890), 1:272–275, and George Hodder, *Memories of My Time* (London: Tinsley, 1870), pp. 211–213. Two reviews of these performances appeared in the *Morning News* on 11 April 1857, and on 28 June 1857.

25. Quoted in Spielmann, p. 268.

26. Ibid. Mayhew was apparently always thinking up schemes for various projects, both for himself and others. R.G.G. Price says that he suggested to Samuel Smiles the project *Lives of the Engineers*, published in 1861. See Price, p. 27.

27. John L. Bradley, "Henry Mayhew and Father William," *English Language Notes* 1 (September 1963):42.

28. Ibid., p. 41. Mayhew published only one part of this manual. In 1851 he tried to exhume it as "The Classic Spelling Book." An advertisement on the wrappers of *London Labour and the London Poor* announced its publication on 15 February 1851, but if it was actually issued, no copies are in the British Library.

29. Henry Mayhew, *The Upper Rhine and Its Picturesque Scenery* (London: George Routledge, 1858), p. 319. He repeated this judgment in *Young Benjamin Franklin* (London: James Blackwood, 1861), p. vi.

30. The novel was published in monthly parts from January through September 1851. Each number opened with a large foldout illustration by Cruikshank, who had worked with Mayhew before, illustrating a number of the novels by the Brothers Mayhew. The first four parts set the scene, and part 5 in May recounted the events surrounding the actual opening of the exhibition on 1 May. On 3 May, Mayhew started his series of weekly review articles for the *Edinburgh News*. He wrote nine pieces for this journal, the last appearing

19 July. An illness then interrupted not only these articles but also affected for a number of weeks his work on *London Labour and the London Poor* and undoubtedly resulted in the collapsing of the last two parts of the novel *1851* (August and September) into one number.

31. The overall statistics, however, show that by the end of the exhibition, shilling tickets had outsold all other priced tickets combined. See C. H. Gibbs-Smith, *The Great Exhibition of 1851* (London: Her Majesty's Stationery Office, 1964), p. 33.

32. "The Shilling Folk," *Edinburgh News and Literary Chronicle*, 21 June 1851.

33. Charles Mackay, *Forty Years' Recollections of Life, Literature, and Public Affairs*, 2 vols. (London: Chapman and Hall, 1877), 2:150.

34. Francis Sheppard, *London 1808–1870: The Infernal Wen* (London: Secker and Warburg, 1971), pp. 248–249; 273.

35. *The Shops and Companies of London, and the Grades and Manufactories of Great Britain*, ed. Henry Mayhew (London: Strand, 1865), p. 14.

36. Charles Mackay credits Mayhew with the idea (2:151). The *Chronicle* in the aftermath of their quarrel with Mayhew in the fall of 1850 denied his role in an editorial (31 October 1850). On the wrapper of part 9 (8 February 1851?) of *London Labour and the London Poor* Mayhew said that he originated the idea in August 1849.

37. Charles Mackay (1814–1889), the brother of Alexander Mackay (see note 38), was subeditor of the *Chronicle* in 1842 and literary and political editor of the *Illustrated London News* from 1848–1852. While he was writing his letters to the *Morning Chronicle* from Liverpool in August 1850, he contributed several articles on Mormon emigrants and Mormonism in general. These letters were later reprinted in book form in 1851 as *History of the Mormons* by the National Illustrated Library. The book went through four editions between 1851 and 1856. The first was published anonymously, but the fourth gave the author as Charles Mackay. Nonetheless the book has been persistently credited to Henry Mayhew by many librarians and scholars, probably because the first edition stated in the preface that the author had done his research in 1851 while engaged on "Labour and the Poor."

38. E. P. Thompson, in "The Political Education of Henry Mayhew," *Victorian Studies* 11 (September 1967):45, discusses the sources of information for identifying the provincial correspondents. Angus Reach (1821–1856) was a reporter at the central criminal court for the *Morning Chronicle* and afterward in the commons gallery. Later he was on the *Punch* staff and in 1850 visited the vineyards of France for the *Chronicle*. Shirley Brooks (1816–1874), dramatist and journalist, was sent by the *Morning Chronicle* to report on labor in Russia, Syria, and Egypt in 1853, and in 1870 he succeeded Mark Lemon as editor of *Punch*. Alexander Mackay (1808–1852) was on the staff of the *Morning Chronicle* and in 1847 was called to the bar. Selections of the provincial letters can be found in *The Victorian Working Class: Selections*

from the Morning Chronicle, eds. P. E. Razzle and R. W. Wainwright (London: Frank Cass, 1974).

39. See the table entitled "Distribution of Occupations: London, 1851," by Lynn Lees in Sheppard, p. 388.

40. Sheppard, p. 325. There has been much debate about the condition of the working classes in England in the 1840s. See J. H. Clapham, *An Economic History of Modern Britain*, 2nd ed., rev., 3 vols. (Cambridge at the University Press, 1930–1932), 1:548–594 for a rosy view. Consult J. L. and Barbara Hammond, *The Age of the Chartists, 1830–1854* (1930; reprint ed., Hamden, Conn.: Archon Books, 1962) for a more pessimistic view. E. J. Hobsbawm has summed up the controversy in three essays in *Labouring Men* (London: Weidenfeld and Nicholson, 1964), pp. 64–104, and come down on the negative side.

41. The unattached money was spent on goods for worthy cases, buying them blankets or fuel, or redeeming things in pawn or paying back rent or furnishing stock money for street traders. When the "Labour and the Poor Fund" closed in early summer 1850, the number of people relieved was around 360, 60 of whom were "special cases" for whom money was especially donated and 300 casual recipients.

42. Mayhew's discussion of his break with the *Chronicle* is contained in "Labour and the Poor," *Report of the Speech of Henry Mayhew, Esq., and the Evidence adduced at a Public Meeting Held at St. Martin's Hall, Long Acre, on Monday evening, Oct. 28, 1850 . . .* (London: Bateman and Hardwicke, 1850), pp. 2–7. The censored material on the bootmakers is quoted on p. 4. On the wrappers of the weekly numbers 15 and 34 of *London Labour and the London Poor* (22 March 1851 and 2 August 1851), Mayhew compared his proofs of Letter LVIII on the timber trade with the "edited" version which appeared in the *Chronicle*. See also Thompson, *The Unknown Mayhew*, pp. 35–38.

43. G. F. Young (1791–1870) was a shipowner and merchant in London and chairman of the general shipowners' society. He was M. P. for Tynemouth from 1832 to 1838 when he was unseated on petition. He was the author of *Free-trade fallacies refuted, in a series of letters to the editors of the Morning Herald* (1852).

44. Thompson, in *The Unknown Mayhew*, p. 39, implies that the laudatory article on Nicoll was followed by the reward of the large advertisement, but since the advertisements begin almost a full month before the article appeared it is much more likely that the article was a reward to Nicoll for placing the advertisements in the first place.

45. *Report of the Speech . . .* , p. 3.

46. See Thompson, *The Unknown Mayhew*, pp. 38–41.

47. The publication began sometime in December, probably the same week in which the metropolitan correspondent made his last contribution to the *Morning Chronicle*. Each number averaged eighteen pages; some ended mid-sentence, showing clearly the intention was to publish them eventually as a

book. The first dated weekly number of *London Labour and the London Poor* is 10 (15 February 1851). Subsequent issues were published every Saturday. If the first nine numbers followed this pattern, the journal would have started 14 December 1850. The date of numbers 1–9 is followed by a question mark in the following text. The last number appeared 21 February 1852.

48. James Grant, *The Great Metropolis*, 2nd ser., 4 vols. (London: Saunders and Otley, 1837), 1:188–190.

49. Quotations from Jerrold's letters are from Walter Jerrold, 2:529; 547; 548.

50. William Blanchard Jerrold, *The Life and Remains of Douglas Jerrold* (London: W. Kent, 1859), p. 343.

51. The article is referred to and apparently quoted at length in Walter Jerrold, 1:248 ff. He referred to it as being in "a forgotten magazine."

52. *Comic Almanac* (London: David Bogue, 1851), p. 350.

53. Bradley, Introduction, p. xxi, says "in the sixties, when he spent long periods in Germany, she remained in England." But Mayhew's account of his stay in Germany in the early 1860s in *German Life and Manners*, makes clear that his wife and two children were with him.

54. The Coumbe ms.

55. Louis James, *Fiction for the Working Man* (1963; reprint ed., Harmondsworth: Penguin University Books, 1974), p. 10.

56. James defines literature sold at a penny as "lower-class," p. xvii. *London Labour and the London Poor* cost twopence per weekly number, ninepence per monthly part.

57. James, pp. 46, 52.

58. Advertisement for *London Labour and the London Poor* on the wrapper of "The Great World of London," March 1856.

59. He is reported in *John Bull*, 5 February 1853, p. 89, speaking in favor of the opening. His speech provoked a sharp counterattack by John Hall, in *The Sons of Toil and the Crystal Palace. In reply to Mr. Mayhew* (London: John Snow, 1853).

60. Bogue was assistant to Thomas Ireland of Edinburgh, a bookseller, until 1836, and then assistant to Charles Tilt of London, a publisher, until 1840 when he became a partner, an association which lasted until 1843. He was bookseller and publisher in his own right from then to his death. His firm was at 86 Fleet Street.

61. According to Clement Scott and Cecil Howard in *The Life and Reminiscences of E. L. Blanchard*, 2 vols. (New York: Brentano's, 1891), 1:157, Blanchard saw "How We Live in the World of London" in April 1856. It was "a threading together of scenes of which Henry Mayhew had written." In it were Shepherd, H. W. Widdicomb, Miss Sarah Thorne, and Miss Marriott. This play, if by J. B. Johnstone, first appeared in March 1854, as did J. Elphinstone's *London Labour and the London Poor; or, Want and Vice.* See Sally

Vernon, "Trouble Up at T'Mill: The Rise and Decline of the Factory Play in the 1830s and 1840s," *Victorian Studies* 20 (Winter 1977), p. 137.

62. Henry Vizetelly, *Glances Back Through Seventy Years*, 2 vols. (London: Kegan Paul, Trench, Trübner, 1893), 2:407.

63. Bogue's death as a reason for the termination of "The Great World of London" is given in an anonymous biography of Henry Mayhew dated 1860 in the manuscript collection of the British Library. It is headed "Biography for W. C. Griffin *Handbook of Contemporary Biography*, 1860." Corrections of the manuscript are in a different hand; neither the manuscript nor the corrections seem to be in the autograph of Henry Mayhew.

64. There is conflicting evidence about the regularity of the monthly publication of "The Great World of London." The British Library copy, made up of nine bound monthly parts of sixty-odd pages each, has nine parts running March through December 1856. Part 7, which could have been the September issue, is smaller in size than the other parts because the margins are cut by a half an inch, and it also has no date stamped on it. An imperfect copy of "The Great World of London," belonging to Michael Wolff (and to whom I am grateful for calling it to my attention) has a note on one of the wrappers dated 1 November 1856 which states that "a severe attack of illness rendered it necessary that he [Mayhew] should abstain from all mental exertion, and it is only very recently that he has been permitted by his physician to resume his literary labours. Now that his health is re-established, he feels that he can promise the completion of his account of the Prisons of the Metropolis during the present year, and at the same time publish the Index and title-page to the First Volume of the work." In this copy part 7 is dated August; part 8, November.

65. The 1865 edition is identical in text to the 1851–1852 and 1861–1862 editions. It does however have different pagination since it numbers prefatory material and illustration pages, which the earlier editions did not. It also contains several additional illustrations.

66. Arthur A. Adrian, *Mark Lemon: First Editor of Punch* (London: Oxford University Press, 1966), p. 35.

67. George Augustus Sala, *The Life and Adventures of George Augustus Sala*, 2 vols. (New York: Charles Scribner's Sons, 1896), 2:161–164.

68. Bradley, Introduction, p. xxxi.

69. The first edition of this work was published anonymously in 1870, but that version had none of Mayhew's material. The second edition of 1874 was expanded by the addition of reprinted material by Mayhew and his name is on the title page, *London Characters* by Henry Mayhew. (A third edition, identical to the second, appeared in 1881.) It seems highly unlikely that if Mayhew wrote the "new" material in the first edition, he would not have put his name to it. More likely is that he had nothing to do with the first edition but that he and the publishers (Chatto and Windus) decided to exploit his name in the

second edition by adding some of his old material. If this is true, he did not conduct any new investigations for *London Characters*.

70. Bradley, Introduction, p. xxxi.

71. "The Late Mr. Henry Mayhew," *Illustrated London News* 91 (6 August 1887):158.

72. "True to Life," *New York Review of Books*, 17 March 1966, p. 5.

Chapter 2 · The Metropolitan Correspondent

1. Quoted in D. P. O'Brien, *J. R. McCulloch: A Study in Classical Economics* (London: George Allen and Unwin, 1970), p. 97.

2. This appeared in the column "Answers to Correspondents" on the wrapper of number 10 of *London Labour and the London Poor* (15 February 1851). Future references to Mayhew's remarks on these wrappers will be made parenthetically in the text (the wrapper number and the date) with the date of the first nine undated numbers shown with a question mark. (See chapter 1, note 47). These wrappers are available in the British Library copy of the 1851–1852 text of *London Labour and the London Poor*.

3. Gertrude Himmelfarb, in "Mayhew's Poor: A Problem of Identity," *Victorian Studies* 14 (March 1971):308, points out this disjunctive sense in Mayhew's title for his next work, *London Labour and the London Poor*. The confusion is sometimes real, but Himmelfarb lays too much stress on it, particularly since that title was not intended as one solely for the street folk. She repeats her charge in her article "The Culture of Poverty" in *The Victorian City: Images and Realities*, ed. H. J. Dyos and Michael Wolff, 2 vols. (London: Routledge and Kegan Paul, 1973), 2:707–736.

4. Asa Briggs, "The Human Aggregate," in Dyos and Wolff, *The Victorian City*, 1:84.

5. McCulloch, "State and Defect of British Statistics," *Edinburgh Review* 61 (April 1835):175.

6. *Chartism* (London: Chapman and Hall, 1842), pp. 14–15.

7. See n. 40 in chap. 1.

8. Letter I, *Morning Chronicle*, 19 October 1849, p. 5. Mayhew's letters normally appeared on pages 5–6 of the paper. His letters have not been reprinted in their entirety, but two different volumes of selections have appeared, Thompson and Yeo, eds., *The Unknown Mayhew* and in Anne Humpherys, ed., *Voices of the Poor* (London: Frank Cass, 1971). Further references to the letters will be given parenthetically in the text by letter number and date.

9. Quoted in *Report of the Speech* . . . , p. 6. During this period the terms *science* and *philosophy* were used more or less interchangeably.

10. I have been unable to trace this book. The Smirke brothers, Sydney and Edward, were well-known architects of the period; Sydney designed the

British Museum. They both published a number of books on London architecture, but none so far as I have been able to determine which would classify as a "History of London."

11. See Eileen Yeo's essay "Mayhew as a Social Investigator" in *The Unknown Mayhew*, pp. 90–95, for a comparison of Mayhew, Booth, and Rowntree.

12. See "The Morning Chronicle on the State of the Poor," *Spectator*, 27 October 1849, p. 1018.

13. Robert Heilbroner, *The Worldly Philosophers* (New York: Simon and Schuster, 1953), p. 122.

14. Hodder, pp. 106–107.

15. Arthur Hamilton Gordon, Lord Stanmore, *Sidney Herbert*, 2 vols. (London: John Murray, 1906), 1:120.

16. Thompson, in *The Unknown Mayhew*, p. 33, suggests that Mayhew may have given in to his antagonism against Ashley in his attack on the ragged schools.

17. J. J. Tobias, *Urban Crime in Victorian England* (1967; reprint ed., New York: Schocken, 1972), p. 175. Richard Altick, in *The English Common Reader* (Chicago: University of Chicago Press, 1957), noted that "one of the favorite occupations of the newly founded London Statistical Society in the 1840's was to demonstrate, in elaborate charts, the relationship between ignorance and the crime rate" (p. 142). An example of the prevalence of this belief comes from one of Mayhew's colleagues, Charles Mackay, in his surveys of Liverpool. In his discussion of education in that city he asserted that "the partially and imperfectly instructed multitudes, even if they have mastered no more than the first elements, or tools of learning, give less trouble, and cost the state less money and care, than those who have received no instruction at all" (19 August 1850).

18. Tobias discusses the difficulties of determining what the exact rates of juvenile crime were at midcentury. There did seem to be a drop after 1850. See *Urban Crime*, p. 127. In his final chapter Tobias discusses the various reasons for the apparently high rate of juvenile crime between 1810 and 1850.

19. I have been unable to find any more information about Henry Wood. The London City Mission was begun in 1835 by David Nasmith (1799–1839) with the object of "evangelization of the vast mass of heathenism in our midst, commencing with the very poorest and most neglected portions of London. It seeks to effect this object by a system of visitation of the poor at their own dwellings." R. W. Vanderkiste, *Notes and Narratives of a Six Years Mission, Principally among the Dens of London* (London: James Nisbet, 1852), pp. xiii–xiv. Richard Knight was apparently one of the men who worked for this project.

20. Quoted in Strathearn Gordon and T. G. B. Cocks, *A People's Conscience* (London: Constable, 1952), p. 178.

21. [J. M. Ludlow], "Labour and the Poor," *Fraser's* 41 (January 1850):3;

"Waiting at the Station," *Punch*, 9 March 1850; *Eclectic Review* 94 (October 1851):424–436.

22. Steven Marcus, "Reading the Illegible," in Dyos and Wolff, eds., *The Victorian City*, 1:263. See also his *Engels, Manchester and the Working Class* (New York: Random House, 1974).

23. Friedrich Engels, *The Condition of the Working Class in England*, ed. and trans. W. O. Henderson and W. H. Chaloner (1958; reprint ed., Stanford: Stanford University Press, 1968), p. 31.

24. Robert A. Nisbet, *The Sociological Tradition* (New York: Basic Books, 1966), p. 42.

25. Thompson, "The Political Education of Henry Mayhew," p. 56.

Chapter 3 · The History of a People

1. Volume 1 (numbers 1–26) appeared between the approximate date of 14 December 1850 and 7 June 1851; volume 2 (numbers 27–63) continued through 21 February 1852. From 23 August 1851 Mayhew published on odd weeks what he then called "The Extra Volume" (odd numbers 37–61), a survey of prostitution, which in 1862 became the early pages of volume 4 of *London Labour*. The thirteen numbers of the extra volume appeared between 23 August 1851 and 7 February 1852.

2. Kellow Chesney, *The Victorian Underworld* (1970; reprint ed., New York: Schocken, 1972), p. 49.

3. *London Labour and the London Poor*, 4 vols. (1861–1862; reprint ed., London: Frank Cass, 1967), 1:10. Further references to these four volumes will be given parenthetically in the text by volume and page.

4. Alfred R. Bennett, *London and Londoners in the Eighteen-Fifties and Sixties* (London: T. Fisher Unwin, 1924).

5. See Eileen Yeo's essay "Mayhew as a Social Investigator" in *The Unknown Mayhew*, pp. 51–95, for a discussion of the ideas Mayhew developed on the wrappers to *London Labour*.

6. G. H. Martin and David Francis, "The Camera's Eye" in Dyos and Wolff, *The Victorian City*, 1:227–246.

7. My correspondence with Helmut Gernsheim, one of the most important collectors of nineteenth-century photographs, has confirmed the apparent disappearance of these originals.

8. Mayhew used the word *scavenger* and the word *scavager* interchangeably. The OED calls such usage of "scavager" rare.

9. In the appendix of *The Diary of Dr. Andrew Smith*, ed. Perceval R. Kirby (1939), the editor lists all Smith's known works. None has exactly the title Mayhew notes as his source although in 1829 Smith published an article on "Contributions to the Natural History of South Africa" and another in 1830

"On the Origin and History of the Bushmen." His major work was *Illustrations of the Zoology of South Africa, Consisting Chiefly of Figures and Descriptions of the Objects of Natural History, collected during an Expedition into the Interior of South Africa, in the years 1834–1836.* 4 vols. (London, 1838–1849).

10. Himmelfarb made this point first in her article "Mayhew's Poor: A Problem of Identity" in *Victorian Studies* and again in "The Culture of Poverty," in Dyos and Wolff, *The Victorian City*, 2:707–736.

11. The first six classifications include the street sellers; buyers; finders; performers, artists, and showmen; artisans; laborers. The sellers are subsequently covered more or less completely if not systematically in *London Labour*, volumes 1 and 2 (to p. 103); the street buyers become the subject of volume 2 (pp. 103–135); the street finders appear in volume 2 (pp. 136–179); the performers, artists, and showmen were not covered until 1856 in volume 3 (pp. 43–220). (One subcategory of the street performers, "the proprietors of street games" which is given in *London Labour*, 1:4, is not covered in volume 3 at all, which indicates the abbreviated form of that volume.) The fifth and sixth groups were never covered.

12. These figures of Mayhew's included not only the costermongers or sellers but also their wives and children. He makes this distinction in 1, 4–6 but fails to do so in 2, 1.

13. *Selected Writings in Sociology and Social Philosophy*, trans. T. B. Bottomore; ed. T. B. Bottomore and Maximilien Rubel (New York: McGraw-Hill, 1956), pp. 169–170.

14. *Latter-Day Pamphlets*, in *The Works of Thomas Carlyle*, ed. H. D. Traill, 30 vols. (New York: Scribner's Sons, 1895–1907), 20:58.

15. *Chartism*, p. 111.

16. Robert Blake, *Disraeli* (New York: St. Martin's Press, 1966), p. 81. Chesney (pp. 190–194) has a discussion of common prejudices against east end Jews.

17. Eric Trudgill, "Prostitution and Paterfamilias" in Dyos and Wolff, *The Victorian City*, 2:699.

18. *The Critic*, 1 April 1858, quoted in the *Morning News*, 5 April 1858.

19. Oscar Lewis, *The Children of Sánchez* (1961: reprint ed., Harmondsworth: Penguin, 1964) p. xii.

20. John L. Rosenberg in his introduction to the Dover edition of *London Labour* (New York, 1968) suggests Mayhew's identification with his subjects. See p. v.

21. *London Characters*, p. 396.

22. Mayhew and Cruikshank, *1851; or the Adventures of Mr. and Mrs. Sandboys* . . . , p. 154.

23. *Young Benjamin Franklin*, p. 250.

24. I have not been able to find out anything about John Binny beyond his

connection with Henry Mayhew. Bracebridge Hemyng was a minor novelist; the British Library has thirty-six works by him all written after 1860. Andrew Halliday (1830–1877), who contributed the section on beggars to volume 4, was an essayist and dramatist connected with the *Morning Chronicle* in 1849; he also later wrote for *Cornhill Magazine* and *All the Year Round*.

25. In answering a letter to the *Morning Chronicle* in 1850, he acknowledged a mistake in some statistics, "but the calculation was not my own, and in the hurry of the moment the error escaped me" (14 January 1850).

26. Written sources that he mentions include, in addition to McCulloch, Porter, and government reports: T. C. Banfield and C. R. Weld, *Statistical Companion*; Samuel Salt, *Facts and Figures* and *Statistics and Calculations*; and Peter Cunningham, *Handbook of Modern London*. Banfield and Weld published two books of collected statistics, *Statistical Companion to the Pocket Book* (1843–1854) and *The Economy of the British Empire*, "containing a condensed tabular survey, with appropriate discussion of the territories, population, resources and government of the British Empire and its dependencies" (1849–1850). Salt's *Facts and Figures* concerned railways and commerce. Cunningham's *History of London* appeared in two volumes in 1849 and contained in dictionary-form information about the history and development of various buildings, clubs, monuments, and streets in London.

27. Peter Quennell, Introduction, *Mayhew's London* (London: William Kimber, 1951), p. 21. Jonathan Raban, "The Invisible Mayhew," *Encounter* 41 (August 1973):69, makes the same mistake, as have others.

28. *Sketches by Boz* (London: Oxford University Press, 1957), pp. 641–642. The Mudfog Papers originally appeared in *Bentley's Miscellany* (1837–1839) and were included later in *Sketches by Boz*. All quotations from Dickens in the following text are from the Oxford Illustrated Dickens.

29. *The Criminal Prisons of London* (1862; reprint ed., London: Frank Cass, 1968), p. 37n. In *London 1850–1851*, a compilation from his *Geographical Dictionary* (London: Longman, Brown, Green, and Longmans, 1851), McCulloch stated that "with the exception of coal, and one or two other articles, there are no means by which to arrive at anything like a correct conclusion" about the consumption of food and other goods in London (p. 55). He then went on to quote "a curious and apparently authentic statement" from the *Morning Chronicle* on the sale of poultry and game at Leadenhall, taken from the last series on London markets by the metropolitan correspondent.

30. Thompson, "Political Education . . . ," p. 58.

31. *Low Wages, Their Causes, Consequences and Remedies* (London: at the office of *London Labour and the London Poor*, 1851), p. 15. Further references are made parenthetically (the abbreviation LW followed by the page).

32. From the Manifesto of 1839. Quoted in William Lovett, *Life and Struggles of William Lovett*, new ed. (London: Macgibbon and Kee, 1967), p. 174.

33. On the same wrapper he hints that taxation might be an answer, but he

does not develop this idea any further. An editorial (probably written by Mayhew) in the *Morning News* for 12 January 1859 says that a "wise" government may have to interfere "with the natural operations of trade and industry."

34. In his preface to *Paved with Gold* (1858; reprint ed., London: Frank Cass, 1971), Augustus laid claim to the survey of crossing-sweepers in volume 2, and the section in volume 3 entitled a night at rat-catching. See my introduction to the reprint for a short discussion of the relationship between *Paved with Gold* and *London Labour and the London Poor*.

35. Advertisement dated 23 September 1856 on the monthly wrappers of "The Great World of London."

36. Volume 3 begins with a forty-two page survey, "The Destroyers of Vermin," a section difficult to place since it has little relation to the street folk—proclaimed by the title page to be the sole subject. An internal date in an interview with a beetle destroyer of February 1855, indicates that the material was collected for the 1856 attempt at publication. This opening section also repeats some of the material in volume 1, where Mayhew surveyed the sale of fly-papers and beetle-wafers (chemical devices for trapping these bugs) (1:435) and the art of rat-catching (1:451–452). There is no evidence that this was meant to open a new volume; no introduction, as was given in volumes 1 and 2, is provided.

37. The illustrations of crossing-sweepers in volume 2 and the illustrations in volume 3 say "from a Photograph" rather than mentioning Beard specifically, as had the earlier ones. Some of these photographs must have been done in 1851–1852. Old Sarey is dead when her story is told in 1856. Since the 1851 Harper American edition of *London Labour* uses the picture of Old Sarey as its title page, her photograph must have been taken at Beard's studio as early as January 1851. Where Harper Brothers got the picture is unknown.

38. Mayhew's *German Life and Manners* states that he was in Germany for two years, while the preface to *The Criminal Prisons of London* remarks that John Binny had to finish the survey of prisons because Mayhew was out of the country; internal evidence points to Binny's having done his research during late 1861 or early 1862 (see the chart dated 29 September 1861 on p. 532). An article in *The Shops and Companies of London* suggests that Mayhew was in Germany through a good part of 1863 (p. 77).

39. Since many of these reprinted letters contain variations of the words, phrases, and in some cases the order of presentation of the material, it may be that Mayhew or someone did revise them slightly.

40. This last addition brings even more confusion to the unwary reader. It begins: "I shall now pass to the labourers at the docks," despite the fact that the preceding sixty-seven pages had already dealt with dock laborers, and it continues: "This transition I am induced to make, not because there is any affinity between the kinds of work performed at the two places; but because

the docks constitute, as it were, a sort of home colony to Spitalfields, to which the unemployed weaver migrates in the hope of bettering his condition" (3:300–301). This sentence refers to an earlier letter (II) in which Mayhew surveyed the Spitalfields weavers but which is not reprinted in volume 3 of *London Labour*. The reader of volume 3 has no way of knowing this, however.

41. Part of Letter XXVII is combined with part of Letter XXIX; this is followed by part of Letter XXVIII combined with part of XXX; next come more parts of XXVII and XXX; then XXVII again, followed by XXVIII, and more of XXIX and then back to XXV.

Chapter 4 · The World of London Prisons

1. *Young Benjamin Franklin*, p. xiv.
2. Prospectus for "The Great World of London" on March 1856 wrapper.
3. See chapter 1, n. 64.
4. Evidence for Vizetelly's presence occurs not in *Criminal Prisons* but in Vizetelly's *Glances Back*, 1:405.
5. Mayhew refers to this ascent in *The Boyhood of Martin Luther* (London: Sampson Low, 1863), p. 150n.
6. "Model Prisons," *Latter-Day Pamphlets*, p. 53.
7. "The Demeanor of Murderers," *Household Words*, 14 June 1856.
8. Tobias, pp. 206–208.
9. *Shops and Companies of London*, p. 46.
10. [William] Hepworth Dixon, *The London Prisons: with an account of the More Distinguished Persons who have been Confined in Them* (London: Jackson and Walford, 1850), p. 161.
11. "On Capital Punishments," in *Three Papers on Capital Punishment* (London: Cox and Wyman, 1856), p. 44.
12. Tobias, p. 11.
13. See Margaret May, "Innocence and Experience: The Evolution of the Concept of Juvenile Delinquency in the Mid-Nineteenth Century," *Victorian Studies* (17 September 1973):7–29.
14. Sheppard, p. 367.
15. Jean Etienne Dominique Esquirol (1722–1840), whose investigations of French lunatic asylums contributed to the reform of those institutions, published his report *Des Maladies mentales, considérées sous les rapports médical, hygiénique et médico-légal* in 1838.
16. In the publisher's preface, dated April 1862, they state "in consequence of Mr. Mayhew's absence from England, they placed the completion of the volume in the hands of Mr. Binny, who supplied all after page 498." This preface is not reprinted in the Cass edition.

Chapter 5 · Attitude as Style

1. Richard M. Weaver, *The Ethics of Rhetoric* (Chicago: Henry Regnery, 1957), pp. 187–188. In "Henry Mayhew's Rhetoric" Thomas has an interesting chapter on Mayhew's relationship to the social writing of the period.

2. *The Upper Rhine*, pp. vi–vii. We should be grateful that Mayhew's intentions for *London Labour* prevented him from writing in this last "higher" style, for the examples he gave of it are without exception dreadful: fields "smile," brooks "murmur," and the "jocund morn" stands "tiptoe on the misty mountaintop."

3. *Young Benjamin Franklin*, p. 229.

4. *Letters of Thomas Carlyle 1826–1836*, ed. Charles Eliot Norton. 2 vols. (London: Macmillan, 1888), 2:123.

5. "Common Lodging Houses," in *Life and Labour of the People in London*, by Charles Booth et al., ser. 1, 3rd ed., 4 vols. (London: Macmillan, 1902), 1:209. In using the work of Booth and his colleagues I do not mean in any way to impugn the justifiably high reputation of Booth's work in general nor to denigrate its scope or statistics. I am interested only in the implications of style in the passage. Also one might note that Booth's own notebooks have much of Mayhew's quality of vividness, immediacy, and preciseness. In the process of turning his note book entries into a formal report however, Booth lost many of these qualities of effective reporting.

6. Weaver gave as the second major weakness of social scientific writing a "pedantic empiricism" or a fear of commitment which clutters the writing with hedging phrases. He speculates that this hedging was ultimately to cover the contradiction between language which merely describes and language which commits the writer to a position about what he reports (p. 193).

7. W. Weir, "St. Giles Past and Present," in *London*, ed. Charles Knight, 6 vols. (London: Charles Knight, 1841–1844), 3:267.

8. P. J. Keating, *The Working Classes in Victorian Fiction* (London: Routledge and Kegan Paul, 1971), p. 250.

Chapter 6 · Mayhew and the Literature of His Time

1. Vizetelly, 1:408.

2. Angela Hookum makes this point in an M.A. thesis, "The Literary Career of Henry Mayhew" (University of Birmingham, 1962).

3. Bradley, Introduction, p. xi. First developed in Bradley, "Henry Mayhew: Farce Writer of the 1830's," *Victorian Newsletter* 23 (1963):21–23.

4. Keating, p. 40.

5. Aina Rubenius, *The Woman Question in Mrs. Gaskell's Life and Works* (Cambridge: Harvard University Press, 1950), pp. 159–174.

6. A more recent commentator, John Geoffrey Sharp, in *Mrs. Gaskell's Observation and Invention* (Fontwell: Linden Press, 1970), p. 149, speculated that the increased concern was due to Mrs. Gaskell's personal experience. The earliest known letter from Dickens to her (in 1850) referred to a young dressmaking apprentice who had been seduced and whom Mrs. Gaskell was helping to emigrate.

7. Stanley E. Baldwin, *Charles Kingsley* (Ithaca N.Y.: Cornell University Press, 1934), p. 76.

8. *Yeast: A Problem,* in *The Life and Works of Charles Kingsley,* 19 vols. (London: Macmillan, 1902), 15:165–166.

9. R. B. Martin, *The Dust of Combat* (London: Faber and Faber, 1959), p. 111.

10. *Blackwood's* 68 (November 1850):598.

11. Bradley, Introduction, p. xxxv.

12. In December 1849 he wrote to J. M. Ludlow asking him to "borrow or buy the *Morning Chronicle* articles . . . at least send me the *Tailor* one by return of post. I will come up after Christmas and help." Quoted in Frances E. Kingsley, *Charles Kingsley: His Letters and Memories of his Life,* 2 vols. (London: Macmillan, 1901), 1:233.

13. *Cheap Clothes and Nasty* (London: William Pickering, 1850), p. 22.

14. Thompson, in *The Unknown Mayhew,* discusses Mayhew's connection with the group (p. 31).

15. *British Quarterly Review* 11 (May 1850):492.

16. Sheppard, p. 241.

17. Frances Kingsley, 1:246.

18. Aytoun, *Blackwood's* 68 (November 1850):608.

19. *Yeast,* p. 98.

20. *Alton Locke* in *The Life and Works of Charles Kingsley,* 7:215.

21. Bradley, Introduction, pp. xxxv, xxxvii.

22. A further parallel implied by Bradley—the vulgarity and lowness of the cheap theatrical entertainments—seems unlikely to me since Mayhew's major attack on these entertainments appeared in *London Labour and the London Poor.*

23. *Literary Gazette and Journal of Belles Lettres,* 5 July 1851. The excerpts from the *Christian Watchman and Reflector* and the *New York Evening Post* were on the covers of the 1851 American edition of *London Labour and the London Poor.* Hugh Massingham, "Victorian Poverty," *Sunday Observer,* 4 February 1951, p. 7; W. H. Auden, "An Inquisitive Old Party," *New Yorker,* 24 February 1968, p. 122; Sheppard, pp. 345–346.

24. For Dickens's views see Philip Collins, *Dickens and Education* (1963; reprint ed., London: Macmillan, 1965), pp. 143, 188.

25. *Dickens and Crime* (1962; reprint ed., Bloomington: Indiana University Press, 1968), pp. 180–181.

26. See *Figaro in London*, 13 January 1838.

27. Edgar Johnson, *Charles Dickens: His Tragedy and Triumph*, 2 vols. (New York: Simon and Schuster, 1952), 1:115.

28. An account of the theatrical appears in the *Illustrated London News*, 29 November 1845, with a picture of Mayhew in costume.

29. My correspondence with the editors of Dickens's letters, Madeline House and Graham Storey, confirms that there is no mention of Mayhew in Dickens's letters.

30. "The Ruffian," *All the Year Round*, 10 October 1868.

31. Harland S. Nelson, "Dickens's *Our Mutual Friend* and Henry Mayhew's *London Labour and the London Poor*," *Nineteenth Century Fiction* 20 (December 1965):207–222. Thomas ("Mayhew's Rhetoric") has an extensive discussion of Mayhew's influence on *Our Mutual Friend*.

32. Richard J. Dunn, "Dickens and Mayhew Once More," *Nineteenth Century Fiction* 25 (December 1970):348–353. Harvey Peter Sucksmith found "echoes" of Mayhew's "The Great World of London" in *Little Dorrit*. See *Nineteenth Century Fiction* 24 (December 1969):345–349. His argument seems unconvincing to me; furthermore he mistakenly attributes *The Mormons* to Mayhew rather than to Charles Mackay.

33. "Gin Shops," *Sketches by Boz*, p. 186.

34. See Philip Collins, "Dickens and London," in Dyos and Wolff, *The Victorian City*, 2:550.

35. "The Dickens World: A View from Todgers," in *The Dickens Critics*, ed. George H. Ford and Lauriat Lane (Ithaca: Cornell University Press, 1961), pp. 213–232.

36. *The Prelude*, 1850 ed., book 7, ll. 722–730.

37. See "The Topicality of Bleak House," John Butt and Kathleen Tillotson, *Dickens at Work* (London: Methuen, 1957), pp. 177–199, and Michael Slater, "Dickens's Tract for the Times" (on *The Chimes*), in *Dickens 1970*, ed. Michael Slater (London: Chapman and Hall, 1970), pp. 99–123. Answering charges against the naturalness of Nancy's devotion to Sykes, Dickens said he found it "useless to discuss whether the conduct and character of the girl seems natural or unnatural, probable or improbable, right or wrong. IT IS TRUE" (preface to *Oliver Twist*, p. xvii).

38. *Life of Charles Dickens*, ed. J. W. Ley (London: Cecil Palmer, 1928), p.11.

39. In *London Characters* (p. 349) Mayhew lists a number of personal experiences he had had in his investigations of the poor, among them a stint on the treadmill and the interview with the blind man.

40. The constable and the ticket-of-leave meeting is in *London Labour* (3:430); the tour of Ratcliff Highway is referred to in Mayhew's report on working men's clubs, p. 24.

41. Harry Stone, ed., *Charles Dickens's Uncollected Writings from House-hold Words 1850–1859*, 2 vols. (Bloomington: Indiana University Press, 1968), 1:49.

42. In his essay "The Fiction of Realism: *Sketches by Boz, Oliver Twist*, and Cruikshank's Illustrations," in *Dickens Centennial Essays*, eds. Ada Nisbit and Blake Nevius (Berkeley and Los Angeles: University of California Press, 1971), J. Hillis Miller demonstrates Dickens's tendency to fictionalize the lives of people in the *Sketches*. See pp. 116–118.

43. "On an Amateur Beat," *All the Year Round*, 27 February 1869.

44. "Bill Sticking," *Household Words*, 22 March 1851.

45. In a letter to Wills dated 16 October 1851, in Stone, *Uncollected Writings*, 1:33.

46. See Butt and Tillotson, *Dickens at Work*, p. 46.

47. Stone, 1:44.

48. See Michael Steig, "The Whitewashing of Inspector Bucket: Origins and Parallels," *Papers of the Michigan Academy of Science, Arts and Letters* 50 (1965):575–584, for a discussion of this aspect of *Bleak House*.

49. "On Duty with Inspector Field," *Household Words*, 14 June 1851.

50. "A Small Star in the East," *All the Year Round*, 19 December 1868.

51. Ibid.

52. *Charles Dickens. A Critical Study* (New York: Dodd, Mead, 1898), p. 96.

53. "A Visit to the Cholera Districts of Bermondsey," *Morning Chronicle*, 24 September 1849. Mayhew used the description several times but with re-visions consisting of different wordings and the shifting of blocks of material from one place to another. In both my volume of selections from the *Morning Chronicle, Voices of the Poor*, and my essay "Dickens and Mayhew on the London Poor" in *Dickens Annual* 4 (Carbondale and Edwardsville: Southern Illinois University Press, 1975), I used a version reprinted in *Meliora*, ed. Viscount Ingestre (London: John Parker, 1851). I noted the revision only in the essay in *Dickens Annual*. Bradley in his introduction apparently used a third version although he does not say what it is.

54. "Night Walks," *All the Year Round*, 21 July 1860.

55. Collins, *Dickens and Crime*, pp. 184–185.

Afterword

1. T. S. and M. B. Simey, *Charles Booth* (London: Oxford University Press, 1960), p. 254.

2. Thompson, "Political Education," p. 58. Himmelfarb, in "Mayhew's Poor: A Problem of Identity," p. 316, picks up the same phrase and has the same reaction as Thompson.

3. A. H. Wells, *The Local Social Survey in Great Britain* (London: George Allen and Unwin, 1935), pp. 80, 14.

4. Charlotte Elizabeth [Mrs. Tonna], *Helen Fleetwood* in *The Works of Charlotte Elizabeth*, 2 vols. (New York: Dodd, 1849), 1:611.

5. *The English Common Reader*, p. 94.

Bibliography

Works by Henry Mayhew

"Answers to Correspondents." *London Labour and the London Poor*. Wrappers for weekly numbers 5–63 (1851–1852).

The Boyhood of Martin Luther. London: Sampson Low, 1863.

German Life and Manners as Seen in Saxony at the Present Day. 2 vols. London: William Allen, 1864.

"The Great Exhibition." Nos. 1–9. *Edinburgh News and Literary Chronicle*, May-July 1851.

"The Great World of London." Pts. 1–9. London: David Bogue, 1856.

"Home is Home, be it Never so Homely." In *Meliora: or, Better Times to Come*, edited by Viscount Ingestre. London: John W. Parker, 1851.

"Labour and the Poor." Letters I–LXXXII. *Morning Chronicle*, 19 October 1849–12 December 1850. (For selections see Humpherys, A. and Thompson, E. P.)

"Labour and the Poor." *Report of the Speech of Henry Mayhew, Esq., and the Evidence adduced at a Public Meeting Held at St. Martin's Hall, Long Acre, on Monday evening, Oct. 28, 1850. . . .* London: Bateman, Hardwicke, 1850.

London Labour and the London Poor. 4 vols. 1861–1862. Reprint. London: Frank Cass, 1967. (For paperback edition see Rosenberg, J.; for selections see Bradley, J., Quennell, P., Rubenstein, S.)

Low Wages, Their Causes, Consequences and Remedies. Pts. 1–4. London: At the office of *London Labour and the London Poor*, November-December 1851. (Reprinted in part in Thompson, E. P. and Yeo, E.)

"On Capital Punishments." In *Three Papers on Capital Punishments*. London: Cox and Wyman, 1856.

The Prince of Wales's Library. No. 1. London: Office of the Illuminated Magazine [1844].

Report Concerning the Trade and Hours of Closing Usual Among the Unlicensed Victualing Establishments Now Open for the Unrestricted Sale of Beer, Wine, and Spirits at certain so-called "Working Men's Clubs," distributed throughout the metropolis. London: Judd [1871].

The Rhine and Its Picturesque Scenery. London: David Bogue, 1856.

The Story of the Peasant-Boy Philosopher; or, "A Child Gathering Pebbles on the Sea Shore." London: David Bogue, 1854.

The Upper Rhine and Its Picturesque Scenery. London: George Routledge, 1858.

The Wandering Minstrel. 1834. New York: Samuel French, n.d.

What to Teach and How to Teach It: so that the Child may become a Wise and Good Man. Pt. 1. London: William Smith, 1842.

The Wonders of Science; or, Young Humphry Davy. London: David Bogue, 1855.

Young Benjamin Franklin. London: James Blackwood, 1861.

Editor. *The Comic Almanac*. London: David Bogue, 1850–1851.

Editor. *Figaro in London*. Vols. 4–8. London: W. Strange, January 1835–August 1839.

Editor. *The Morning News*. London: January 1859.

Editor. *Only Once a Year*. London: Stevens and Richardson, 1870.

Editor. *The Shops and Companies of London, and the Grades and Manufactories of Great Britain*. London: Strand, March-September 1865.

And John Binny. *The Criminal Prisons of London and Scenes of Prison Life*. 1862. Reprint. London: Frank Cass, 1968.

And George Cruikshank. *1851; or, The Adventures of Mr. and Mrs. Sandboys and Family, who came up to London to "enjoy themselves," and to see the Great Exhibition*. London: David Bogue, 1851.

And Athol Mayhew. *Mont Blanc*. London: privately printed, 1874.

And Others. *London Characters. Illustrations of the Humour, Pathos, and Peculiarities of London Life*. 2nd ed. London: Chatto and Windus, 1874. (The other authors are unknown: see note 69, chapter 1.)

Works by the Brothers Mayhew (Augustus and Henry)

Acting Charades. London: David Bogue, 1850.

The Fear of the World; or, Living for Appearances. New York: Harper and Bros., 1850. (The only English edition I located in the British Library was an 1855 reprint under the title *Living for Appearances*; the novel was serialized in the *Illustrated London News* in 1849–1850.)

The Good Genius that Turned Everything into Gold; or, the Queen Bee and the Magic Dress. London: David Bogue, 1847.

The Greatest Plague of Life; or, the Adventures of a Lady in Search of a Good Servant. London: David Bogue [1847].

The Image of His Father; or, a Tale of a Young Monkey. London: H. Hurst, 1848.

The Magic of Kindness; or, the Wondrous Story of the Good Huan. London: Darton and Co., 1849.

Whom to Marry and How to get Married! or, the Adventures of a Lady in Search of a Good Husband. London: David Bogue [1848].

Works about Henry Mayhew
(Starred items have discussions of significant length)

à Beckett, Arthur William. *The à Becketts of "Punch."* London: Archibald Constable, 1903.

*[Account of Mayhew's bankruptcy.] *London Times*, 12 February 1847, p. 8.

Adrian, Arthur A. *Mark Lemon: First Editor of Punch*. London: Oxford University Press, 1966.

*Auden, W. H. "An Inquisitive Old Party," *New Yorker*, 24 February 1968, pp. 121–133. (Review of *London Labour and the London Poor*.)

*Beale, Thomas Willert. *The Light of Other Days*. 2 vols. London: Richard Bentley, 1890.

Beames, Thomas. *The Rookeries of London*. 2nd ed. 1852. Reprint. London: Frank Cass, 1970.

*"Biography of Henry Mayhew for W. C. Griffin Handbook of Contemporary Biography." Manuscript of 1860 in the British Library.

*Bradley, John L. "Henry Mayhew and Father William," *English Language Notes* 1 (September 1963):40–42.

*_____. "Henry Mayhew: Farce Writer of the 1830's," *Victorian Newsletter* 23 (1963):21–23.

*_____. Introduction. *Selections from "London Labour and the London Poor."* London: Oxford University Press, 1965. (The standard biography.)

*Briggs, Asa. "The culture of poverty in 19th-century London," *Scientific American*, July 1966, pp. 123–126. (Review of *London Labour and the London Poor*.)

Cazamian, Louis. *The Social Novel in England 1830–1850*. 1903. Trans. Martin Fido. London: Routledge and Kegan Paul, 1973.

Chesney, Kellow. *The Victorian Underworld*. 1970. Reprint. New York: Schocken, 1972.

*Clayton, Herbert. "The Henry Mayhew Centenary." *Notes and Queries*, 11th ser., 5 (1912):145, 317–318, 433; 6 (1912):71–72.

*Coumbe, Mrs. L. M. "The Mayhew Brothers." Manuscript in the possession of Patrick Mayhew, London.

"Distressed Populations." *Economist*, 16 November 1850, pp. 1264–1265. (Unfavorable review of *Morning Chronicle* series.)

*Dunn, Richard J. "Dickens and Mayhew Once More." *Nineteenth Century Fiction* 25 (December 1970):348–353.

*Edwards, [Henry] Sutherland. *Personal Recollections*. London: Cassell, 1900.

Forshall, Frederic H. *Westminster School, Past and Present*. London: Weyman, 1884.

Glass, Ruth. "Urban Sociology in Great Britain: a Trend Report." *Current Sociology* 4 (1955):5–19, 27–76.

Hall, John. *The Sons of Toil and the Crystal Palace. In reply to Mr. Mayhew*. London: John Snow, 1853.

*Himmelfarb, Gertrude. "Mayhew's Poor: A Problem of Identity." *Victorian Studies* 14 (March 1971):307–320.

*———. "The Culture of Poverty." In *The Victorian City: Images and Realities*. Ed. H. J. Dyos and Michael Wolff. 2 vols. (London: Routledge and Kegan Paul, 1973) 2:707–736.

*Hodder, George. *Memories of My Time*. London: Tinsley, 1870.

*Hookum, A. M. "The Literary Career of Henry Mayhew." M.A. thesis, Birmingham University, 1962.

*Humpherys, Anne. "Dickens and Mayhew on the London Poor." *Dickens Annual* 4, ed. Robert Partlow. Carbondale and Edwardsville: Southern Illinois Press, 1975, pp. 78–90, 175–179.

*———. Review of *The Unknown Mayhew* by E. P. Thompson and Eileen Yeo. *Victorian Studies* 15 (December 1971):243–245.

*———, ed. *Paved with Gold* by Augustus Mayhew. 1858. Reprint. London: Frank Cass, 1971.

*———, ed. *Voices of the Poor*. London: Frank Cass, 1971. (Selections from Mayhew's *Morning Chronicle* letters.)

Jerrold, Walter. *Douglas Jerrold: Dramatist and Wit*. 2 vols. London: Hodder and Stoughton [1914].

Jerrold, William Blanchard. *The Life and Remains of Douglas Jerrold*. London: W. Kent, 1859.

Kingsley, Charles. *Alton Locke*. Vols. 7–8 of *The Life and Letters of Charles Kingsley*. 19 vols. London: Macmillan, 1902.

———. *Cheap Clothes and Nasty*. London: William Pickering, 1850.

*"The Late Mr. Henry Mayhew." *Illustrated London News* 91 (6 August 1887):158.

[Ludlow, J. M.] "Labour and the Poor." *Fraser's Magazine* 41 (January 1850):1–18.

Mackay, Charles. *Forty Years' Recollections of Life, Literature, and Public Affairs*. 2 vols. London: Chapman and Hall, 1877.

Massingham, Hugh. "Victorian Poverty." *Sunday Observer*, 4 February 1951, p. 7.

*Mayhew, Athol. *A Jorum of "Punch."* London: Downey, 1895.

"Mayhew's London." *Times Literary Supplement*, 24 August 1951, p. 522.

Men of the Time. London: David Bogue, 1856.

"The Morning Chronicle on the State of the Poor." *Spectator*, 27 October 1849, p. 1018.

*Nelson, Harland S. "Dickens's *Our Mutual Friend* and Henry Mayhew's *London Labour and the London Poor*." *Nineteenth Century Fiction* 20 (December 1965):207–222.

"New Serial, The Great World of London." *Spectator*, 8 March 1856, p. 275.

Obituary of Mayhew. *London Times*, 27 July 1887, p. 5.

Obituary of Mayhew. *Punch*, 6 August 1887, p. 53.

Price, R.G.G. *A History of Punch*. London: William Collins, 1957.

*Pritchett, V. S. "True to Life." *New York Review of Books*, 17 March 1966, pp. 5–6. (Review of *London Labour and the London Poor*.)

Quennell, Peter, ed. *London's Underworld*. London: William Kimber, 1950. (Selections from volume 4 of *London Labour and the London Poor*.)

*———, ed. Introduction. *Mayhew's London*. London: William Kimber, 1951. (Selections from vols. 1–3 of *London Labour and the London Poor*.)

———, ed. *Mayhew's Characters*. London: William Kimber, 1951. (Further selections from *London Labour and the London Poor*.)

*Raban, Jonathan. "The Invisible Mayhew." *Encounter* 41 (August 1973):64–70.

Razzell, P. E., and R. W. Wainwright. *The Victorian Working Class: Selections from the Morning Chronicle*. London: Frank Cass, 1974. (Selections from the other series of "Labour and the Poor.")

Review of "Labour and the Poor." *Eclectic Review* 94 (October 1851):424–436.

"Review of the 'Morning Chronicle' Correspondent on the State of the Poor in the Metropolis." *British Quarterly Review* 11 (May 1850):491–493.

Roberts, F. David. "More Early Victorian Newspaper Editors." *Victorian Periodicals Newsletter* 16 (June 1972):15–28.

*Rosenberg, John D., ed. Introduction. *London Labour and the London Poor*. 4 vols. New York: Dover, 1968.

Rubenius, Aina. *The Woman Question in Mrs. Gaskell's Life and Works*. Cambridge: Harvard University Press, 1950.

*Rubenstein, Stanley, ed. *The Street Trader's Lot*. London: Sylvan, 1947. (Selections from *London Labour and the London Poor* with an introduction by M. Dorothy George.)

"St. James Theatre—The Amateurs." *Illustrated London News*, 29 November 1845, p. 348. (An account of Dickens's production of *Every Man in His Humour* with a picture of Mayhew in costume.)

Sala, George Augustus. *The Life and Adventures of George Augustus Sala*. 2 vols. New York: Charles Scribner's Sons, 1896.

Scott, Clement, and Cecil Howard. *The Life and Reminiscences of E. L. Blanchard*. 2 vols. New York: Brentano's, 1891.

Sheppard, Francis. *London 1808–1870: The Infernal Wen*. London: Secker and Warburg, 1971.

*Spielmann, M. H. *The History of "Punch."* New York: Cassell, 1895.

*Sucksmith, Harvey Peter. "Dickens and Mayhew: A Further Note." *Nineteenth Century Fiction* 24 (December 1969):345–349.

Thackeray, William Makepeace. *The Letters and Private Papers of William Makepeace Thackeray*, ed. Gordon N. Ray. 4 vols. Cambridge: Harvard University Press, 1945–46.

*Thomas, Alan Cedric. "Henry Mayhew's Rhetoric: A Study of His Presentation of Social 'Facts.'" Ph.D. thesis, the University of Toronto, 1971.

*Thompson, E. P. "Mayhew and the 'Morning Chronicle.'" In *The Unknown Mayhew*, eds. E. P. Thompson and Eileen Yeo. New York: Pantheon, 1971. (Primarily a selection from Mayhew's letters to the *Morning Chronicle* and his pamphlet *Low Wages*.)

*———. "The Political Education of Henry Mayhew." *Victorian Studies* 11 (September 1967): 41–62.

Tobias, J. J. *Urban Crime in Victorian England*. 1967. Reprint. New York: Schocken, 1972.

*Vizetelly, Henry. *Glances Back Through Seventy Years*. 2 vols. London: Kegan Paul, Trench, Trübner, 1893.

Wells, A. F. *The Local Social Survey in Great Britain*. London: George Allen and Unwin, 1935.

*Yeo, Eileen. "Mayhew as a Social Investigator." In *The Unknown Mayhew*, eds. E. P. Thompson and Eileen Yeo. New York: Pantheon, 1971.

Index

Numbers in boldface indicate pages where definitions of unfamiliar occupations that Mayhew surveyed are to be found. *London Labour and the London Poor* is abbreviated *LLLP* in all entries.